Life is an Amazing Song

Life is an Amazing Song

John (Juha) Raikkonen

To my family

And

In memory of all our loved ones

And

Our Son in law, Ross Vigeant

1

1942

T HE TASTE OF BURNED SHOESTRING still lingered in my mouth and is to this day firmly fixed in my memory. I can even feel and taste the thick, acrid smoke clinging to the surfaces of my mouth. It was my first smoke, and I remember it vividly enough to feel the tightness in my chest as I inhaled that suffocating smoke.

It was 1942 and I was in Oulu, Finland. World War II was raging and I can still recall the thunder of the bombs exploding around the city as the Russians worked to devastate our small but resilient country.

My family and I were jolted from our sleep that morning around 3:00 a.m. to the shrillness of the now horribly familiar air raid sirens. We could hear the drone of the oncoming planes as our grandparents woke us up to hurry us to the bomb shelter. The basement of our apartment building had been modified into a bomb shelter at the beginning of the hostilities with the Russians. My grandparents ran downstairs from the third floor, pulling my cousin and me the entire way. The residents of our small apartment building were shoving and pushing against everyone else. The rush to reach shelter first became a match of strength and will as people clawed their way downstairs in order to be the first ones to safety.

My cousin, Rake was staying over that night. He was my older cousin, worldly and wise at the age of seven. I was only four and looked to him as a mentor and a best friend.

On this night, of all nights, amidst all the bombs and the palpable fear, I would learn something new from his endless supply of wisdom.

As bombs exploded around the city, Rake and I huddled in the corner against the cold wall of the narrow, damp basement. I was terrified. The walls reverberated with each blast and there was an unspoken fear that each bomb that was dropped drew closer and closer to the safety of our shelter. The more distant bombs sounded like a dull thud. But the closer they came, louder.

The light from the single lamp brought down to the basement barely penetrated into our far corner. We sat next to each other, separated from our grandparents. I was shaking from cold and worry. He huddled against me as he showed me his secret. He carefully pulled out a crumpled page of newsprint, carefully looking around before he unfolded it in his lap. This secretive show had distracted me from the bombing. I could not wait to see his secret treasure. I was disappointed when he showed me the contents of the crumpled newspaper. On it sat four short cuts of shoestring and a box of wooden matches, nothing else. I could not imagine what Rake had planned with this odd set of items.

He cast a furtive glance over his shoulder once more. Even at the age of four, I remember noticing everyone else was in their own private world of fear. The shrill alarm still rang and everyone tensed at the earth shaking explosions, visibly worried about the chaos that reigned outside. Rake nudged me and motioned me to come closer, handing me one of the short cuts of shoestring and told me to put one end in my mouth. As usual I did as he did and put one of the strings in my mouth. I tried to copy his knowledgeable actions, wondering what insane idea my cousin had planned now. Carefully with no one watching, he lit one of the wooden matches and shielded the flame from the huddled tenants. He brought the glowing flame to the end of his string and inhaled deeply. The tip of his string glowed in the dark. He drew in a deep breath, holding the smoke inside of his chest for a moment before exhaling it from the corner of his mouth, grinning wickedly at the same time.

"It's fun, Juha" he whispered. "Just do as I do." His cheeks puffed wide with another breath. Rake looked so calm and even sophisticated beyond his years that I was afraid to even attempt to copy his actions.

With a wavering voice I told him, "Okay. But I don't know what I'm doing." I was not even sure why we were doing it.

"Nah, nah. It's easy. And it tastes good," he promised me with a wink. He gave me another sly smile, letting more smoke escape from the corners of his mischievous mouth.

He lit another match, bringing the warmth of the flame close to my face where the string hung from my lips very limply. He told me to suck, as hard as I could, as he lit my first, "smoke." As soon as the shoestring-smoke entered my mouth, I was ready to faint. The thick smoke attacked every taste bud on my virgin tongue. As the smoke entered my lungs, my chest seized and I coughed violently. A girl sitting not far from us snapped her head toward us and frowned. I tried not to throw up. Rake laughed and was sucking on his shoestring like a pro, trying to urge me to continue. By now, tears were running down my cheeks and the smoldering shoestring dropped from my mouth and landed in my lap, burning a small hole into my pajama bottoms. I jumped up with surprise, trying to swat the smoking shoestring into submission. I immediately ran back to my grandparents who then questioned the tears on my face.

"The bombing," I lied, "I'm scared of the bombing." They looked at each other knowingly and pulled me in close against them while Rake came to join us. How could I tell them the truth, much less explain why I had just smoked a piece of shoestring? Or that Rake had indulged me with my first smoke in the middle of the Russian's bombing of our city? It was the most horrible tasting experience yet one of the very early memories from what would be an exciting and adventurous life.

* * * *

Still now, in my old age, I can taste that burned shoe string and can smell and feel that pungent smoke in my nostrils. Years passed and Rake and I graduated to our grandfather's cigarette butts, which he had saved for rolling more cigarettes. A few years after that, we would raid the tobacco leaves from his garden at the farm outside Oulu. We would carefully dry them in the warm sun and would roll them into fat cigarettes. We used a fresh tobacco leaf for the outer cover. We were children and already viewed ourselves as connoisseurs of good smoke.

As I sit back and think about these days, truly the "good days," my mind wanders. There were plenty of hard times during the war. But there were good times as well. What I remember most is a strong zest for life and an enthusiasm for the discovery of all things new. Even in the rough times, even during the devastation of our country by the Russians, were things proven to be wonderful in their own right. The day the Russians came and bombed our city was the day that my cousin and I first discovered the "joys" of smoking. Even with the devastation, things worked out for the best, sooner or later. This fact has been proven to me a thousand times as being a gift from God.

* * * *

After what seemed like an eternity, the sirens finally stopped and we slowly and cautiously emerged from our shelter. Reaching the street level, fires could be seen burning within a block of our apartment building. Everyone, the young and the old, looked upon the scene with heavy hearts. Our faces were a fixed expression of sorrow. Some wept openly, but most moved along, dragging their feet against the ground, in complete silence and disbelief. This most recent bombing was one of many in a campaign that was slowly but surely crumbling our city. We were left with numbness as though we had become immune to this wreckage. Almost everyone moved trancelike.

The air was silent now except for the slow shuffle of feet against the earth. We had finally reached the safety of our apartment. Both Rake and I were sent to bed, thankful for the warmth of our blankets and that our apartment building had been untouched in this latest attack. I was still able to taste burned shoe string coating every surface of my mouth. Falling off to sleep, in my mind I could still hear the reverberations of the bomb blasts.

* * * *

The Finnish-Russian war (The Winter War) was fought between the years of 1939-1940. Russia had assumed that Finland would be no match for them. However, Finland's resistance came as a surprise to the Russian forces, as our people displayed more obstinacy than Russia could have anticipated from our small country. Finland fought gallantly for as long as they were able, but our small country was no match for the Russians' air bombardments and well prepared frontal attacks.

Early in 1940 events on the Karelian Isthmus brought the Finnish resistance to the verge of collapse. In the peace treaty signed in March of that year, Finland ceded part of Karelia, Viipuri and several border territories to the USSR, but the fighting was not to end there.

The "Continuation War" began in June 1941 and lasted till 1945. Here Finland began fighting again against the Russians, but not alone. We had signed an agreement to let Germany attack the Soviet Union across the Finnish border. Our country entered into this conflict with the determination to get back the territories in Karelia and the North, which we lost in The Winter War. The attack was stopped in Karelian Isthmus at the old border line from the war before, only some ten kilometers from Leningrad.

After two and a half year of trench warfare, the Soviet Union started their counter attack in June 1944 on Karelian Isthmus as well as at the Lake Ladoga. Because of the threat of military collapse, the Finnish troops were withdrawn quickly and retreated back towards the border line after The Winter War.

Meanwhile, the German troops were fighting against the Russians in northern Finland, mainly in Lapland. When the cease fire agreement between Finland and Soviet Union was signed, one of the terms in the agreement stipulated that the unwanted German presence in Finland must leave in two weeks with all their equipment. Because it was impossible for the Germans to leave, especially on such short notice, the Finnish troops invaded the Finnish coastal towns that were under German control. This caught the German troops by complete surprise but as revenge for these attacks the Germans conducted a scorched earth policy with Lapland receiving the brunt of it. As the Germans retreated, they burned every village they came to destroying all bridges and as a last ditch revenge, sowed mines throughout the North. Within a short period of time, the Germans inflicted more damage to Finland than the Russians ever did.

The Germans left, but with the Russian peace treaty, Karelia and part of Northern Finland was taken over by the Russians. They also commandeered a small part of southern Finland, west of Helsinki called Porkkala. This area did provide Russia a strategic harbor in The Gulf of Finland which was to be turned back to Finland after fifty years. The peace treaty came with a large price tag but at least Finland would be independent once more.

After the war, our little country borrowed money for re-building from the United States just as most other countries ravaged by the war had done. It is on record, which we are very proud of, that Finland was the only country who ever repaid the United States their war debts. There is a word in the Finnish language *sisu* which translates to "internal strength and fortitude" and the Finns claim the suffering brought this about making them strong and proud.

* * * *

Our home was in the city of Hameenlinna, just north of Helsinki. My mom was home with my sister, Inga who was born just a year after I was. We lived in a small house next to the famous Hotel Aulanko with its national park and lookout tower. That is where my mother worked as a food and beverage checker. Everything that emerged from the dining room must be checked by her before it was delivered to the guests. Inga was only three and was being taken care of by our next door neighbor who was running a small nursery. It was difficult for my mother to take care of us with her busy work schedule, so I was often with my grandparents.

The war had ravaged Finland and no one had the needed money or supplies to live on due to the war. My father was stationed along the Karelian border where most of the heavy fighting took place. Left alone with two small children, my mother made the difficult yet necessary choice. Inga would be staying with my mother in Hameenlinna while I was sent to live with my grandparents on their farm north of Oulu. She simply did not have the resources to care for both of us. My grandparents stepped in gladly. I would miss my mother, but even at that age I could remember understanding why I must go. Admittedly, I was excited to spend time on the farm with my grandparents.

* * * *

The following morning, my grandfather made his announcement to the family. We would be leaving immediately for Rantala, their farm fifteen miles northwest of Oulu. I was to stay there until the war was over. Rake was not happy for this news as he was losing me, his friend and co-conspirator, but my grandmother did her best to make him forget his sorrow.

We left that morning, in the winter of 1942, to start our journey to the farm.

2

IT WAS A FIFTEEN MILE-DRIVE over a frozen country road. It had been well plowed, but icy ruts still covered the whole distance making the ride slow and jarring. My grandfather's prized 1938 Model Ford, his pride and joy, had been packed to the maximum for this trip. To me, the jet-black car looked like a big box on four wheels. The inside was a marvel of dials, switches and handles. This, of course, fascinated me the most. Grandfather had bought the car in Helsinki a few months earlier. He could often be seen with his handkerchief, wiping off some small mud specks on the hood. Worried about possible spills, he admonished us not to eat or drink anything while riding in his car.

He drove slowly and carefully, trying to avoid the biggest ruts, only to hit ones even bigger than the last. I was in the back, squeezed in amongst bags of clothes and other items, trying to look out of the frosted window. I saw nothing but a frozen snake of a road meandering between the snow banks and a telephone pole every so often. The tops of the pine trees were visible in the distance. We occasionally passed clumps of birch trees. The black patches on their trunks stood out sharp against the otherwise white, snow-covered world. It was rather flat with only a few small hills and a smattering of red farmhouses here and there. The smoke from their chimneys wafted lazily into the sky. The colder it was, the straighter the smoke and today, it was straight as an arrow.

After a seemingly endless ride, my grandfather, Ukki, as I called him turned the car right onto a small, unplowed side road. The only tracks to be seen in the deep snow were from a horse drawn sled. Between the two runners, I could see the hoof marks from the horse. Ukki expertly guided his Ford onto the path of the runners and slowly made his way down the drive. Soon, we stopped by a small cabin nestled within some pine trees. Ukki got out and walked to the front door and knocked. A bearded, slightly stooped, old man greeted him. He motioned Ukki inside while my grandmother and I waited in the car.

I sat inside patiently with Fammu, as I called my grandmother. It was beautiful there, stopped alongside the cabin. Outside was a winter wonderland. The small cabin was nearly buried up to two small dark windows, with a heavy load of snow on the roof that seemed to push the cabin into the ground. All the surrounding tree limbs were drowsily drooping from the weight of the snow piled on them. The only visible sign of someone living here was the cabin and the nearby barn. Smoke rose from their chimneys. It was eerily quiet.

Finally, the front door opened again. The man limped with Ukki toward the car. He was bundled up in a heavy parka and wore a colorful four star, blue, red, green and yellow Laplander hat. I could see the bread crumbs on his beard when he came to greet us. Ukki told us that we would have to leave the Ford here until the road to Rantala would be plowed. The man would be taking us by horse and sleigh for the next two miles to the farm. My heart jumped. I was excited. It would be a sleigh ride like in the picture on the Christmas cards I had seen.

The man shuffled toward the barn to fetch his horse. At least ten minutes went by before he led out a very large, furry, dark brown, Northern working horse by the bridle. Steam was rising from the warm horse as it hit the cold air. Its breath billowed like smoke. The horse was hooked up to the sleigh and was working to free it from the ice and snow. I could see the energy that it was expending to free the sled. With one final pull, the sled was free and the man muttered something in the horse's ear and tenderly rubbed its nose.

There was plenty of room in the sleigh. In the back half of the sleigh, my grandparents stacked up their belongings, leaving plenty of room for all of us. We were dressed warmly of course, but the cold left us with our teeth chattering. We sat down on the flat bottom on a pile of multi colored quilts and the old man handed us three more large thick ones which each of us wrapped around ourselves. We were cold through and through by now, but as the sleigh plunged forward with a sudden yank, the quilts began to slowly warm us up. We were moving toward the woods on a wooden bridge over the frozen creek draining from Jaalen Lake, the Lake at Rantala.

After a while, we joined a deep rutted snow road with countless hoof marks and sled tracks. To our left I could see more of Jaalen Lake. The road showed heavy use circling the lake toward the small community of Jaali with its few homes and small farms, post office, general store and a blacksmith shop. I knew we were very close to Rantala.

Last summer, my grandmother had taken me for a long walk to purchase some groceries and to pick up the mail. There was not much to buy due to the war shortage, but they always had a lollipop for me, making the long trek worthwhile. The strawberry flavored lollipop lingered on my tongue all the way back to the farm.

The sun was still struggling to shed some light, but it was losing the battle. It was early afternoon but dusk was settling in when I saw the farm ahead. A tall red house peeked out through the pine trees as we got closer. Other buildings began to appear. A large woodshed, the main barn with the two silos next to it painted bright white, which blended in with the snow almost making it completely disappear except for the black trim around the windows and doors. As we entered the yard, I could see the ever important sauna by the lake with a wooden pier jutting out into the ice covered lake. A shoveled path from the main house led up to it.

To the left of the main building was a small idyllic two story chalet, built in the Swiss Tyrolean style with a porch on each floor. This was the *aitta*. Downstairs were the storage for grain, wheat, rye and an underground cellar for potatoes, vegetables, jams and berries for the winter. Upstairs were small quarters used for guests during the summer. Behind the aitta was the all important outhouse painted the same barn red. From the main house, there was a well traveled foot path between the two.

In the middle of the yard towered the tall well structure. We had always been warned not to play around the well and scary stories had been told of what happened if we did not listen. Children had fallen into wells and drowned, so stay away, the grownups had said. Over the years, however, it happened to careless grownups too.

There was still another building. It was a massive long roof with no walls, only supported by one pillar after another, sheltering hundreds of cages. This was the mink farm my grandparents had started a few years back. Over six hundred minks were kept underneath this roof. The cold weather here was perfect for growing healthy, furry minks. They were elegant creatures with their silk like fur, their long, arched, slender bodies glimmering against the snow. But they were vicious. They would try to attack anyone that approached, baring a mouthful of razor sharp teeth against intruders. Had I been foolish enough to stick a finger in the cage, I would not get my finger back. Ukki had told me that this was the last season for minks. Although profitable, the work was too much work. After this lot would leave, that would be the end of mink farming.

The main barn housed a dozen milk cows, pigs, four working horses and one riding horse, named Juha, after me. This was my horse. My grandfather had given him to me as a present against Fammu's wishes. She was worried that I was too young to ride. Fortunately, he did not listen and began teaching me how to handle the horse and how to ride confidently. It was daunting because the horse was gargantuan compared to me. But in a short time, I learned how to ride on my own in the yard. I was proud sitting atop this massive animal. After riding alone for a month or so, one of the farmhands and I went for a ride in the woods, stopping for a short break. He had to help me back on the horse after our break. He had just put me in the saddle when out of nowhere, my horse decided to kick. The farmhand had been passing along the rear of my horse when it happened. Its hoof landed square on the young man's jaw, throwing him several feet. I was so scared I don't know how I managed to ride home alone for help. That night, I visited the boy in the hospital. The poor lad was in agony and Ukki informed me that his bones would never heal correctly and most of his teeth were broken. All my life I have thought about this boy, feeling guilty because it happened when he was helping me, always wondering how he made it through the ordeal. I never saw him again but always hoped that the hospital had been able to help him.

We had reached the main house. The long peaceful ride was over. The old man halted the horse by the kitchen entrance and Ukki called out to someone in the house. The caretaker Mr. Kolli and his wife and three children lived on the lower level of the farmhouse. They had been employed by my grandfather for over four years doing most of the chores around the farm. They were evacuees from the Eastern front, having escaped the anticipated war with the Russians. From day one at Rantala, they proved to be a tremendous asset to my grandparents, assuring that the farm ran smoothly. Someone peeked through the kitchen

11

window. I could see the face of a young girl, mouth open, looking surprised. Shortly, Mr. Kolli was buttoning his heavy jacket and coming out to greet us. He looked startled, not knowing that we were coming. The telephone lines had been down for several months otherwise Ukki would have called ahead.

"Terve tuloa,"--welcome, he greeted us and reached to shake Ukki's hand. Their faces lit up at seeing each other. Mr. Kolli nodded to Fammu and me and repeated the greeting. His accent was Eastern Finnish. He was a stout and rather short man. He looked very heavy all bundled up in his brown puffy parka with a reindeer fur collar protecting his neck. Ukki explained to him that we were going to stay there for the rest of the winter and upcoming summer, perhaps even longer.

We made our way up the stairs to our living quarters. The stairs were covered in snow and two of the older sons appeared with shovels in order to clear the steps for us. Both of them looked like their father, strong and sturdy and well suited for the work required at Rantala. Mr. Kolli told us later that he could never do the work at the farm without the help of his boys. His wife Kaisa and their young daughter also did their fair share, more so in the house and in the garden in the summer.

We emptied the sleigh of our belongings and Ukki bid farewell to the old man and his horse. I saw him slip him some money for his time and transportation. The old man thanked us and shushed the horse for a leisurely trip back home. I was happy to have reached this point, settling our belongings inside the house. We would be safe from the bombings and I would be safe from any further experiments that Rake had in mind for me. Although I missed my companion and associate in troublemaking, I was looking forward to the rest of the winter and of course the summer, which was the best time to be at Rantala. But now, it was time to eat. Kolli's had invited us for a welcoming feast.

3

KAISA, KOLLI'S WIFE, WAS BUSY in front of the old black wood stove in her colorful long apron. She was holding a large homemade wooden ladle. In the other hand she was holding a pot holder and resting on the rim of a black skillet. She turned her head towards us and greeted us. Her genial warm smile reached her small eyes which twinkled. She wore her life of hard work on her face now wreathed in wrinkles on her forehead and under the eyes. Her light brown hair was tied into a bun hanging over one of her strong shoulders. She was not a large person but you could see her strength and her determination from her stature.

Still holding on to the pot, glancing at it at the same time, she said, "Please go to the dining room. I am almost done with dinner. We are having moose stew tonight," she said cheerfully," my husband shot it a couple of weeks ago," she continued, in the dialect of eastern Finland, which was so deep and hard to understand at times. Before stepping into the dining room, Fammu handed a pot of berry soup to Kaisa with careful instructions how to serve it. She was very particular with her creations.

It was warm in the kitchen from the wood fire in the stove, and the air was mixed with the wood smoke from the fire and the aromas of the cooking foods. We were famished from our journey that day and ready to eat. We were led to the dining room, where the rest of the family had gathered around a large rough wooden table. Benches surrounded it. Anja, their young daughter was still finishing setting the table. She took her eyes away from the table and nodded, saying "Hei, as she continued her task. She was a small girl with a very pretty face framed by long blond curly hair. Her eyes were emerald green. She was simply beautiful for her age and resembled her mother in many ways. The boys sat at one side of the table on a long bench and Mr. Kolli was seated at the head, waving for us to come and join. After greeting everyone, Ukki sat down opposite the boys, but Fammu continued walking to the far side of the room and I followed her towards a large metal bird cage, where "Goia" resided.

Goia was a tall very colorful parrot that had been brought to her parents from Venezuela by a sea captain friend. Her parents had passed Goia along to Fammu when she was in her twenties which meant that she had been caring for the parrot some forty years. Seeing Fammu, the parrot made some funny parrot sounds. It did know how to say thank you in Swedish: "tack so mycket," but that was the extent of its vocabulary. My grandmother only spoke to the parrot in Swedish and for that matter, to us also, even though she knew, how to speak Finnish. I was never quite sure why my grandmother adhered to strictly to the Swedish language instead of Finnish. Even I did not speak Finnish well because the common language even with my cousins was Swedish. Goia had been left in the Kolli's care from the previous summer and looked as healthy as ever. He continued to squawk a few words and sounds here and there while preening his glamorous feathers. After talking with the parrot for a while, we went and joined the table, Fammu sat next to grandfather and I joined the boys.

They had set a small pillow on the bench for me. Jussi, Kolli's robust son, was sitting next to me chewing on a piece of dark brown bread called limmpu, the true Finnish soul food bread, made with rough rye flour and molasses. He reached out and offered the bread basket to me, explaining that his mother had baked it earlier in the day. I took a piece of the thinly sliced bread slathering it with a big chunk of dark yellow homemade butter which had been made by Kolli in the barn. It was a delicious, hearty, earthy slice. A hint of molasses spread over my tongue when I bit into it. My stomach growled. I was so hungry. Bread had never tasted so wonderful. The boys and I were munching on the bread, as Ukki was talking with Kolli about the winter and the live stock.

Dancing flames from the fireplace were casting shadows and warmth from the fireplace, creating a very comfortable mood. The table was set with thick

14

white ceramic plates with faded blue rims with some chips, which showed years of use. The gleaming silverware was old and heavy, which probably was used only on special occasions. A tall glass sat in front of everyone and a huge pitcher of milk next to a smaller pitcher of buttermilk, in the center of the table. Typical country fare, legend said that butter milk gave you strength and kept you warm in the winter. Looking at Mr. Kolli and his strapping young sons, I had no doubt that this was true. Even Ukki swore by the stamina he gained from buttermilk.

"Dinner is ready," Kaisa called out coming from the kitchen followed by Anja, each carrying a large blackened cast iron pot. They set the pots on the table, one on each end.

"I hope you like my cooking?" she said looking at Fammu, a bit nervously.

"Kaisa, we know that you are a superb cook, having had dinner with you many times before," Fammu answered giving the hostess a friendly and assuring smile. Kaisa seemed to relax as she continued to put food on the table, with a slight smile of relief.

Now Kolli himself had to agree, "She is the best, let's eat," he continued reaching for the pot close to him.

"You are now going to eat my catch, a moose-, which I shot three weeks ago in the woods right behind the mink farm," he announced with a hint of pride. "It was a monstrous animal -taller than a horse," he continued with a broad smile. "I had been stalking it for many weeks and finally got lucky. The antlers are huge, hanging on the wall in the wood shed," he told us, spreading his arms out in an attempt to show us how big they were before spooning his first serving on a plate.

With Mr. Kolli continuing his adventure with the moose, everyone began eating, passing beets and carrots, the moose stew, bread and milk. Kaisa, who sat next to me at the end of the table, ladled a big heaping of meat, potato and onion, and beets which had been cooked in the stew pot. She set it in front of me. I stared at the plate. It contained so much food. It scared me. I looked at Fammu for help, but all she did was just nod her head, saying, "Juha, be a good boy and eat," in Swedish. I picked up my fork and tasted the moose and liked it. It tasted a little different from the regular beef which I was used to, but this was good, and so tender. As the dinner proceeded, the food in the pots and on the table seemed to disappear. For a while, we could only hear the silverware clanging and a slight hissing noise from the kerosene lantern hanging over the table that cast a yellowish light. I was staring into my dish which looked untouched, even though I had been eating and forcing down some more. I was hoping that my food would magically disappear, but it didn't. I could not eat any more. Heikki, the younger brother, nudged me whispering into my ear "Don't worry the dogs will get the rest."

"Kaisa, you have outdone yourself," Ukki said looking up from his plate. He leaned back in his chair and patted his stomach. "I have eaten plenty of moose dinners, cooked every which way, but this is the best," he said with a big grin looking at Kaisa.

Kaisa smiled, blushed, looking around the table turning her gaze to Grandfather "Thank you, Heino." This was my grandfather's name. The Kolli's addressed my Grandparents by their first name, Fammu's first name being Edith, whereas they called Mr. Kolli, as just Kolli. His first name was Ilmari. I had never heard anyone call him by that name. "The recipe is from my grandmother who lived in Itajarvi, located almost directly east of us and now in Russia after they commandeered that part from Finland." There was a sad tone in the last part of her comments. "We used to cook many wild animal meats back home, we even ate bear sometimes, When we got married, Ilmari enjoyed this type of food. Now here at the farm, we of course have the luxury of eating pork, beef, chicken and lots of seafood, but once in a while wild game tastes good and it is fun to cook. Brings up memories," Kaisa said, looking at her husband with her bright blue eyes and loving smile.

Kolli stretched his arm, laying it on his wife's shoulder and looking at her tenderly, "You are so right, but I do enjoy the farm food much better, yet hunting is still in my blood. I only kill what we can eat. I even skinned the moose. The hide is enormous. I have not decided yet what to do with the pelt," Kolli pondered aloud.

"We could make some moccasins from the moose pelt," Jussi said chuckling.

The father looked at him and said," Are you going to chew the hide to cure it, just like the Eskimos used to do?" and with a grin he added, "first you piss on it to get the salt and acids to soften the hide and then you chew and chew. What do you think about that?"

"I will make the moccasins, but Heikki can do the chewing and pissing," he said looking at him with a crooked smile, knowing full well that the moccasin idea was not accepted by his brother.

"Forget it," Heikki growled back. "You piss and chew yourself. It is your idea," he said, moving a bit closer to me.

"I will ask my son at Astrom leather factory if they are willing to cure the hide for us," Fammu interjected. "I think he will have them do it. He owns the factory, so I don't see why he would not help" she said nodding her head.

Ukki was just sitting there and listening to the conversation, but finally joined in.

"Kolli, tell me about the winter so far," he said, not having been to Rantala since last October. "How did the animals survive the cold weather?" he inquired.

Kolli looked across the table thoughtfully and said."Well, we had no major problems. Twice we had to drive to Jaali and bring back the veterinarian, once for one of the cows suffering from breach birth while delivering. We made it back just in time. The cow is well, but unfortunately the calf did not make it." He looked sad as he told this. The trauma of this delivery had affected everyone, when they are so helpless in these cases. He continued, looking at me. "Juha, your horse, suffered from some ankle sprain which the veterinarian was able to bring under control with medicine and a tight bandage. The horse seems to be fine now."

"What about the minks?" Ukki asked.

"All the minks are healthy with shiny fur. I believe that the sunflower seed addition to their diet was a big improvement. There had been some wolves prowling around and we were worried that they would try to get to the minks, but so far they have not. I shot one wolf about a month ago, perhaps this scared the rest of them off," he said nodding.

"Aren't we all glad that this is the last season for the minks," Fammu commented, looking around the table, noticing everyone nod their head. "I think that the time for some dessert is in order. I will help you with it, Kaisa," she said rising up from the bench.

Anja and the boys also got up to clear the table of the dinner dishes. Jussi was holding on to his stomach after eating too much. I could hardly move from so much food, but managed to collect the glasses and take them to the kitchen. Goia was babbling in the cage. The men remained seated, conversing about the on-going war and the bombing raids on Oulu, so close by.

Kaisa and Fammu left for the kitchen returning shortly with the pot of berry soup and colorful bowls. The pot and bowls were placed in front of Fammu, who proceeded to ladle the hot soup with a theatrical flair, lifting the ladle slightly higher than necessary letting the soup cascade into a bowl and passing it along. All eyes were glued to this show, knowing that it was important to give her some extra recognition, which she of course loved. I must say, it was good and sweet. Everyone else joined in announcing how much they enjoyed it. My grandmother was beaming and happily uttered, "Thank you. I am glad you like it," she said reluctantly, in Finnish, as Kollis did not speak Swedish.

I left the table to talk with Goia. It was babbling something in parrot language moving to the end of the perch, bending its head so the beak rested on the thick wooden rod. This meant for me to scratch its colorful head. I did, as it was a ritual, Goia sounding like it was purring in a short guttering gargle. This went on for a while. Goia would have liked it to last for hours, but it would be time to leave soon, so I bid the bird good night and walked back to the table.

"Looks like Juha is tired and ready to leave and you get up so early in the morning to feed the livestock. You must be tired. It has been a long day," Ukki commented using me as a good excuse to end the dinner party, getting up at the same time.

"Kaisa and Kolli, this was just a fine evening. Thank you." We shook hands with the family. Kolli's hand was rough like sand paper and huge. I was only able to squeeze one of his fingers.

"Oh- I almost forgot, please have the horse and sled ready by eight thirty tomorrow morning. I will meet the company car at the main road. I must go back to the office. I will have the road plowed to Rantala tomorrow, so that we can drive all the way. Thank you again. See you in the morning, "Ukki told Kolli.

We bid the Kollis good night and proceeded into the mud room for a heavy dress up, all this just for a few minutes' walk around the building. I was tired and grumpy by now, secretly hoping that Ukki would carry me, which he actually wound up doing after Fammu's coaching. I was happy. When he picked me up I mellowed down a few degrees.

The stars shone like diamonds in the sky. I could see the Big Dipper and had learned to look for the North Star. As we crunched our way around the building, I was imagining that the North Star was guiding us home. The moon hung in the shape of a lemon peel.

4

I SLEPT WELL THAT NIGHT. THERE were no wailing sirens or bombs exploding nearby. This first night back at the farm, I was finally able to sleep well. I dreamed of fishing and hunting.

Late August, last summer, Rake and I had set a noose trap, a simple "hang man's" thin wire snare across the path of some plump hares we had seen. They had created such a noticeable trampled path with its telltale signs of droppings. We were sure to catch one.

Early next morning we left to check the trap, anticipating our catch. Approaching the trap slowly, coming around the last bend, we could see that our trap had worked. A large plump snow hare was limp, caught in the noose. We could see the disturbed pine needles and dirt beneath the poor creature as it fought against the trap for its last breath. We both were sad and elated at the same time as we took it off the noose and carried it home, taking turns. The following day the hare was our dinner. Fammu had skinned and cleaned the meaty hare, oven roasting it under slow heat, with potatoes, carrots and onions. It was delicious. We were mighty hunters, which in itself made the wild gamy meat melt in our mouth.

That night however, I dreamt the hare was a gorilla, but it was still alive in the trap as I was tiptoeing closer. I could see that the gorilla was friendly as it looked at me with tearful eyes, beckoning for help. I was not afraid of it. I walked up to it talking in a peaceful voice, telling it that I was a friend and felt sorry for having set the trap and that I would help it get out. After I carefully cut the noose off, as to not hurt the gorilla any more, I sat down on the soft cushion of pine needles next to a hefty stump. The gorilla joined me and sat on the stump, looking down at me in a smiley way telling me how thankful it was for my help and assured that it would always protect me from harm. I hugged it and it hugged me back tenderly. We would always be friends.

As I woke up, I kept thinking about this gallant dream and wondering if it really lived in the woods.

As I was laying there stretching and looking at the ceiling, it occurred to me that this was the same bed and the same room where I had laid for over one month, close to death with serious second degree burns and infections after accidentally pouring extremely hot water on myself. How fearful this serene room felt, during the recovery period, when in horrible pain I had cried myself to sleep only to encounter nightmares. My jaw, throat, stomach and upper inner arms were raw with the skin peeling off in sheets as pus and ugly smelling matter poured from my wounds. The memories were so vivid, never be forgotten and as reminder to this day, I still carry the scars on my stomach and inner arms, luckily not on my face. I was only a year and a half old at the time and still carry the horrible memories of this event with me as though it were a movie to be played over and over again.

Shortly before the accident, I had learned to walk and run, being wild like any other toddler at that age. On this particular evening, I was standing by the picture window in the living room overlooking the lake, holding a large crystal vase in my hand precariously close to the window. Grandmother came out of the kitchen carrying a pitcher of boiling water for the washroom. Seeing what I was doing she became scared that I might break the window with the vase. She set the pitcher on the coffee table, running over to me to retrieve the missile from my hand. As she pried it away, I turned around and scooted to the table, picked up the pitcher without knowing how hot the water was, and began to drink it. No sooner than when the scalding water hit my lips, my instant reaction was push it away and in so doing, the whole pitcher spilled with the boiling water running down the front of my body. I screamed from the instant, searing pain. Fammu ran over immediately grabbing hold of me and lifting me to her bosom, holding me tight as she ran to the kitchen to splash cold water on my chin. This was during mid winter and I had been bundled up in heavy woolen clothing. As she is hugging me, she did not realize that the water had run down my clothing and her desperate attempt to soothe me and attend to my face she was baking my upper body with the boiling clothing. When she realized this, it turned out to be too late. The clothing had glued itself onto my raw skin which could not be removed without the skin peeling off at the same time. I do not remember exactly what happened after that. I must have passed out from the pain. I later woke with the doctor's face hovering over me. I was lying naked on the bed in excruciating pain with some hideous smelling salve covering half of my body. That night, the doctor stayed in the room with my grandmother. They were so worried that it might be the end of me. I kept hallucinating in and out of a turbulent interrupted sleep, which seemed to go on endlessly night and day. Soon the infections came, which the doctor was able to bring under control somehow. The ceiling was my view which I kept staring noticing every small blemish in the paint.

My mother had been rushed to Rantala having been devastated by the news. She told me many years later that she had a premonition of something fearful happening to me, just at the time when it did. She stayed with me at my bedside and prayed and read aloud hour after hour and comforted me as much as possible. After a week she had to return back to Hameenlinna. Inga had been born five months earlier and had been left with my mother's good friend as she rushed up to my bedside.

The longest month in my memory had passed. Somehow, I was now able to get out of bed for a few weak steps all bandaged up, whereas while in the bed I had been covered only with a loose layer of gauze. It felt wonderful to be up and about even so my legs hardly were able to support me. I had become a skinny little boy, but determined to soon be able to run around again.

After about three months, I was feeling rather well but the memory of this ordeal would never go away, nor would the scars.

Almost directly above me on the ceiling was still the old paint blemish which looked like a mouse with a curled up long tail. I had named this mouse Mikko, after someone's name in one of the stories read to me by Fammu while recuperating from the burn. I said good morning to Mikko as I finally got out of bed. I had asked Fammu last night to wake me up early enough to see Ukki off, but being excited after my first night at Rantala, I had woken up on my own.

Ukki and Fammu were sitting in the kitchen having coffee and crackers with cheese; a typical Finnish breakfast. We used to eat so much cheese and other dairy products including heavy cream with coffee, until years later when the country became alarmed over the high heart attack rate. The doctors and media began a strong promotion concerning the health hazards of these items. It eventually sank into people's mind, and the number of heart attacks were cut in half. During those times, no one knew about these dangers, thinking that these heavy foods would ward off the cold during the freezing winters.

Ukki, dressed in a business suit and tie, was ready to leave. He had always commented how much he enjoyed being casually dressed or in his hunting out-fit around the farm. His retriever dog named, Jasse that had its own kennel by the wood shed, apparently could read what was going to happen that day from Ukki's dress code. When he usually approached the dog in his hunting clothes, the dog went wild. Today Jasse would have a melancholy look on its face, and perhaps the tail would wag just a little.

From the kitchen widow, I could see Kolli approach with the horse pulling a small but ornate two person sleigh, painted black with a golden color scroll along its edges. The horse pulled the sleigh with ease and shook its mane loose in the frigid air. Kolli headed down towards our entrance and would wait there for Ukki. I was hoping that my grandfather would ask me to come along for the ride, but after few moments went by and he had not asked, I did. "Of course," he answered, smiling down at me. "I was hoping that you would want to come." He looked at his pocket watch. "Dress warm, we'll leave in five minutes." I rushed to my room, got dressed with the speed of a fireman and ran back to the kitchen. Fammu handed me a napkin tied into a bag, which she said contained some crackers and cheese for the trip. It was time to leave. Ukki hugged Fammu giving her a long kiss and told her that he would be back in two days. He often stayed in the apartment in the past, instead of traveling back and forth daily. Now that the bombing was going on, it was scary. Fammu told him to be careful. Many times his job required for him to work late hours or travel to other locations.

Kolli greeted us and helped me up. This was so much more comfortable than the previous ride the day before. After getting settled and bundled up in quilts, we took off. Kolli had harnessed the horse in the "Sunday" harness with several small shiny bells. The horse set out at an even trot with the bells ringing and sled runners shushing through the bright white landscape. The ride back to the old man's cabin, and the car, was fast. The Ford was covered in frost and a light layer of delicate white snow. We continued up a gradual slope to the main road. Ukki's chauffeur was waiting there, sitting in the car with the motor running. The car was a French Peugeot which Ukki had ordered, on behalf of the government, for his personal company car. A chauffeur went with it. The car and his pictures were written up in The Oulu newspaper, the car being the first Peugeot in Finland. In the picture he was leaning against the car with a big, proud grin on his face.

Ukki's employer was the Finnish Government Forest Department. He was the head of the Forest Department for the Oulu region. This region was quite large, reaching up north almost to Rovaniemi. Kemi was to the east, and some one hundred miles south. He was on the road often, traveling through the region on various inspections. North of Oulu a new hydroelectric power station was in the planning stages. This project occupied much of his time in the office and on the site. Other travels took him to visit farmers in distant locations, who had requested his presence and help to iron out pressing land problems. Very often he returned home with presents of meat, vegetables, and chickens and once with a live piglet as a token of appreciation of his help. Fammu never knew what he would bring next.

One of these "gifts" was the worst food I ever remember tasting. Some farmer down south had sent along with Ukki some pickled river leeches. They tasted as badly as they sounded and looked awful. The leeches looked horrid in a glass jar that illuminated them from every angle and magnified them as well. They were dark brown, fat and long like a cigar and tasted slimy, rubbery and muddy. Ukki had cut me a good size chunk on a dish and setting it front of me, urging for me to taste the "morsel." I put it in my mouth and chewed it only once, immediately throwing up on the table. I began to cry, looking at the mess I had made. Ukki laughed but, Fammu scolded him, ordering him to take the rest of his leeches out and dump them. "Eat them on your way out," she shouted after him.

"Juha," She said, "that was the most disgusting food I have ever seen or tasted," while she wiped off my tears, the front of my shirt and the mess I had made on the table. "Don't feel bad, I tasted a little bit of it and almost threw up like you," she said patting me on the head. "Ukki is probably throwing up in the snow bank," she chuckled.

The chauffeur saw us coming so he got out of the car and opened the back door for my grandfather. Grandfather bid farewell to me and Kolli and climbed into the car. We waited for them to leave and I waved as the car pulled away.

"Juha, do you want to drive back?" Kolli asked me, knowing the answer.

"Yes!" I said all excited, climbing onto the front seat next to him.

Kolli handed the reins to me and I urged the horse to move with "aha" as I had heard being done and at the same time giving the horse a gentle smack on the rump with the reins. It took off slowly first but began trotting as soon as we reached the woods. I felt so proud and confident sitting there with Kolli. The horse responded to the slightest tension on the reins. Kolli kept telling me what to do, but never reaching for the reins, explaining the horse's sensitivity to the slightest pressure and verbal command. It seemed to me, as we moved along at an even trot, that these animals know the way, especially when the direction is home bound. The bells were ringing, with me at the helm.

As we were approaching Rantala, Kolli told me to drive directly to the barn, where he would un-harness the horse and leave the sleigh under a lean-to at the far end of the barn.

Kolli took over and backed the sled under the roof. He uncoupled the sled walking the horse through the barn door and into its stall, where he would un-harness it. I loved the smell of the horse barn. I had always liked the smell of a horse barn. To me, it was somehow a stimulating smell that always seemed to clear my mind. For some reason, the mixture of the horse and the smell of the manure had this effect on me. I remembered the crackers in my pocket and dug out the napkin bag, untied it and scooped the broken pieces into my hand offering them to the horse, who did not hesitate to reach for the morsels. Its tongue left a wet trail in my hand as it licked every crumb. I scratched its forehead and uttered thanks for obeying my commands and making me look good in front of Kolli. This experience was so exciting for me.

After attending to the horse, Kolli walked out without saying anything. He actually was a rather quiet person, speaking only when necessary. I decided to follow him where ever he was going. He was in the front and I tagged along behind him headed towards the mink building. Jussi and Heikki were there already feeding the large hungry lot. They must have been there for a while because I could see them in the center of the long rows of cages. Jussi called out and motioned for his father to come over where they were, lifting both arms up to indicate which direction they were preceding. To me it was thrilling to be surrounded by so many ferocious animals, ready to bite if given the chance.

They were fed every morning a nutritious slop of high protein animal byproducts mixed in cereal. The byproducts were purchased from many local farmers but the ingredients were mixed to a carefully controlled formula by Kolli himself at the end of the building, where a small room acted as a kitchen. He combined fish, poultry, egg shells and other animal byproducts into a huge iron kettle with tall legs and a wood burning fireplace under it. All this was boiled and later mixed with cereal consisting of wheat, rye and oats. Ukki had sent Kolli and Jussi for several days up north to a large mink farm, to learn all they could about minks, their diet requirements and mating habits and anything else they should know.

Both father and son had become proficient mink farmers over the past few years. Several books in Ukki's library were also available and he himself had made a point of learning about mink farming as much as possible.

Ukki had told me that the female minks were more valuable because they had a more lightweight fur with a thick under fur than the males. The buyers were critical of the color and the softness of the fur. There are many varieties of breeds, but our minks were mainly mahogany colored animals which seemed to be the most popular and brought the most money. Even at my young age, I had learned quite a bit about these animals making it interesting.

In the spring time, it was fun to see the baby minks hover around their mother. They grew quickly in just a few weeks and were soon moved to two in a cage. In September the minks were separated onto their individual cage so the fur would be damaged by their pen mate.

I left the Kollis to finish their chores. On the way to the house I had to make a stop in the outhouse located by the woodshed. It was bitter cold and seemed even colder inside as I closed the door and pulled down my pants, sitting down on the hole. My behind felt like I was sitting in the snow bank or on the ice covering the lake. Sitting there shivering, the light coming in through a heart shape opening in the door, I noticed that someone had carved their initials on the wooden wall just above the pile of old newspapers. There were other carvings here and there but I could not make out what they were. It was important to do your business as fast as possible in the winter, but in the summer I often sat a long time daydreaming and listening to all the animal sounds outside. The paper was rough old newspaper and this too was cold. It felt like sandpaper. I wondered if some of the news print had rubbed off on my behind. I chuckled at the thought if someone wanting to read the news, and having to look at my behind.

All of a sudden, there was a loud roar coming from outside. Swiftly I finished pulling up my pants and ran outside still buttoning up to see what was going on. It was the plow truck, which I guess Ukki had sent. It was driving into the yard snow shooting up in the air on both side of a large V-shaped plow, as it continued towards the barn. There it turned and plowed the front of the long barn coming up towards the house, circling it and driving away in the direction from which it came. All this took only some fifteen minutes, leaving us with a wide and well plowed roadway. Now Ukki could bring the car all the way to the farm.

Fammu was fixing lunch when I arrived inside, standing by the stove in her red and blue long apron.

"Juha, I saw you driving the horse when you came back," she said in a pleasant tone, while attending to the pot on the stove. "It takes a big man to drive the horses," she continued. "You looked so proud. It was nice of Kolli to let you drive."

My chest swelling a bit, I answered, "I am glad you saw it. It was exciting to steer the horse. Not hard at all. I want to do it all the time."

"Here, come and have some hot porridge," she said, ladling it into a bowl.

I was hungry after all the "work" and from the cold as I sat down for the hot meal. It was rough oatmeal porridge with milk and sugar and cinnamon sprinkles. The steam was rising, smelling delicious. After all the work I had done, it tasted very good and warming as it traveled down to my belly.

"Now there are just the two of us. Ukki probably will come back in a day or two," said Fammu, as she sat down to eat with me.

I could hear Goia babbling in the living room. Someone must have brought it up from Kolli's. The house already felt empty, not having Ukki around and yet it had only been a few hours. On many occasions last summer, there had been just the two of us but the summer time seemed different from now because there was so much to do and everyone stayed outside as much as possible. Even the mood in the summer differed from the winter mood. In the winter, people all over the country in general seemed to be in a surly mood due to the long darkness and cold weather. In the summer, it was just the opposite. People were happy and smiling like the buds that woke up from the long winter. The sunshine and gentle rain did miracles for everyone. We were already anticipating spring.

We moved into the living room where Fammu sat down at the piano and gently lifting the keyboard cover. I rolled Ukki's office chair next to the window, close to the grandfather clock, which I must remember to wind, sitting down and staring out over the lake. I could see something run across the field between the house and the sauna. As it came closer, I saw that it was a silver fox. It stopped, looked around and speedily took off for the far woods, its bushy tail swinging. The wildlife around the farm was a natural zoo with so many different animals. Many times the bears came out of the woods looking for something to eat around our dump. Moose roamed close to the farm, Wolves were not uncommon visitors, but unwelcome visitors. Fox, squirrels, hare, hawks and smaller birds of every kind moseyed or flew around all year long. The migrating birds, ducks and geese, had flown south a long time ago.

The room filled with the piano concerto of Beethoven's fifth, as Fammu's fingers glided across the keyboard in a skillful delicate touch. She played from memory after years of studying classical music. In her younger days, she had played a solo in a concert in the Antwerp Philharmonic orchestra. She grew up in Belgium when her parents moved there from Finland when she was a young girl. She had also played at the Helsinki Philharmonic Hall when visiting her home country. She was a concert pianist. Her upbringing was a fascinating journey. Her parents; the Von Hooks, lived in Belgium for many years, where she had attended a private exclusive girl's prep school and later the Musical Institute of Antwerp. Her father was a well known industrialist from an aristocratic family. Her mother was a celebrated gentile social lady. Growing up in this blue blood environment my grandmother inherited their traits and snobbishness, hence wanting to speak Swedish only, which was nothing but snobbery. Finnish, in her opinion, was considered below her dignity. Yet these facts put aside, she was a kind woman, even though she held on to her heritage.

She had an uncle, Captain William Hook, who sailed his cargo vessel to Vladivostok in Russia at the turn of the century. One thing after another led the captain into staying in Russia where he also became a wealthy business man, mainly in gold mining. He got married to a Chinese woman and as the history goes, they had a baby boy, who was born apparently at the same time that the Dalai Lama died in Tibet. A rumor circulated that the boy was kidnapped and had been taken to Tibet to become the new Dalai Lama because he was born at the same moment of the death of the ruler. The captain spent many years trying to search for his son in China and Tibet, without success. He was not welcome at the holy city of Lhasa, where he believed their son to be, so with sorrow he gave up the search. He visited Finland twice during this time. He died in Vladivostok, but not before opening a university in his name and donating it to Russia.

The captain's brother was also in Asia. He was a Lutheran missionary for many years until he was arrested by the Chinese and thrown in jail. The Chinese accused him of being a spy. They kept him imprisoned for eighteen years without any outside contact. He was released finally, an old shriveled up man with a long straggly beard and sent home to Finland where he was greeted with open arms. Everyone had thought he had died somewhere many years ago. He had enough strength left in him to tour Finland and Sweden to speak and write a book of his ordeal.

Fammu had met her first husband while in Belgium. He was a Swedish business man by the name of Sandelin. They had two sons, Borge who lives in Helsinki, involved in international commerce and Runar, who lives in Oulu and owned the Astrom leather factory, which had been founded by his father.

Fammu's first husband was an avid sailor, who I had believed had drowned in a severe spring storm off the coast of the Aaland Islands between Finland and Sweden. I came to learn later that Fammu had actually divorced her first husband due to his three weaknesses: the glee club in which he participated fanatically, port wine and ballerina girls. Rake, Anna-Lisa and Harri are my cousins here and in Helsinki there are three more cousins by Borge and his wife. Ukki was Fammu's second husband, an up and coming forester, who she met in Finland at a government dinner party, twenty eight years earlier. A few years later they got married, my father being their child. They also had a daughter, Elsa, who lived in Sweden, married to a Lutheran minister. There are two more cousins there.

The music of Chopin, Tchaikovsky, Mozart to Sibelius, was filling the room, with Fammu's playing without cease, switching from one composer to the next. She could sit there for hours without ever glancing for help from sheet music. The notes were imbedded in her mind. I sat and listened, looking out the window contemplating the upcoming summer with Rake and other cousins and friends who would be visiting. I was hoping that Inga also would be able to come to Rantala for the first time. I had not even met her yet, and she was my sister.

I was imagining how she looked. I had her painted as a beautiful young blond girl, giggly and happy. I had seen photographs taken of her as a small baby, but by now she was over three years old. I must ask my grandparents to arrange for her to come.

The time went by peacefully the following couple of weeks. Ukki came and went to work, sometimes staying for a few nights in the city. He had brought the car to the farm, leaving it in the wood shed after Jussi had cleared a spot for it. The chauffeur came and picked him up after he had spent a day or two with us, bringing him back again after his days at Rantala. The daily chores were attended to by the Kollis with me often tagging along, which they did not seem to mind. I learned how to milk a cow and what to feed the various animals. I spent most of my time with the horses and in particular with Juha, my horse. He still glanced at me questionably, with his big sad eyes, wondering if I had forgotten the mishap with the farm hand. Whenever I could snatch an apple from Fammu's fruit basket, I fed it to him. We had become good friends. Very rarely Kolli's wife or daughter was to be seen. The only time I saw Anja was early in the morning when she went to collect the eggs. It must have been her daily chore. Once I went to help her, but wound up playing with the small chicks instead. In the afternoons the family was indoors with the boys and Anja attending home school taught by the mother. The closest school would have been in Kiiminki, which was some ten miles away, which meant that it was impossible for them to attend without transportation, so Kaisa had taken on the task of home schooling the children. From what I had heard, the children were doing very well and were attentive students.

Life went on without any major problems. Everyone was looking forward to the arrival of spring. The temperature was slowly becoming warmer. The bombing of Oulu, thank God, had stopped, after such a long siege. We would be having visitors shortly. No one would tell me who was arriving or when. "Soon," they said. It was a surprise. I just had to wait and see who these secret people were. This was gnawing at me. Who could they be? I tried to coaxing the information from Fammu, but she just smiled in a sly way, shook her head, and said, "I don't know, we just have to wait."

What a liar, I thought.

5

A FEW MONTHS HAD GONE BY. I could feel some warmer weather arriving as the days became longer and could see the buds on the pussy willows beginning to blossom, and bare spots in the snow began to appear.

One sunny afternoon, Ukki surprised us by coming home early with two other people alighting from the car. Fammu and I rushed outside to meet them and to our great astonishment, one of them was my father. Joyfully I ran to him jumping up into his outreached arms for a bear hug. This hug was the first one in over a year. He looked stronger than I remembered and so handsome in his captain's uniform decorated with two medals and many stripes. The second man was a stranger. My father put me down and turned towards the stranger. His name was Stranos Kolmynsky, a Russian prisoner of war who had been assigned to Ukki's custody as a minimum security prisoner. My father had arranged for him to be left at Rantala for the duration of the war. Bowing deeply, Stranos greeted us in Russian, with a big grin that displayed two stainless steel teeth. He only spoke Russian my father told us. He was unshaved, the stubble protruding in uneven patches on his face; his clothes were baggy and dirty, his boots worn and dried into cracks. Standing there in front of us he appeared to be friendly, perhaps a little scared and uncertain of his new surroundings. He was studying us as much as we were wondering about him. This was a new experience to us, having a prisoner around. I faltered a little bit at greeting this man, wondering if I should have reason to fear him. The word "prisoner" was a terrifying word to me. I kept studying him, trying to figure out what type of person he was and wondered if he had any children at home. His bright brown eyes shone in a peaceful way and his smile seemed genuine. He looked so shabby and tired having fought in the war and having been a prisoner in some terrible camp. His hands were large and dried up, chapped from the cold. His worn appearance tended to disarm my concerns a bit. I decided that I would do everything to make him feel at home with us, maybe even teach him some Finnish. I would be his friend.

Fammu, with a puzzled look, finally asked my grandfather where this stranger was going to sleep, as she sized Stranos up and down, a critical expression on her face.

"We will clean up the wood working shop in the barn by the horses," he answered, his plan already formed. "That room will be perfect for him. There is a working brick stove for heat, all we need to do is get him a bed and some blankets. On top of it, I understand that this man is a very gifted wood worker, the tools and work bench are there ready if he wants to use them. He will be an extra farm hand for us," Ukki declared, starting to walk towards the barn, motioning for Stranos to follow. Stranos reached into the car grabbing a bundle of clothes heaving it over his shoulder and lumbered behind Ukki. Father and I went along.

Fammu still looked uncertain about these arrangements when she called out to us, "Don't stay too long, I will have some lunch ready soon. Come up—" she paused for a moment "and bring Stranos also."

To the left of the entrance leading to the horse barn was a small room, fitted as a wood shop with a long solid work bench and various tools neatly hanging on the wall. A tall cabinet stood against the far wall, next to a floor to ceiling wood stove made out of bright red bricks. The floor was covered with saw dust, wood chips and curled up shavings from the plain. The air was crisp with the smell of recent woodwork. To the right as we entered, was a stack of old planks and beams leaning against the wall. Ukki pointed at this pile, mentioning that he would have Kolli move it in and bring a bed from the house for him. This room would be his home. For how long, no one knew.

I was watching Stranos' expression while he was eyeing his new quarters. I could see that he was happy with a big smile and a friendly twinkle in his eyes. I felt another twinge of fear and could not help thinking about his countrymen bombing our country and killing our solders. I felt assured however that Father would not bring him to Rantala if he was not to be trusted. But it still worried me, still remembering the nights spent in the bomb shelter. This would be different from the prison camp where he had spent many months. Here he would have heat, a comfortable bed, and tools for his wood working knowledge and, of course, food. The food at the camp had been almost nonexistent. He had endured starvation and goodness knows what else.

"Da!- Da!." he kept repeating over and over, nodding his head. Walking around the room, he was picking up and inspecting a few tools, laying them back gingerly. Suddenly he reached out and shook my father's hand with a determined grip, nodding his head. He then turned to Ukki and repeated the same motions. He patted me on the head. One could see that he was relishing everything he saw. He set his meager bundle on the work bench when Ukki motioned for him to follow. There would be plenty of time for Stranos to discover everything about the farm. It was time for lunch. Fammu was waiting.

During lunch, my father was telling us about the heavy fighting his battalion had been involved in on the Eastern front. They had lost several of their comrades, and endured severe hardship. He had been granted one week leave of which he had already used four days at home with my mother and Inga, making this visit just an overnight stop. He would be leaving tomorrow. Hearing this, I became concerned about his safety. Would he return? Would he be wounded? I kept thinking about him fighting the enemy, wishing the war would end soon. The conversation around the table continued about the war, Ukki and Fammu's life on the farm, and of course about me. I assured him that he would have nothing to worry because I was a good boy, helping as much as I was permitted. It was a lively fun reunion. Father had no idea when he would be able to come back again. Stranos was eating and enjoying the food, not understanding a thing that was said. His appetite was never ending. Dressed in a worn and torn gray woolen turtleneck sweater with snowflakes knitted on the front, he did not deter the gathering, but instead seemed to add some color to it. So far everyone's apprehensions seemed to disappear. Stranos appeared to be well-liked. He devoured the food and kept nodding his head in genuine appreciation. I know I liked him.

That evening father carried me to bed, sitting down telling me about Mother and Inga and how nice it was to see them again after such long time. He told me how much he had missed all of us and hoping that the war would be over before long. Later he read me a book about children in Lapland living in tents and looking after reindeer. I must have fallen asleep, because when I woke up during the night, he was sleeping next to me. I hugged him, snuggled up and felt so safe and soon fell back into a deep peaceful sleep.

The following morning Fammu and I said good bye to my father wishing him safety and quick return. As Ukki's chauffeur drove the car away on the snowy road, I ran behind it as far as I could, wave and yelling that I loved him. I tried very hard not cry, but it was very difficult to hold the tears back.

Life turned back to a peaceful normality. Once in the while, we could hear airplanes fly over close to the tree tops. One day, five planes flew very low directly over the farm as the boys and I were standing in the yard. We waved at them, and one pilot even waved back, until we realized that they were Russians on their way to Oulu on a bombing mission. I wondered if Stranos had been a pilot. I hope not. With our experience with them dropping bombs on Oulu, I had a strong dislike for Russian pilots. We were petrified that they might drop bombs on us. Ukki assured us later that they would not bother dropping bombs on a farm. The bombing still took place in the city, but with less frequency.

Stranos was becoming familiar with his assigned duties, which in the winter consisted mainly of feeding the animals and keeping the barn clean. I tagged along with him often, and when working in his shop, I would sit for hours watching him repair and create wooden objects. We had become good friends. He was learning few words in Finnish and I a few in Russian but mostly we talked in some kind sign language. The first thing Stranos built in his shop was a large truck for me. I could actually sit in it and use my feet as pedals. It was painted blue and white; the Finnish colors. I was so happy and proud of my truck, running it around in the barn terrorizing the cows and pigs. The pigs retreated to the far corner of their pen, the cows were trashing around in their cubicles and mooing in unison. I was having so much fun, laughing out loud. When the snow completely disappeared, I would take it outside. Stranos was working on some other project which he would not show to anyone until finished. This he was able to make us understand in his own version of sign language running his finger over few months on a crude calendar. We wondered what it could be.

He ate with the Kollis daily. About two months later, he arrived for the evening dinner carrying something rather large wrapped in a blanket. He treated the bundle very gently. The Kollis tried to get him to reveal what was in the wrapping, but he shook his head and pointed up to the ceiling uttering, "Ukki."

After dinner, he came up the steps and knocked on our door. I ran down and opened the door inviting him in. Fammu and Ukki were in the living room reading, when he walked up to the coffee table, laying down the bundle, and carefully unwrapping it. To our amazement, there sat the most beautiful violin we had ever seen. This delicate instrument was sitting on top of a worn brown blanket. The box, varnish, strings and the neck with its scrolled end were perfect. He picked it up like a baby, tenderly, handing it to Ukki, who was standing next to him in utter disbelief. How in the world had he been able to build such a masterpiece with the crude tools and the wood available to him? Where did he get the strings? Later we learned that the strings were "borrowed" from one of our largest horse's tail. Stranos stood quietly watching our reaction, saying something in Russian which we did not understand. Ukki admired the violin, turning it and inspecting it from every angle, Fammu retrieved a bow that she had leaning in the corner by the book cases. She reached for the instrument, first looking at it closely in admiration also, setting it under her chin, bringing the bow to it. A soothingly beautiful sound emerged, as she was playing it eyes closed. I did not know she played the violin as well. Setting the violin down on the blanket she uttered her wonder at such a fine creation by our unknown war prisoner Grabbing Strano's large rough hands, she squeezed them looking into his eyes and proclaiming in Swedish how fine his instrument was. Stranos just stood there knowing from the tone of her voice, that it was a compliment.

Over the tenure of the Russian's stay with us, he built four more violins and gave them as gifts to my grandparents. Each one was a superb masterpiece. They became heirlooms to the whole family. To this day, my father treasures one of them. From the moment Stranos gave Fammu the beautiful violin, he was accepted as part of the family. Her attitude towards him was no longer cool or snobbish. His gesture had definitely warmed the icy demeanor she had toward him in the beginning.

6

I T WAS SAUNA NIGHT, JUST as it had been always at least once a week for
all Finns. It was an important ritual for cleanliness and relaxation both
mentally and physically. It did not matter what weekday one chose for this
important event, but here at the farm it normally was on Friday evenings.

Earlier in the afternoon, Kolli had announced that he would go down to
start heating the sauna. Hearing this I wanted to go along and help him, his
sons also joining. There was an important order of things to be accomplished
in preparing the sauna for the evening's enjoyment. Yes, to be in a state of enjoyment was right when it came to looking forward to this warm and soothing
experience later that night. Normally the whole family, parents, children, grandparents included, made it a social event. Sometimes neighbors, good friends or
other communal individuals joined. Modesty never entered anyone's mind. Having been brought up in such fashion, it was normal for everyone to get totally
undressed and enjoy themselves.

Years later, when my wife and I were visiting my mother, who by now lived
in Helsinki, there happened to be a documentary on the television called, One
Day in the Life of President Kekkonen, who was the Finnish president for some
twenty years. The camera followed the President from the time he got up in the
morning until bed time. A long segment took place in his sauna that evening.

We were shocked to see our President stark naked with four cabinet members, also stark naked taking the sauna with sweat running down their ample hairy frames, discussing the country's affairs. They ended the event by running into the swimming pool, steam rising from their hot bodies. After swimming or just standing in the water, they finally climbed out and toweled off. This was shown on public television. My mother and I were most embarrassed. All she could say repeatedly was, "hyi-hyi," meaning, "oh-my." Needless to say, we never forgot these fat men frolicking naked on Finnish television.

The sauna at Rantala was typical of any other sauna, perhaps a little larger. Kolli carried a bucket full of kindling for lighting the two stoves. Light snow was falling off and on this afternoon. The path had begun to thaw from the many warm days. At times, our steps had to skirt mud puddles, which to us was a welcome signal of springtime. Before entering the sauna, Jussi led us to the back of the building where we loaded up with wood for the stoves. As I stepped in through the doorway, the familiar odor of smoke and cedar hit me. Kolli was already in the hot room setting the kindling into the fireplaces as we dropped the wood next to him.

It was a very old and well used sauna. The cedar planking on the graduated seating showed aged wear. The walls by the stoves were covered in a thin layer of soot, but otherwise the place was very clean. One stove had an immense, black, cast iron hot water pot, for wash water and throwing over the rocks for steam. A large oak barrel for cold water stood in the corner. The other stove, in place of a pot, was built up into a mound of lake stones which would become very hot after proper heating, casting soothing dry heat into the room. It was an unwritten rule, that the sauna stones had to be from your lake and that it was the only way to attain suitable steam when doused with water. The top tier seating always received the brunt of the steam. This was my favorite spot and I would often have to double up from the intense heat. Kolli finished lighting the stoves and ordered us to grab the wooden buckets and go to fetch water from the lake.

Next to the dock, a hole had been chopped into the thick ice for just this purpose. Since last use, the opening had frozen into a thin sheet of ice that Jussi chopped open. The water was crystal clear as we dipped the buckets and carried them in. Jussi and Heikki filled their buckets. I was only able to carry half full buckets. It took us many trips back and forth, before Kolli announced that it was enough. Good thing because by now, I was tired and my muscles were crying out. With our combined efforts, the room had already become noticeably warmer.

The other room in the building was the dressing room which was also the room for relaxing and socializing. It was the place when one came to escape the intense heat and cool off for a short while before returning to the steam room or to enjoy cold water or homemade beer. In our case, we usually went back and forth three times, stretching the bath to over an hour. Before leaving the sauna, it was important to stoke the fires for the next attendees. A few hardier souls may run out and roll in the snow between the sessions in the steam room. I had done this a few times, but before even understanding what a heart attack was, I thought I was going to have one. From extreme hot to extreme cold was an awful shock. In the summer, the lake was an open invitation for extended dips.

Later in the evening, my grandparents would take the first sauna, the boys and me the next, Kolli and his wife and daughter last. Tonight I would join the boys for a change. Normally, I bathed with my grandparents.

Jussi threw two ladles full of water over the hot rocks as we were perched on the top bench. We sat on towels, careful not lean back against the wall which had become very hot. The steam rushed up from the heated rocks towards the ceiling. When it reached us, it took our breath away, smacking against our bodies like hundreds of needles pounding into us. I leaned down putting my head between my knees, breathing slowly and waiting for the steam to subside. Soon I was sitting upright. After about ten minutes, sweat was running profusely down my body forming puddles at my feet. From the changing room, Heikki had brought three bunches of dried young birch branches laden with leaves, which had been set in warm water to become pliable. They were made during midsummer last year and hung up to dry for winter use. I could smell summer from the still green leaves.

I poured warm water over the bunch and began the "self torture" of slapping the bundle all over my body, but not very hard. The scent from the birch leafs was intoxicating and soothing; soon all aches and pains disappeared. This was the ultimate sauna experience which everyone enjoyed and always came back for more. In-between the steam room sessions, we relaxed in the cool dressing room. Jussi braved us to run and jump into the ice hole for a quick dip, which Heikki and I declined. We watched him through the window as he sprinted out on the dock and jumped into the icy water. He splashed around for a brief moment of bravado before climbing up to the dock and speeding into the steam room, his face contorted with pain, and joy.

Finally, we washed ourselves, scrubbing with hard bristle brushes and home-made soap, with an evergreen aroma. The soap smelled good, but was harsh and left a burning sensation. The sweat had brought out every single dirt particle from our pores and many toxins from our bodies, which were now being washed away. I could see myself shining, I was so clean and smelled of soap, birch, cedar and smoke. My muscles and mind were in total harmony and peace.

It was amazing what therapeutic value a sauna session brings to one's being. That night or any night after the sauna, I slept so peacefully and had pleasant dreams. Several other countries around the world have their own version of a steam bath, but none of them compare to the true Finnish sauna. In the rural country side, some old fashioned smoke saunas still exist where all the smoke enters the steam room, escaping through a small square hole cut in one wall. We had a friend who actually had a smoke sauna, which Ukki and I tried once. Neither one of us liked it. It was very black and covered in soot and the smell of the smoke was too strong. It was hard to breathe in the room. It took many days for the smoke odor to leave our bodies and clothes.

The temperature had dropped and the snow had stopped. A full moon was rising above the tree tops and the stars glimmered as we headed back to the house. By the time I reached the front door, my hair had frozen into a stiff ice hat. Fammu had fixed a pot of hot chocolate and a fruit tort, which I devoured thanks to a healthy appetite. The sauna always made me hungry. Now I was content.

7

EARLY SUMMER HAD ARRIVED. WE had taken several trips back to the city to shop and visit my uncle and cousins. Oulu had been bombed rather seriously. The city was littered with ruins and the black shells of some buildings but somehow our apartment building had survived the bombing. The bombing had thankfully ceased by this time but the fighting with the Russians still continued at the border. Evacuees had been dispersed in large shelters in the outskirts of the city. Various food items and supplies were scarce. The air was filled with quiet despair and could be seen in the eyes of the people who shuffled along the streets from store to store, hoping to be able to find some type of food for their families. We stood in many lines wishing that something was left on the shelves by the time we reached them.

Fammu of course continued to talk to me in Swedish, which was terribly embarrassing. I tried to stay away from her, actually hide, so that she would not say anything to me. I hoped that the people in the lines who looked so sullen did not hear this snobbish language. They did not take kindly towards it. In Helsinki, Swedish was common but not here in Oulu. No, here in Oulu we spoke Finnish only. The people in these lines or stores glared at my grandmother and me too if I happened to be close to her. Needless to say, I did not like shopping with her.

My Uncle Runar and his family lived on a small island next to the Astrom leather factory. The island was connected to the sprawling factory grounds by a bridge over a narrow river, which also served as the water supply for the factory. Their home was an imposing large structure with vast spaces. It had polished granite stairways and a formal dining room, a large living room overlooking the river and factory beyond, also six bedrooms, too many bathrooms, and a large kitchen with server's quarters next to it. I had spent many days and nights with them in the company of Rake and the rest of the family. I always enjoyed these visits because Rake and I somehow managed to get involved in some mischief.

Rake's older brother Harri was not interested in our escapades. He was a studious chap and more interested in reading, but mainly collecting and sorting stamps. At this time, he had already accumulated a sizable stamp collection, from correspondence around the world. In later years I learned that he had become a well known philatelist and possessed one of the largest stamp collections in Finland, if not in Scandinavia. Rake had a collection also, but he was not too serious about it. It seems that Harri discarded unwanted stamps to his brother.

It is terrible, but when people ask me now, "When did you start smoking?" I cannot answer truthfully. How could I answer that I was only "close" to six years old when I started, even though it was only sporadic? It was still a start. Of course now I regret it, having smoked practically all my life, unable to quit. Well, every time I stayed with Rake, he managed to produce some cigarettes that he had stolen from his father, hiding them for our meetings. The garage with the big shiny Buick sitting in it was our smoking room. We sat in the car puffing on the butts, listening to music on the radio and pretending to be driving. It was exhilarating. We never got caught even though twice the battery had "mysteriously" drained to nothing.

The old man in the guard house for the factory had become our friend. He had been my uncle's chauffeur for many years, but lost his license for five years, having had enjoyed one beer before driving. Finland was very strict with drinking and driving laws and he had been caught. Now he was a watchman, and many hours on Saturdays and Sundays were spent in his small guard shack and on his long inspection walks throughout the immense factory. Rake and I tagged along climbing on the mountains of animal hides and finished leather slabs. We had glue fights, sampled color watts, checked half finished goods, tried on finished boots and shoes, over all making ourselves a bit of a nuisance.

We had fun horsing around, being scolded now and then by the old man as he punched in on his round watchman's clock in building after building. We were playing inside of Scandinavia's largest leather factory.

I must have been about eight years old when we went through a stage of shooting pigeons on the roofs of the factory. Rake had an old air gun which we cleaned and oiled for our hunting expedition. The pigeons were everywhere, and it was no challenge for us to shoot hundreds of these unsuspecting plump birds. Now when I think about it, it was so cruel for us to kill them, but at that time we were in a frenzy to shoot as many as possible, leaving them where they fell. Once we brought a friend of ours for the big hunt, who somehow fell from one roof to another, dislocating his right leg. He was in severe pain laying there. Somehow we were able to get him back on the ground, holding him up between us as he hopped, crying, on one leg to an old gypsy woman's house some five blocks away. We had heard rumors that this woman was some type of "witch doctor," and thought that maybe she could help us. The boy screamed when the woman yanked, but in an instant the leg was back in place. We thanked the woman and helped our friend to hobble home.

There was one thing that scared me when we sat down for formal dinners at my uncle's house. It seemed that every dinner was formal. The table was long. My uncle sat at one end, my aunt in the other, both looking stiff and stern. The cook and servant hovered around the table, serving various foods. There were at least ten to twelve people always, but many more often taking part in good food and hushed conversation. Perhaps it was the tense atmosphere that created loads of gas in my stomach. Throughout every dinner, I had to lay farts. I tried to hold them back but it did not work. I looked around innocently, hoping that my fart would come out quiet, which worked most of the time. But often I burst into a coughing spell when I realized that it would be a noisy one. With my napkin, I would disburse the smell around, still looking blameless around to see where that whiff came from. It never failed. These dinners were a torture for me.

On our shopping and visiting trips to the city, Grandfather had always arranged for his driver to pick us up at Rantala, take us where ever Fammu would direct him, and finally return us. Sometimes these trips were stretched over two days if we stayed overnight at the apartment or at my uncle's. Driving back, when we had reached the country side, the driver would often pull to the side of the road and let me jump in his lap to steer the rest of the way. I was ecstatic doing this as we slowly made our way back to the farm. Fammu would be sitting in the back seat issuing instructions, but I did not pay any attention to them, because I knew how to drive. The most challenging stretch was the narrow road between the highway and the farm, meandering its way through the woods. There were still high snow banks and some slippery spots, making the ride unhurried, the chauffeur being cautious and ready to grab the steering wheel if needed. I was so proud when we finally reached the farm, without having hit anything on the way.

8

I T WAS LATER IN LIFE when I thought about growing up with my grandparents, that I came to the conclusion of having been born with the "golden spoon in my mouth." The reason I say this is that any time I stayed, which was often, with Ukki and Fammu, I was totally spoiled rotten. I had everything I wanted any time I wanted and much love also at the same time. My grandparents, uncles and aunts were well off compared to my poor mother in Hameenlinna, who worked so hard to take care of my sister and Brother Kari, who was born in September. My mother pampered us with love, but she was not able to spoil Inga and Kari and myself like I was spoiled by my grandparents. She could not afford it. With my father being in the war and her working long hours, the money was tight. I was the fortunate one who was living on Easy Street having been sent to my grandparents. I loved every minute of it, yet often thought about them, wishing that they would be able to share in the life that I was living. Later moving back home, I found life to be great in an opposite way. Having to work from an early age during summers and not to be able to have everything was just fine. It was different, somehow more exciting because it was demanding, and so wonderful to be together as a family.

Summer finally came. The snow was gone and the weather was warm. The lake was glistering in a blue green color with the waves gently slapping the shore.

Around the farm the bustle of early summer work had begun. Extra help had been brought in by Ukki for cultivation of the fields. The plowing and seeding of wheat, rye and oats was taking place next to the farm and at the same time in the fields across the highway. Fammu had begun planting in her vegetable garden. Tomatoes, cucumbers, lettuce and many other vegetables were planted, including a large patch of potatoes. This was her domain except for weeding, which somehow had fallen into my lap. Kolli's wife was also a great help in maintaining the garden. My grandfather had also been busy planting seeds for his tobacco crop.

The horses and cows were put out to pasture and the minks were finally gone. The chickens had access to an outside corral totally covered in chicken wire to keep the hawks from attacking the flock. Often in early morning I would help to drive the cows to their pasture which was past the forest immediately by the farm. There they had a large electrically fenced pasture for endless grazing and in the evenings I helped the drive back to the barn for milking. It was a dream type of life.

I learned how to ride my horse well, trotting and galloping around the neighboring woods and fields. Often I would ride the horse to the edge of the lake where it would drink and munch on the shore grass. I even tried to coax it into the lake, but it was stubborn and would not do it. When finished riding for the day, I rode the horse to the pasture where we stopped by a platform built for me for the purpose of mounting and dismounting the horse.

I was still hesitant with the memory of the previous summer's accident, but I was told by Ukki not to let the horse know that I was scared of it. I tried very hard and apparently it worked.

One day when I was roaming around the barn I came across a rather large rat which I cornered in the milk room. Even though the rat was hissing and spitting, I quickly reached out grabbing its tail and holding it up in the air. The rat was thrashing, trying to get loose, but I held on carrying it proudly towards the house, thinking that I should show my catch to Fammu. All of a sudden the rodent swung around locking its jaws in my thumb. I screamed from the pain trying to shake it off, but the rat would not let go. Ukki had heard the scream, running to see what was wrong. He could not get the rat to open its jaws. He darted to Kolli's kitchen, rushing back with a butcher knife. Only after killing the rat was he finally able to release its locked jaws from my thumb. The doctor was called. He gave me a tetanus shot and some pills for infection, telling me never to corner a rat again because they have been known to attack. I had learned my lesson the hard way. The pain lasted for many days, but the scars for many years.

By now the fish were biting which meant that I spent many hours on the dock trying to lure them with plump worms. Rake and other cousins came and went. Some of them liked to fish but he seemed to be the best fisherman in that group, the others growing restless very quickly. Between the two of us we caught many dinners and had fun just sitting on the dock and talking. We dared each other to jump into the water for a quick swim, the water temperature still being rather chilly. Rake had all types of plans for the future; he was going to become a sea captain, a pilot, an auto mechanic and so on. His dreaming and thoughts changed from week to week. Eventually he graduated from college and became a business manager for a corporation in Helsinki. I again, listening to him, really did not have any thoughts yet about the future, but having read several Tarzan books, I was secretly hoping to become like Tarzan in the jungle. I tried to practice some Tarzan type of traits around the farm with the cows and the pigs, but that is where it ended.

Kolli was in the wood shed with a chicken tucked under his arm holding it by its neck. In the other hand he had an ax. He placed the chicken's head on the chopping block and with one quick move swung the ax down and cut the neck. The head dropped to the ground between his feet, the chicken taking off running for a short distance before dropping. The sight was shocking because this was the first time I witnessed it. The poor chicken running without a head was a thought which rolled around in my mind for a long time. How awful.

Later in the summer I heard the terrible squeal by a pig which was being slaughtered. I did see the aftermath when the pig had been hoisted up by its hind legs to bleed into a bucket before it was cut up. It was also one of those everlasting memories, with the taste of the blood pancakes, served with bitter sweet lingonberris that same evening. Slaughter and I did not mix at all. It all was so cruel. Even though I ate the pork and the chicken, I did not want to think about how it came to our dinner plates.

Stranos the Russian went about his duties and had become an intricate part of the farm family by now. The communication with him was easier as he had learned some Finnish and all of us had learned some Russian. He was full of surprises. Not only had he made all the violins and my big truck, he also had another surprise for me. One day in the middle of summer, he had called Heikki to the barn to help him bring out something. We were by the vegetable garden under a very tall and old birch tree sitting at a picnic table, when the two of them came out carrying a small row boat. They brought it in front of me, setting it on the ground, him uttering, "Juha," and motioning with his hand that it was for me. It was also a masterpiece of woodwork, just like the violins. All of us sat with our jaws agape, totally surprised. Stranos, seeing this, was beaming with pride and rightfully so. I clambered off the bench and climbed into the boat, which was perfect for my size. It would carry two people safely in its lapstreak construction with bent cedar ribbing, painted shiny white. The two oars were lying on the bottom of the boat and it even had a small anchor made out of cast iron with a rope attached to it. This man was an absolute magician in the things he could build. I never wanted him to leave us. On many nights his lantern had stayed lit past midnight, glowing in a subdued yellow cast in his window. These must have been the nights he worked on his creations. As it turned out, Stranos would be staying until the end of the war. Over time I had been able to understand that he had a boy back in Russia about the same age as me and this was probably why he was so kind towards me.

We all were in a hurry to launch the boat. Kolli's sons carried it to the dock and carefully placed it into the water where it floated gracefully. All of us took turns in rowing it, I initiated the boat by being first. It rowed and cut the water so well, it seemed like a feather floating through the air. I was so happy, now I had a horse and a boat, what else would be coming my way? I ran up to Stranos who had been the second in line to try out the boat. As he was climbing up to the dock, I grabbed him in a big hug while his feet were still in the boat, and thanked him over and over.

Not very far from the house, hidden in the pine forest, Rake and I had proclaimed a sand pit as our club hideaway. We would track through the pines to the pit, carrying food and drinks with us. Our steps were quiet, on the thick cushy carpet of pine needles. We knew it would be a while before returning home, and we wanted to be comfortable. Our treasure box had been hidden, under a loose chunk of reindeer moss containing a note book, pencil, butts and matches. It was a square metal cookie box which we found in the woodshed attic, looking old and mysterious. The box was opened with care and placed on a wooden crate we had brought along last summer, to serve as a table. The food and drinks were laid under the crate.

The sun was beaming down casting shafts of sunlight through the tall pine trees as we sat leaning into the warm sand pit wall. We could hear the light breeze in hushed tones blow through the forest and a multitude of birds chirping. A woodpecker was pecking an old pine almost above our heads. Rake lit one of the half smoked butts, offering one to me, which I turned down telling him that I would have one later. They made me dizzy. I grabbed for the note book and pencil, handing them to him in the event that we would come up with some good ideas. The note book contained lots of scribbles by him from our previous "meetings," important and secret to us boys.

There had been something on my mind for long time which I did not understand, nor to which had I been able to get an answer. I thought that my wise and learned cousin could help me with this question.

"Rake, where do babies come from?" I asked suddenly.

He thought for awhile answering, "From Mom's stomach."

"How can the baby get out?"

"How would I know?" he snickered in a sly smile.

When he gave me a brief explanation, I still did not picture what he meant. How could this be?

"No way," I said.

"Juha, believe me. Harri told me about it, he knows."

I did not understand how this was possible. Maybe he was pulling my leg or had wrong information from Harri. I had asked my grandfather the same question and he just told me something about a bird and changed the subject. Perhaps it was an egg like the chickens lay? I could see that Rake was not interested in talking about the subject any longer, so I gave up. I would find out for sure very soon.

The afternoon was spent stretched out on the warm sand, staring at the sky, listening to the wind in the pines and the chirping birds. At one point a curious silver fox ventured close to the pit, stopping momentarily looking at us and scurried back into the woods, the thick gray tail mopping the ground. We ate the lunch of sliced ham and cheese on the dark bread limppu, and for dessert, an apple each. To drink we had brought only one large bottle of milk, which we shared. My grandmother did not mind when we took our excursions, knowing that we would be safe and stay out of trouble. Over time both of us had learned simple navigation, which made it unlikely of getting lost. Behind the pit, the forest stretched far and that was the area where Ukki came to hunt at times. There were bears and moose around and beyond our pit, but we had never seen any, nor were we worried of running into them. An owl hooted in a nearby tree making me wonder if it was the same one that kept me company at the outhouse. The "kuku" bird was calling in the distance. We had named it this from its sound, not knowing what type of bird it was.

The sun had dropped rather low by now, still the rays were shining through the woods but not into our sand pit. It would disappear below the horizon only for a few hours tonight, the night never getting dark, but remained dusk, until rising again around four in the morning. We were located just south of the Arctic Circle. In June the sun barely sets, hence the country of midnight sun.

In July, the summer had reached its peak. The vegetables were growing fast, it seemed as the nature knew the season was so short thereby speeding the growth cycle. The seeds for the flowers had matured into tall green fields, the sun and the rains nurturing the plants to grow high and wait for the autumn harvest. Over the years, Ukki had planted several apple and pear trees, their branches hanging heavy with fruit, not yet ripe. The blackberry and wine berry bushes were just about ready for picking, which Fammu always did, carrying her full baskets back home for preserving. The aura of growth could be felt and seen. It was felt by everyone as strength from the sun. Happiness and well-being from this season was also being stored up for next winter.

My cousins from Helsinki came to visit, staying two weeks with us. The rooms in aitta had been refreshed from the long winter, with crisp linens and blankets. They had stayed in this building before, and told me how much they had looked forward to their visit again. We spent the days boating, fishing and swimming. Cousin Niels constructed a sail for our larger row boat and on any given day someone could be seen sailing across the lake in a gentle breeze. It only blew hard when a threatening thunderstorm was pending. When the black clouds were approaching, all the boats needed to be pulled ashore before the high winds and torrential rains that accompanied the storm.

My little rowboat was a joy. One calm day when Fammu told me of having to go to the community store at the head of the lake in Jaali, I offered to row her, instead of going by horse and carriage. She agreed, asking me if I was sure that I had enough strength to row such a distance, to which I of course answered, that I did. Well, by half way there, I had run totally out of steam, not being able to row even one more stroke. With very careful maneuvering my grandmother and I changed seats, the small boat almost tipping over. She took the oars, continuing rowing to the store which seemed so far away. I could see that she was exhausted by the time we hit the shore and walked to the store. She told me that she had not rowed since she had been a young girl. The first thing she did was to ask to use the phone and called Kolli, telling him to harness the horse and wagon and to come and pick us up. Kolli came to fetch the boat, groceries and us. Fammu never wanted to go rowing with me again.

Father had sent us mail often, but he was not able to visit. At least I felt good knowing that he was safe and well. Inga was to have come that summer if my father was able to, but sadly it did not work out. I would have liked so much to see her. My mother also wrote throughout the summer, sending photographs of her and my sister and brother. We were a separated family, with father and I being away from home.

It was late August when I found out what had been planned by my grandparents for me. Finland was still in full war with Russia and the future did not look good in the eyes of the grown-ups, which had led to scores of children being sent to Sweden for safety. Most children were temporary foster children, sent to strange families who had volunteered to take a child into their home until it was safe to return to Finland. This was to become my fate also, except I was to be sent to live in a home of friends of my grandparents in Orsa, central Sweden.

Hearing this, I was devastated. Now I would be further away from my mother and also away from my grandparents. For how long? What kind of people would I be living with? Why? Life here seemed so serene. I cried myself to sleep many nights, shining to my grandparents that I did not want to go to Sweden.

The reason Orsa had been chosen, was because my Aunt Elsa and her family lived there and were also good friends with the people with whom I would be staying. Elsa's husband was the pastor of the local Lutheran church and they had two sons, my cousins, whom I had never yet met. After finding this out, I did feel some relief of not being thrown to some total strangers, at least some relatives and cousins would be around. No one seemed to know yet, but after my arrival there, my sister would be arriving also and would be staying with our aunt's family. Fammu and Ukki kept telling me how happy and safe I would be in Orsa and they would be coming often to visit. We shall see, I thought.

9

THE DAY HAD ARRIVED WHEN we departed for Sweden. Ukki had arranged for us to leave by ship from Oulu to Gavle in Sweden, continuing from there by train to Orsa in central Sweden. Next we would travel to Mora in the Dalarna region, where the "Mora Nisse" ski races were held each winter. From Mora to our destination, was a half hour trip in a small single car electric train that looked like a trolley car.

It was early September, when we boarded a tramp steamer in the port of Oulu. The sky was overcast, drizzly and raw. The ship was large, towering above us as we rambled up the steep gang plank. The captain met us aboard his ship. From the way he acted with my grandparents, I think that they knew each other well. He was a tall distinguished man in a captain's uniform with a hat to match. He greeted us, welcoming us aboard and escorted us to his private cabin, which was warm and furnished comfortably. Eyeing the ship from the dock, I had already surmised of having to sleep in some dungeon close to the bottom of the ship. Here in the captain's quarters we would be very cozy for the two day trip. It looked already more promising to me as I stared though the port hole down to the docks where people and cranes were busy loading the ship. We were so high up, everything on the ground looked small.

The captain invited us to come to the bridge after getting unpacked when he would take us for lunch in the officer's dining room. While my grandparents went about organizing and getting settled, I spent the time looking around, even venturing out on the upper deck, looking out towards the turbulent gray sea. The mist was hanging heavy with intermittent showers, but the work in the harbor continued with ships leaving and others waiting to be docked. The port of Oulu was a major shipping depot for ships from around the world, yet during the war it had slowed down for fear of bombing. The war had changed many things.

The captain had explained that after lunch we would be casting off. He wanted to be able to navigate from the harbor and the many islands beyond before darkness. The captain turned out to be distantly related to Ukki, therefore the luxurious accommodations and warm hospitality.

At about four in the afternoon, the loud steam whistle blew three long blasts signaling our readiness to leave. The thick ropes were cast off by the dock crews. The engine was rumbling, pushing us towards the open sea in calm water, but even I surmised that this would change once away from the protected harbor. The three of us had been invited to stay on the bridge as the captain directed the ship out. Ukki had told me to behave and not to touch anything as I walked admiring the large wheel, compasses, radios and piles of charts. The captain was telling my grandparents that his cargo consisted of raw paper materials and wood pulp, destined for Rio de Janeiro, after stopping in Sweden for twenty new Volvos. Through the window I could see the whole front of the ship as we cut through the water speeding up and creating a foamy wake. Looking behind me through a large round porthole, I could see the rest of the ship and the men still working on the deck securing the cargo holds. Oulu was disappearing on the horizon into a gray mist.

Later in the evening after a delicious dinner with the captain, I walked around the whole ship, poking into various rooms on different levels. It was a Finnish ship with a foreign crew from many countries. I met the engineer in his greasy overalls, who was a kind Swedish man, telling me that he wanted to show me his engine room. We climbed to the belly of the ship, into an ear splitting thumping and hissing cavernous room, occupying the largest steam engine I had ever seen. I did not think that such monsters existed. Puffs of steam were shooting about from an array of black, red and white thick pipes running across the room. Dials and valves were everywhere with two men attending to them. The things moving up and down were the pistons, the engineer told me. We stood on the second floor cat walk overlooking the madness, the sound and power vibrated the iron walk way. I was holding on to the railing, until my knuckles turned white. I could stay here for hours, it was so interesting. Later when telling Ukki and Fammu about my adventure aboard and how huge the engine room was, they told me I was fortunate to see that room as most people were not welcome there.

The next morning was still gray and rainy. The wind had picked up during the night rocking the ship from side to side. During the night I had woken up wondering where I was, until the rhythmic motion and tight bunk reminded me, lulling me back to sleep. I dreamt about Mother and Inga and my horse.

Later that morning, after breakfast, I could feel a different sound and vibration, seemingly slowing the ship down. As I made my way to the bridge, I noticed that we actually had stopped in the middle of the ocean, close to a tug boat pulling a large barge behind it. The tug with its truck tire fenders maneuvered itself to the side of our ship, one of the crew casting a thick rope to us to be tied up. The two captains were yelling to each other, the tug's captain calling out that he needed to transfer one of his passengers aboard our ship. Meanwhile, the barge had floated to the back of the tug, resting against us, bouncing up and down with the wave action and hitting with a thump, metal to metal.

The sight facing us from the barge was just unbelievable. We were standing by the railing looking down at hundreds of sad, crying blue eyes peering back at us, tears running down many cheeks. The barge was loaded with small children huddled against each other, girls and boys, all bundled up in raggedy clothes, each one with a large name tag hanging around their neck printed in bold black letters. These were children who were being sent to Sweden, just as I was, but these were orphans of war. We were staring down at youngsters, my grandmother in her mink coat, Ukki all bundled up in fur collar coat and myself in warm new clothes. My face burned with guilt. Why was I here and not with them? Looking at them, I became sad just like they were.

Oh God, why am I here-
Why not with them, looking up, as they are
With tearful blue eyes and broken hearts,
Whimpering of loneliness. Fearing for the future.
Displaying a card of identity against an unnourished small chest,

The breeze lifting it in air, beckoning-
"This is I", please read-
"Who I am - where I'm going?"

This poem was written many years later, but at the time, these were my feelings.

The youngster who had taken seriously ill was lifted aboard our ship for care and warmth, after which the tug was let loose, continuing its trip to Sweden. The boy brought aboard was suffering from high fever, but the mate would be take good care of him. Soon the tug, with its human cargo, blended into the gray mist. My eyes had followed it as long as possible.

The weather had cleared up but it had become much windier, the waves still hitting us broadside making the ship rock heavily from side to side. It made me wonder if we would recover from some of the steeper angles. The white caps looked vicious churning atop the tall waves, creating a rumbling and groaning sound as they struck the ship. My grandparents looked rather peaked sitting in the cabin trying to read. I felt fine and enjoyed the constant rocking. It would be early the following morning when we would reach Sweden. Many thoughts and questions still occupied my mind concerning my new life.

By the time I woke up the following morning, I could not feel any motion nor hear the engine sounds. I jumped up from the bunk, rushing to the port hole I peered out to find that we were already docked. This must be Sweden, I thought. My grandparents were still asleep when I woke them up with excitement, declaring that we had arrived. Running up to the bridge, I saw some items being unloaded, at the same time a tall crane was swinging a new automobile through the air, lowering it gently into one of the holds. The captain was standing on the deck overseeing the work, when I walked up to him asking if this was Sweden. Motioning with his hand to the crane operator to slow down with the hanging car, he said, "This is Sweden, young man, as soon as we get the cars loaded, we will be casting off. Please go and tell your grandparents that we will depart in about two hours."

I rushed back to the cabin, where my grandparents were already packing up, and relayed the captain's message to them. Shortly thereafter we carried the luggage to the deck, thanked the captain for his wonderful hospitality and bade him a safe journey before starting down the steep gangplank. Ukki helped grandmother on the shaky stairway. One of the crewmen carried the luggage down to the dock. We stood by the ship and waved to the captain who was still directing the loading operation.

It was a warm autumn morning as we walked to a nearby office where Ukki called a taxi for a ride to the railroad station. From this city, the next step was to take the train to Stockholm and there change trains for one going to Mora. We had no idea of the schedules but luckily only had to wait an hour at the station before being whisked towards the capitol. We were traveling in second class and had our own small compartment. Having traveled on the Finnish trains, this one looked the same with black and gray striped upholstery. I started to think that perhaps all the trains around the world used the same color scheme? The ride to Stockholm went fast. We had a quick breakfast in the dining car, relaxed in our compartment gazing at the country side as it sped by. There was no difference between the two country's landscapes, except for small towns which appeared to be more prosperous than back home. I don't know what I was expecting to find in this country but so far it looked like Finland. Soon we began to see the outskirts of Stockholm, the dwellings evolving from low houses to higher and higher buildings and then into a congested metropolis. The train pulled into the enormous railway station, full of people rushing every which way, and we mixed in with them, looking for information for trains to Mora. We found out that the next one would be leaving six hours later and the trip would be an overnight journey, arriving in Mora nine o' clock in the morning. Ukki bought the tickets for that train, securing a sleeper compartment.

We were strolling the streets of "Old Town" Stockholm with six hours to wait before our departure. Fammu had declared that there would be no way we would be waiting that long in the train station so here we were, amongst the idyllic, centuries old buildings and narrow cobblestone streets, passing the time. I enjoyed it. Now I was in a big city compared to Oulu and this part of the "Northern Venice," as Stockholm was often referred to, was interesting, full of shops, full of merchandise with no lines. Fammu could speak Swedish to me all she wanted, without me having to be embarrassed and trying to hide. We came to a gun shop. Ukki could not pass it without going in to see what they had. I went with him, Fammu disappearing into a clothing shop next door. We were admiring the large collection of hunting rifles and shotguns, Ukki asking to inspect several of them, pointing out too that many of them were made in Finland, which was rather well known around the world for its quality fire arms. It was Fammu, carrying a big bag that finally came and dragged us out. For us the time had stopped, browsing amongst the gleaming weapons. Continuing the walk, we stopped for lunch in a small restaurant, taking our time trying to spend the remaining hours somehow. At the restaurant, Fammu had them prepare a "picnic" bag with sandwiches and fruits, to take along for the train ride. After some small knick knack shopping, we returned in plenty of time for the trip ahead.

The train for Mora left exactly on time. Our accommodations were fine for just one night's trip. There were two berths, one above the other, a small table and wash basin with hot and cold water inlayed in a recessed cabinet. The bathrooms were on either end of the railway car. It was still full day light outside as the train was speeding northwest towards the district of Dalarna. The countryside was woodsy and flat with farms and fields scattered here and there. Birch trees seemed to be prominent here, but as time went by more pine forests appeared. The wheat fields had turned into a light golden hue undulating in the breeze. Fammu was taking a nap, Ukki was reading and I was glued to the window, watching the countryside pass. I was still hesitant in my thoughts of the next morning and meeting my new guardians. I hoped they were nice people and lived where there were other children around. They had no children of their own, my grandparents had told me.

After sleeping well with the rhythmical rocking of the train, I woke up again before my grandparents, in anticipation of the day. The wash closet posed a bit of a problem, as I opened the fold down cover, it turned out to be so heavy that I had to let it go, and in so doing it created a loud bang waking up my grandparents, who jumped up alarmed. Seeing what had happened, Ukki came and gave me a hand with it. The water smelled rotten. There was no way I would wash myself with it, I just sprinkled some water over each eye, and for washing my teeth, used some of the soda which Fammu had bought. I felt refreshed enough, and sat to look out the window. The terrain had become much hillier during the night and the population and farms more sparse. We were close to Dalarna.

Arriving in the town of Mora, I noticed the leaves were starting to turn into vivid early autumn colors of reds and gold. The day was sunny but cooler than Stockholm. This was further north and west, inland also where the oceans and seas had very little warming effect. The station was a small, well cared for building, painted in the colorful fashion of the region, with bright blue, yellow and red colors forming the area's designs. The small "trolley" would be leaving for

Orsa within a half hour, giving us a moment to walk around, breathe the fresh air and stretch our legs. It would be a quick trip from here to our destination.

The last leg of this long trip was fun in the small electric car. It reminded me of the trolley cars in Oulu, except now we were traveling through the country. In a short time the large lake of "Orsasjon" was visible to the left which we would be skirting on our way to Orsa. To the right, I could see large meadows and farm fields, all set on rolling hill sides, with well groomed farm houses, barns and silos. Many hay fields had been harvested with the yellow hay formed into a tall cone around a supporting pole. Cows, horses and some sheep were grazing in the pastures. Everywhere I looked, life looked very prosperous, more so than in Finland, I mentioned this to Ukki and he told me Sweden was a much wealthier country than our country, not having had any wars and remaining neutral during this war.

I guess when I was nervous, I had to fart. This happened again, after so many days of anticipation, as the "trolley" pulled up to Orsa station. There were several people waiting outside the small station house. I was trying to guess who was who. Ukki had telephoned from Stockholm, telling my aunt of the arrival time. There was an older couple, well dressed by another couple next to two boys, one my age, the other older, single people and others with small children running around. I pegged my first observation as being the welcoming committee for us and I was right. As we stepped out of the car, they approached us, the boys running to greet, grabbing some of the luggage. The grownups followed. After much hugging and kissing, I was introduced to my aunt, the pastor and the boys. I was more interested in meeting my new "parents," who turned out to be the well dressed couple. My aunt introduced me to them as, Mr. and Mrs. Westholm. They stooped down and gave me a hearty hug, welcoming me to Sweden and their home. The man handed me a small gift wrapped package as a welcoming present telling me to call them Far and Mor, Swedish for father and mother from here on.

My first impression of them was okay. They seemed friendly, yet a little reserved and perhaps a bit like Uncle Runar, refined and dignified. This should not be a problem for me, I was thinking, having been surrounded with these types of people. Far must be a business man, well dressed, slim, stern face but friendly smile. Mor was taller and chubbier than her husband and wore a colorful summer dress, her gentle smile radiating her face. Mor grabbed my hand leading us past the station house to the street, where a taxi was waiting. Ukki and Fammu would be coming with us to Westholm's and would later go to their daughter's house. We bid farewell to my aunt, her husband and the boys.

I was sitting in Ukki's lap. The taxi was small for all of us, squeezing the gift, eyes glued to the surroundings. After crossing the railroad tracks we proceeded up on a long incline. Once reaching the top, we turned to the right through a tall iron gate to a circular crushed gravel drive way, driving to the front entrance of an elegant large brown house in white trim. The ride had only taken five minutes. An iron fence skirted the property and disappeared into the distance. Landscaping was lush and well groomed. Tall oaks and pines with a clump of birch trees stood out in an island of vegetation. The house was two stories high with several chimneys. A wide front door, framed with tall narrow windows and a small balcony on the second floor were prominent Rather close to the main house was another large building, painted barn red. It was built onto the sloping hill side. Between the two buildings, I could see a vegetable garden and the glimmer of Orsa Lake in the distance. My first impression was that of a grand estate. So far, so good, I thought.

Entering through the heavy front doors we arrived into a large hall, furnished with beautiful couches, side tables and chairs. Fresh flowers adorned the room. Countless oil paintings mainly of landscapes and a few portraits adorned the walls. Many open arched doorways led to the first floor rooms. A wide polished staircase led to the second floor. Our luggage was piled up next to the coat alcove. This was the first time my grandparents saw this house and from their expressions I could tell they were impressed. I could see from Fammu's critical looks that she fitted right in here. Well, it was my house now, she was the guest. The Westholms led us to the main dining room, where the table was set with an assortment of cold cuts and sweets, coffee and tea on the side table with some juice for me. I walked up to the open French doors leading to a veranda running full length of the back of the house, where a grand vista emerged. We were high atop a hill overlooking wide valleys and tall wheat fields beyond, the lake. On this clear day, I could see across the lake into the horizon so far away that it just blended with the blue sky.

Everyone was coming out through the doorway carrying plates of food, Mor telling me to get some and come back out to join them. By now my nerves had calmed and I was hungry. I carried a plate full and joined everyone seated on comfortable wicker furniture. To me all this so far was unbelievable. I could see that I would enjoy it here, a nagging thought however would not go away. I would have liked so much to share this with my mother and sister. Somehow I felt very guilty.

I was looking around some more and focused on a hammock suspended between two birch trees down the slope, just this side of a tall hedge separating the yard from the wheat field. I would have to try it soon, maybe take a nap in it. Off to the side of the hammock, in the open, a large black patch of charcoal and burnt branches sat, as a reminder of the midnight festival this past June. By next summer, Far said, it would be built into a tall bonfire again. He also told us about the other building on the premises, which housed the caretaker, his wife and daughter, "By the way Juha," he said, "Kerstin, the daughter is just about your age and a very sweet young girl. You will meet her soon." I nodded to be polite but thinking, *a girl?* I need someone like Rake around. I don't even know what to say to a girl. He continued to talk about how the building was also the wood shed, laundry with a mangle, sauna and garage for the bicycles and kick sleds for winter use. I was happy to hear of the sauna and I wondered if they knew how to take a good Finnish sauna. I had learned to bike a couple of months earlier in Rantala by borrowing Ukki's bike, riding it tilted between the cross bar which was the hardest possible way to learn how to ride a bike. We sat and listened to Far and Mor talk about Orsa and about me especially explaining that they were so happy to have a youngster in the house and also informed me that I would be starting school next week. Rake had always told me that he hated school and now I had to start going to one. That statement did not sound very good at all. Give me at least a little time to get used to the place first, I was thinking.

From my new parents, a sad story emerged. They told us of having had a daughter, who died several years ago from some illness which they did not name. She had lived in this house, after Mr. Westholm had retired, selling his sawmill and lumber yard close to Stockholm, then moving with his family here. I could see tears running down their cheeks, while telling the story, and how much they loved and missed her. It was very sad, I almost cried and so did my grandparents.

10

WHEN I WOKE UP, IT took a long time to figure out where I was. Was it Rantala, a ship or a train? Slowly, very slowly, it finally came to me. I was in Orsa, in my new room. The sun's rays were tickling my face. It must be time to get up. After dressing, I made my way through the upstairs. No one was around. I went to the kitchen steps and tip toed down. I did not want to wake anyone up on my first day. There was an older lady by the sink, older than Fammu and much heavier. She was wearing a brown hair net, a flowery dress and a stiff white apron. The lady was not much taller than I. For whatever reason, she did not look happy. She had a nasty frown on her thin lips.

She was washing some vegetables when I walked in ever so quietly. She must have seen me from the corner of her eyes because she jumped and dropped the vegetables in the sink. She looked me up and down, finally speaking, "Are you the boy from Finland? You frightened me!" she barked and glowered at me.

"I did not hear you. Don't sneak around."

I gazed at her a long time, answering," Who are you? I'm sorry I scared you."

"Young man, I am the housekeeper, you can call me Mrs. Anderson," she barked. She continued, picking up a cleaver. "I run a very clean house. Don't come in with dirty shoes," she said, banging the cleaver on a cutting board.

"My name is Juha," I stuttered in Swedish, "Johan. I won't mess up anything," I said timidly.

This lady scared me, with her tone of voice and angry look. I must watch out for her.

"Sit down, I will get you something to eat," she said, shuffling towards the ice box.

I sat down at a round table by the windows wondering where Far and Mor were. Mrs. Anderson brought a plate with some of yesterday's cold cuts and a glass of milk, slamming them down in front of me. "Eat!" she barked. What a way to be greeted the first day! I ate but I kept a watchful eye on her.

Far came in from outside, walking over and sitting down opposite of me. He was wearing old work clothes and a worn felt hat. He must have been up a long time working. His breath was short and labored, and he looked tired.

"Johan, did you sleep well?" he asked, taking his hat off, setting it on the chair next to him.

I swallowed a mouth full of food answering, "Very well, thank you." The food was leftovers from yesterday's buffet table, dry cold cuts and hard to swallow.

"I see you already met Mrs. Anderson. She is a wonderful housekeeper."

"Yes," but I don't know about wonderful, she is chilling, I thought.

"I tell you what, after breakfast, let's go and meet the caretaker Mr. Sundholm and his family. Ok?"

"I am almost done," I told him. Meeting Kerstin worried me. What would I say to her?

Mrs. Anderson had brought Far a cup of coffee, which he proceeded to pour a small amount onto the saucer, bringing it to his lips and slurping it down. He saw me looking surprised. "When the coffee is hot, I drink it this way," he said with a smile. "The old Swedes drink it this way all the time."

"I like coffee too," I said, hesitantly, having had it only a few times with grandfather.

"Well, Johan, we will form a secret between us. You can have a cup of coffee once a month with me, but don't tell Mor, she will get mad," he whispered.

With a broad smile I answered, "Great. It is our secret."

After we were done and walking towards the kitchen door, I turned around calling out to Mrs. Anderson, "Thank you for the breakfast." She only grunted quietly.

We went outside past the vegetable garden. The green beans were towering above all other vegetables. We were walking towards a small patio door in the red building. Far knocked and a young girl came to open it. She must be Kerstin, I thought. She was a pretty girl. She had blue eyes and curly blond hair and was wearing a colorful summer dress, and teddy bear slippers. I did not know much about girls, but the one standing in front of me sure looked nice. Far introduced us as we entered the apartment, where I met the mother, Mrs. Sundholm. She was dressed in a peach colored house coat and red slippers. She was a petite woman, quite young and seemed like a friendly person. She came over and gave me a big hug, saying that they had been waiting for me for over a month.

"Welcome, you are going to be very happy with the Westholms, they are such delightful people." Kerstin was standing close to her mother, bashful, reaching for her hand.

I did not know what to say, but finally coughed up, "Thank you. I am happy to be here." I could feel myself blushing, trying not to look at Kerstin.

"My husband is at work right now, you will meet him later today," she said with a smile. "He drives big trucks for the town," she continued, holding her daughter's hand.

"See you later. I am showing Johan around," Far said, tugging my hand.

At least I would have someone to play with, I thought about the girl as we proceeded to the other parts of the building. Far explained that Mr. Sundholm had a full time job and only a part time caretaker's position with us. He took me around showing me everything housed here. The wood shed was a long and narrow room, stocked to the ceiling with wood, which I was told would last through the upcoming winter. It smelled so good from the newly split fire wood, reminding me of the shed in Rantala. Next, he took me into a large airy room on the second floor which was the laundry room with a huge ironing mangle for sheets, standing in the center and many washing machines and sinks to the side. Off to the far corner stood a large iron pot over a fire place. All the hot water was boiled there. The last area to see was a garage, without a car, but housing several bicycles and a brand new smaller boy's bike with a blue bow on the handle bar.

"Johan, this bicycle is yours," Far said, wheeling the shiny bike to me. "You will need it to get around. We hope you like it."

My eyes had popped out. "It is beautiful. Thank you!" I burst out excitedly. I was shaking. I hugged Far, not believing that I had my own bike. This sure was going to be different from riding grandfather's bike. I grabbed it, moving toward the door which Far had opened, leading it outside and took off on the crushed rock drive way. It rode so well. I was happy as a lark riding it around the circular drive way, proudly showing Far how well I could do it. All of a sudden, I fell. The loose, crushed stone on the drive way made me slip. How embarrassing. I was hurting and was laying under the bike, moaning. The stones were sharp. Far rushed over to help me. Blood was dripping from my knees, hands and face. Tears were running down my cheeks, but I did not sob. Far lifted the bike off me, setting it down on the grass and helped me up.

Hand in hand we entered the kitchen. Mrs.Anderson had a devious smirk on her lips when she saw me wounded. She probably was concerned about more of blood drops on the floor, than me. She lifted me up to the counter. She looked around, spotting two dishes of soap. A smile appeared on her lips. She chose the yellow ugly looking soap, not the white. She began washing the cuts. The soap stung worst than my cuts. I could not help it, but now I was sobbing. She probably received pleasure in hurting me, I thought. She proceeded to plaster me with band aids. They were everywhere. She wrapped gauze around one knee. Far was watching us with a smirk, without saying anything.

After the torture, Far said, "Johan, be careful, it is hard to ride on the stones, try to stay to the sides or push your bike. I am glad it wasn't worse. You will be fine."

Mor had gone shopping on her bike and when she saw me all patched up, she was very much concerned, wanting to know what happened. I told her, assuring that I was fine, it just hurt a little. I helped her carry the groceries in. On the porch, she began to tell me all about the household.

"Mrs. Anderson," she assured me, "is a nice woman, don't pay attention to her crabbiness." She also told me about Sundholms, upcoming school and Orsa. It all sounded great, but the school business was worrisome. Rake's comments rolled around in my mind. During the conversation, she laid her hand on top of mine, squeezing it tenderly at times, emphasizing her comments. I liked her. Her blue eyes sparkled. Her friendly, assuring smile took away any hesitation I had about being here. I already started to genuinely feel at home. She handed me some coins, explained that the closest little store was just up the road, that I could see it from the house, telling me to stop over there and buy some candy. "Can I take the bike?" I asked. "Be careful, are you sure you are not hurting too much?" she asked as I was already out the door.

I could not believe my eyes when I saw the display of candies and gums. One whole shelf was crammed full of candies and chocolates in colorful wrappers. On the counter, there were eight large glass jars, plumb full of loose candies. In Finland, we were lucky if they had a lollipop now and then. I looked at the coins in my hand trying to figure out what I could get, I had no idea. The owner finally came over having noticed my problem. He was wearing a full length doctor's white coat. "You must be new in the neighborhood?" he asked, looking at me up and down, in a puzzled stare. "You look like you are being held together with band aids. What happened?"

"I fell off the bike. I just came from Finland and am staying with the Westholms," I said.

"They are wonderful people. How is Mrs.Anderson? I love that sweet woman," he said.

Yach…I thought. He counted my coins and told me how many of what I could get with it. After a long time, I wanted everything. I walked out chewing Chiclets chewing gum and stuffing other goodies in my pocket. I still had a few coins left.

I rode around, inspecting the neighborhood. My knees were hurting as I pedaled up and down the roads. Very few cars went by. About two blocks from the house, I saw a small school house, not much larger than the store. I wondered if that was going to be my school. I stopped. A few children's heads were visible through the windows and a woman was walking by. She must be the teacher, I was guessing. Continuing the journey, I pedaled down the hill a ways towards the town but had to turn around, I was even too far by now. Going back, I had to push the bike uphill to the gate. Mor was waiting nervously in the yard, scolding me for being gone so long the first time. I felt bad and told her I was sorry.

Later that day, I was helping Far carry firewood from the wood shed, to the basement of the house. He was stockpiling it there for the winter use. Kerstin came out and tagged along with us, carrying one small piece, setting it on the stacked pile.

"How is Finland?" she asked, peering at me.

I was surprised by this sudden question, thinking for a moment, answering in an authoritative voice, "It is very nice, especially at my grandparent's farm. I have my own, horse his name is Juha." At that point I felt a great relief of having been able to say something to a strange girl.

"Your own horse? I would be afraid to ride."

"I was in beginning, but the horse is really nice. If you ever come and visit, I will teach you," I was gaining confidence by the minute.

"How old are you?" she said, her voice a bit timid. She kept turning her head from side to side, her blond curls shifting from shoulder to shoulder.

"I am almost seven. How old are you?"

She thought for a moment, "I am almost six. Next year I will start school. I cannot wait," she said dreamily.

"My cousin told me that school was like a prison, and I have to start next week." The tone of my voice was not pleasant. My face must have shown agony. She looked at me quizzically. Kerstin probably had not heard the true story about schools. "Why do you want to go there?"

"The teacher is our friend and she is so nice. I want to learn how to read. You will also like her and our school, which is so close," she affirmed.

"We'll see. Girls always like schools, boys don't."

Far had lost his helpers. He was carrying pile after pile of wood into the basement. He looked at us but did not say anything. I got stuck talking to the girl, and wondering if I should help him instead. He must have noticed my wondering expression and said, "Why don't you two go inside? I will tell Mrs. Anderson to give you some cookies and milk. You can sit and talk. Kerstin will tell you all about life here. Come with me," he said, heading towards the kitchen.

Mrs. Anderson stopped what she was doing, annoyed, mumbling to herself as she reached in the cupboard for some cookies, setting them on her prep table with two glasses of milk. There was no way I was going to sit in the kitchen with the tense atmosphere. Kerstin grabbed the cookies, I took the milk, and we thanked Mrs. Anderson, heading out the door, quickly, to the hammock. Kerstin sat in one end facing me in the other end, with the cookies in the middle. It was a beautiful fall day. The birds were chirping in the hedge, the breeze was rustling the leaves which had begun to turn into an autumn display of vibrant colors. The hammock was swinging ever so gently.

I was stretched out with one arm under my head, looking at Kerstin who was munching on a cookie, wondering what Rake would have thought if he would have seen us. Who would start to talk first? I still felt awkward in the company of my new found friend. Sure, I had been with girls before, but it did not count. They were my cousins and I knew them. I guess I was the stiffer of us two, because soon Kerstin started to talk. First she told me all about her mother and father, life here with Westholm's and her father's duties, all about Orsa and the lake. There was a circus coming to town in a couple of weeks, which she was excitedly looking forward to, especially for the elephants. She loved all animals, but had never seen a live elephant before. She invited me to go with her family, doubting that the Westholms would be going. I had never been to a circus, which would be fun. Her tone of voice had a mellow sound to it making listening to her a pleasure. I was more or less letting her do the talking, interjecting a few comments here and there. She looked pretty. Much prettier than my cousin Majja from Helsinki. I had had a crush on Majja for a while, but she seemed to ignore me, perhaps because she was two years older than I, and a bit snobbish. I gave up on her, but still secretly thought about her. Rake and I often talked about girls, deciding they were not very interesting. He did not like Majja either.

It was so comfortable to lay here. I had finished the milk and eaten many of the cookies. When Kerstin reached a delay with her stories, I began telling her about my sister Inga, who was just about the same age as her, about my mother and my father who was fighting the Russians, the bombing and much about Rantala. I told her about the chicken running around without a head, which she did not like hearing, stating, "horrible" and her rosy look, turning into a sad gaze. "Don't tell me such awful things," she said, looking away. I continued talking about fishing, and about my good friend, the Russian prisoner, Stranos and about the wonderful things he had made for me and the violins for my grandparents.

"A Russian prisoner!" Kerstin burst out, looking perplexed. "Weren't you scared of him? An enemy prisoner!" she stared at me like I was crazy.

"No, he is one of the nicest men I have ever met. I miss him very much," I said with a smile that could reach out to Rantala. Then I continued telling my story about driving my grandfather's car. Time went by very leisurely and Kerstin appeared to be much interested in my stories, wide eyed, giving me added confidence and a thought that girls were not so bad after all. Somehow our conversation here had been so different from the conversations which Rake and I often had in the sand pit. This almost made me feel older and wiser now. Our visit was interrupted by Mor's call for dinner.

After sitting down for dinner, Far said grace, adding how happy they were in having a youngster in the house. Mrs. Anderson hovered about, serving soup as appetizer and meatballs with oven roasted potatoes and home grown peas still in the pod. The dinner was very good. Mor commented about Mrs. Anderson having been with them for many years, even in Stockholm and moving with them to Orsa. The atmosphere was relaxed. I did not feel like passing wind, which was a re-assurance of immediate adaptation to this household. I had decided to make the best of it, to be good in school, even though the idea was not pleasant, also to help around the house as much as possible. Kerstin sure added to my well being, I thought of her still being a bit childish, but for her age I had to accept it.

Far served the dessert which was something called "long milk." I had never heard of it. Standing up he ladled the white, heavy, milk into individual bowls, bringing the ladle high up into the air. To my amazement, it stretched like well chewed chewing gum from the ladle to the dish. After sprinkling sugar over it, I brought a spoonful to my mouth with a long length of it reaching the dish. This was weird stuff. It tasted like buttermilk, but behaved like liquid rubber. Far said that it was an old Swedish folk dish. Maybe it would make a good slingshot, I mused.

Later in the evening, we sat upstairs listening to Mor play the organ. She played mainly from a church hymnal book, singing the words quietly. Far hummed along. I almost fell asleep. As I was to find out, the Westholms were very religious with church every Sunday. In fact, it was the Lutheran church where my uncle was the pastor. Once every two weeks, on a Thursday evening, Mor took me along to a Salvation Army meeting, where she was one of the main officers. We sang the same hymns which she had been playing at home, and now playing here. Then we listened to a long sermon and afterwards had some sweets. Everyone in the room was wearing Salvation Army uniforms. There were only two other youngsters with their parents, also in uniforms. This looked scary to me. Sure enough, the first night I attended, one of the ladies came over and began measuring me from top to bottom.

"Why are you measuring me?" I asked surprised.

"Johan, we are going to make you your own uniform," she said smiling adding, "You will also get a hat," she said, playing with my head. I did not like this at all.

The uniform and hat were ready before the next meeting, which one of the members dropped off at the house. They made me stand on a stool after changing into it, "oo-ing and aa-ing", telling me how precious I looked, while I stood there embarrassed. The color of the uniform was green and blue, the hat a ghastly blue, with a red rim and a leather strap under my chin. It sat like an upside down pot on my head. If Rake could see me now, he would die laughing. I was not happy but had to go along with it. I could picture when Christmas came, I would probably be standing at some street comer ringing a bell.

It had been a long active, interesting day and when Mor began reading me Peppi Longstocking I had trouble staying awake and soon fell asleep. During the night I woke up once in a sweat from a nightmare of a malicious school teacher chasing me in the wood shed.

11

WE WERE BIKING DOWN THE long hill to Orsa to visit my aunt and
grandparents who would be staying there until next week. Far was
leading, Mor behind him, and I was last. We made our way, stepping on the brakes until reaching the railroad tracks where the business district
started. Passing small store fronts, coffee shops and office buildings, I could see
a tall white church steeple in the distance, which would be the Lutheran church
where my uncle was the Pastor. I had been told that his church was very large
and the only other in town was Methodist and very small. After pedaling past a
few more blocks and a grave yard, the church was directly in front of us.

It was beautiful, massive and white with a tall steeple. The shining sun
painted the steeple in a bright glow. The bells could be seen in an arched opening atop the steeple, with the cross uppermost. The front door was framed by
tall narrow colorful stained glass windows on each side. The side windows were
equally large and decorative. My aunt lived in the parsonage, which Mor pointed
out was beyond the church.

We pedaled slowly past the church towards the very old wooden building,
painted in the traditional barn red with white window trimming. The house
was enveloped in English ivy, with colorful wild flower beds in front. The fragrance of the flowers and rose bushes in full bloom filled the still air. The yard

had been well manicured with hedges, bushes and apple trees counterpoint to the dark green freshly cut lawn. It was so quiet and peaceful. All my relatives were outside. Fammu and my aunt were attending a vegetable garden on the side of the house. Both ladies stooped, holding a basket and were picking vegetables. They did not see us coming. Ukki and the pastor were picking apples from a fully ripened apple tree. The pastor was reaching up with a long pole, shaking and probing them loose as Ukki tried to catch as many apples as possible, although missing many as they fell. It looked comical with Ukki running around. I laid the bike on the grass and went over to help catch. They were surprised to see me but continued with the task. The apples were coming down so fast that we could not keep up, more than half falling to the ground. Later we collected them into a wooden box. It was almost full as we carted it around the building into a storage shed.

Afterwards, we sat on the back porch, enjoying my aunt's homemade cold apple juice. There was an assortment of pastries from a local bakery. The pastor was a cheerful, well educated and knowledgeable man. He seemed to be a few years older than my father. He radiated self-assurance with his tall stature and motions. His expressions coincided with his conversation, from happy to sad. He told us how much work went into running a church, which very few people realized. He loved Orsa and his position, which prompted him to become one of the "elders" of the town. Their older son Erick was also destined to become a minister. Their younger son Alex who was eight years old, sounded like me. I had met them only for a few minutes at the station and now they were in school. I wish they were here now. To me, it felt like I was always spending so much time with grownups.

My Aunt Elsa, who was two years younger than Father, was a delightful lady. Her laughter echoed through the porch. Her smile was like sunshine. She looked very much like my father, thin and well groomed. In her gardening clothes with a scarf on her head, she reminded me of the farm help at Rantala. She told us of not having seen her brother in over three years, wondering how he was holding up with the war. Fammu assured her that he seemed to be doing very well, having received several promotions and that he looked fit and strong. She commented how much I resembled him, reminiscing about their youth. She also mentioned about the possibility of bringing my sister from Finland to live with them until end of the war. It was not yet certain, but soon they would make the decision. This news piqued my attention telling them and I told them that

I would be so happy if this happened. It was the best news I heard since leaving Finland. Please!

As we were heading back home after a leisurely visit, I had more time to see Orsa. The beach by the lake was very close to the church and being it was such a nice day, Far decided to take a detour to show it to me. Soon we were biking on the beach road overlooking a wide span of Orsa Lake, with a sandy beach skirting the shore. I could see clearly across the shimmering calm lake. The far shore was hilly with the green forest vivid against the blue, blue sky. He told me that in the summer time, the beach was teeming with people enjoying the water and sun shine. A small cluster of shops were located roadside, but were closed now for the season. A few people were walking on the sand, enjoying the clear early autumn weather.

Back in the business district, we stopped at a bakery to pick up some sweets and bread. The bakery smelled so good and showcased mouthwatering delicacies behind its glass cases. I wanted it all bur Mor was very choosy, buying only bread and two pieces of pastry, which she let me pick. It appeared as if the Westholms knew everyone, greeting them as we biked by. The car traffic was sparse and bicycles were everywhere. No one seemed to be in a rush which was so different from any big city. After passing the railroad tracks the hill was too steep to bike up. We had to push the bikes rest of the way, which was very tiresome.

Mor told me that I should take a bath again, after such a long bike ride. The idea did not appeal to me. I would rather take a sauna, I told her. She replied that they very seldom heated the sauna. Why have a sauna if you don't use it, I thought. Perhaps I could slowly change their thinking? I didn't mention this opinion to them, but would work on this idea some time.

Now it was bath time. Mor went upstairs to draw the bath, I followed and got undressed in my room. She had filled the tub standing next to it, waiting for me to jump in. After all the saunas at home, I was used to being naked. However, I always felt funny naked in front of her. She told me to drop my underwear and jump in. I turned my back to her, pulled the pants down and stood naked, shivering in her presence, finally sliding into the tub with a splash. Seeing my modesty, she chuckled, "Johan, you don't need to be embarrassed. I have seen many naked boys in my lifetime." She had a big smile on her face but that did not make me feel any better. Mor stayed and scrubbed my back issuing orders how to scrub myself, specially my feet. I did not need to be told how to get clean, but promised to follow her instructions.

Laying in the water, playing with the soap bubbles, my mind traveled back home to Mother and Inga. By now we had another youngster in the family. Our brother Kari was born in the first part of September. When would I see him? How in the world was Mother coping with a new baby in the house? If I was older, I would surely be at home helping her. Until now, I had spent such little time at home, actually only when I was a small baby.

I was trying to understand, in my short life, why I had been shuffled around from here to there. I could comprehend some of it, but not being shipped to Sweden. It did not seem to have any reasoning behind it. I loved my grandparents, so why did they ship me away? I actually got angry thinking about it. The war was not affecting them very much, so why send me here? Perhaps it was because Inga might be coming to Sweden? If it was to happen, it would be a great reunion for us and I hope she would like it at our aunt's. I wonder what she and Mother thought about this. The water was getting colder. It was time to scrub up and get out.

Far was in the office doing some paper work, sitting behind the massive desk, with a pair of round reading glasses clipped on his nose. He removed the glasses and looked up hearing me enter the room, beckoning me to come over. He explained of still being involved in lumber business, but in a much lesser capacity. He showed some pictures of the huge lumber yard in Stockholm, telling me that they had shipped wood products to many countries around the world. "Let me show you the safe," he said getting up and walking towards it. He stationed himself in front of a large metal door rotating a numbered dial back and forth, finally reaching a handle with both hands, turning it. The massive thick door opened into a small room with shelves crammed full of papers and ledgers and with many locked metal drawers recessed into the wall. I had seen a bank vault in Oulu and this reminded me of it. It smelled exactly the same, very important.

He left the door open walking back to the desk, muttering for me to look around but not to touch anything. I stayed in the room for a while pretending to be a banker, telling myself that the monies were locked in the metal drawers, which was probably true. There was a small desk and a chair. I sat down, found a blank piece of paper and a pencil and began to scribble numbers acting to be rich. The rich air in the vault, in the house and grounds contributed towards this feeling, which I did not mind at all. Meanwhile, Mother was struggling at home, which I did mind a lot, but there was nothing I could do. That made me sad. When I grow older, I will help at home. I wish that she could be here with me, experiencing what I was enjoying. If I could only share it with her, I would be so happy.

12

SCHOOL STARTED THE FOLLOWING MONDAY. Nervous about it I had woken up extra early in the morning in order to get ready. Rake had told me horror stories of school. I was certain now that I was being thrown to the lions. The new clothes which Mor had bought me for school were neatly laid out on the chair. A dark blue blazer with shiny gold buttons, crisply pressed gray slacks, and a white shirt was the first day's wardrobe. A tie! I had never worn one before and did not like the idea. She would have to knot it. I did not know how. The new shoes hurt and they were too shiny. After breakfast, my grandparents arrived for the occasion and escorted Mor and I to the school house. We got there too quickly. I wish it would have been further away.

Many children were playing outside and stopped to look and point at us when we passed them. I heard some whispers and chuckles. I was embarrassed. I was overdressed. I was the only one sporting a tie. I wish I could have hidden under Fammu's skirt. Inside, we were greeted by the only grownup I could see, a pleasant older lady dressed in some type of blue uniform. She introduced herself as Mrs.Bjork saying that she was the head master and the teacher, running the school by herself. She was carrying a long stick in one hand leading us into the classroom to her desk where she pulled out some papers from the drawer.

She turned to Mor and asked, "Is this the boy from Finland?".

"Yes, Mrs. Bjork. His name is Johan," she acknowledged.

Looking down at me, she asked, "Johan, do you speak Swedish?"

"I do," I answered timidly.

"You will like our school and will make many new friends," she said, and adding as an afterthought, "welcome."

I had nothing to say to that. The grownups were talking to the teacher and I began to walk around the room, looking at many colorful paintings by the students. The walls were covered with them. The room had a warm atmosphere, filled with worn, wooden flip up desks. It smelled a bit dusty. By the blackboard, in the corner, stood a big round globe on wooden legs, and in the other corner hung a tapestry showing the full alphabet. Front of the backboard, sat an old wooden teacher's desk, with the Swedish flag on a stand. The blackboard was dark green. The windows faced out into the playground, where I could see more children by now. I wondered which desk would be my, hopefully it would be off to the side somewhere, maybe by the windows so I could look out.

Mor came over telling me that the paper work was done and that they would be leaving, saying, "Johan, don't be scared. The first day is always the worst but I'm sure that you will like the school and Mrs.Bjork is a wonderful teacher." She kissed me on the cheek.

My grandparents did likewise telling me that I was a big boy now, knowing I would like it here. Ukki gave me a wink as he was leaving.

The school bell rang. Immediately there was a storm of children rushing in to their desks. Mrs.Bjork called me, pointing at an empty desk saying it was mine. At least it was in the third row, but not close to the windows. Everyone was standing by their desk, I did the same. After a short prayer, we sat down. The teacher asked me to stand up and introduced me to the class. I could feel my face redden as I stood there looking at my feet and the shiny shoes. She told the class to be friendly with me and to help me in the beginning as much as possible. The class murmured. I sat down.

We started with reading. I knew how to read a little and had no problem following along with the book that had been issued. Mrs.Bjork at one point had me stand up and read five words, which luckily I was able to do. She complimented me, giving me a small amount of confidence in front of everyone. Few boys did as well as I had done, making me feel even better. Each hour had a fifteen minute recess and we rushed out to play. Many boys approached me, telling me their name and asking me to join them in kicking a soccer ball. We ran kicking the ball around the playground, having fun. By now I was starting to feel good by their friendliness. Even one girl with pony tails, just like Peppi Longstocking, stopped to talk to me saying shyly that she was happy to have me at their school. Why had I been afraid of school? Rake was wrong, this was not a prison. Instead it was an enjoyable place. I will tell him.

At midday we sat at our desks for lunch, which consisted of a steaming bowl of oat meal and milk. There was a small kitchen in the back of the classroom. A woman had arrived earlier to cook the lunch, which five designated students went around placing in front of us. It tasted good, even though I had eaten so much oat meal at Fammu's that I was tired of it. Today I was so hungry from nervous tension and running around during recesses, that I would have eaten anything. When lunch was over, we sang a couple of Swedish songs, which I did not know, and went out for some more playing before resuming the class. By now I had no objections of being here.

Walking home after school with two boys my age, we stopped at the corner store to buy some candy for each, which we ate sitting down on the curb outside the store. Mor had given me some coins that morning. The boys wanted to know all about Finland, and so I told them some things, but mainly about Rantala and my horse. They in turn told me they lived just up the road and in their backyard they had built tree house, which was their club house. I could go and visit them whenever I wanted to. The sun was still shining brightly and when the candy was gone, we all headed home.

I ran home, full of excitement and stories of the first day. Far and Mor were sitting on the back porch, when I stormed in.

"I like school," I yelled out, still panting from the run, continuing, "I made a lot of friends."

"Johan, that is wonderful news, but we figured that you would. It is a nice school and you are smart and want to learn," Far said. Mor sat and looked at me with a broad smile.

"My friends have their own tree house. Can I go and visit them?"

"Not today, you had enough excitement for one day. Maybe tomorrow," Mor said.

"Okay," I said disappointedly, but it was true, I was tired and even had some home work to do. I sat down and had some cookies and juice telling them about the day, what we learned, about lunch and the recesses. I told them that I did not like to wear a tie, but Far insisted I should. I'll take it off before I get to school, I decided, put it in my pocket and string it back on before reaching home.

That night when in the bed, I began to read Peppi Longstocking on my own. It was hard but I was able to make out many words and guess the rest. During the night, I woke up from a scary dream about a tree house, which was perched atop a swaying flag pole. I was hanging on tooth and nail in order not to fall, but the house blew away and I slid down the pole winding up at my desk in school. I was happy to wake up.

On Saturday, Mor announced that she was going to go shopping in Mora for the day. This opened the door for our monthly coffee break, just Far and I. He did not need to be reminded. He came up to me hinting that later, us men would sit down and enjoy a cup of brew. I helped him with the garden by collecting baskets full of sugar peas and digging up piles of carrots. At lunch, after Mrs. Anderson was finished serving, we sat on the porch with a cup of coffee in front of us. I felt like a grownup. I tried Far's trick of drinking the coffee off the saucer, but it slipped spilling the beverage down my shirt. Far told me not to worry about it, later I could change. He even added a little more coffee with some milk into my cup, which I drank slowly the normal way. Oh, how good it tasted. We men talked about many important things enjoying the drink. That was my first real cup of coffee and I would never forget. With Ukki there had only been spoonfuls once in a while. Later we continued with the garden and I felt the effects of the coffee. My picking seemed to have speeded up and my energy level had increased.

Kerstin spent time with me every day, now being disappointed that I was going to school. I enjoyed her company but was looking forward to joining the group of boys from school. I had met her father who was a husky, jolly man. His hands reminded me of two large plates and if he would place one on my head, I would surely sink into the ground. He promised to take the two of us for a truck ride very soon. He normally drove a mammoth of a dump truck filled with sand or gravel for a road work project outside the town. That would be exciting.

School went well and in fact I liked it very much. Reading and Math appealed to me, but my favorite subject was Geography. We were studying different countries in Europe, countries which I hoped to be able to visit some day. Belgium was especially interesting because Fammu had told me so many stories about her youth there. My friend Niels was a rather rowdy boy, even in class. He wound up standing in the corner very often. Mrs.Bjork was a sturdy teacher not putting up with any nonsense. The time she caught me chewing gum in class, resulted in the corner for me. That was the first and last time I had to experience this punishment.

Finally I got to see the tree house. On that day after school, Niels and his friends invited me to come along to their house up the hill. Entering the back yard, Niels pointed to an old tall oak tree with thick branches protruding in all directions. High up in the fork of the tree, half hidden in yellowing autumn leaves, I saw what looked like a river raft with railings and a roof above it, carefully woven around the heavy branches. There was a rope ladder hugging the ample trunk leading to an opening in the platform. "Let's go up," Niels said, reaching for the ladder.

I climbed following him, careful not to lose a grip on the wiggly ladder. Once up through the opening in the floor, I had entered a hideaway of boyhood dreams. The floor had been constructed with thick planking, covered with colorful throw rugs, the inside railings with cutup burlap potato sacks. In the center stood a small wood stove with the chimney pipe extending up through the roof. A pile of wood was stacked next to it. A thick comfortable looking worn couch was next to it with pillows and with three wooden fruit crates as tables. On one side sat a beat up bureau with drawers, the top strewn with various knick knacks.

When all four of us were inside, Niels turned to me and asked, "Well, what do you think of our clubhouse?"

I was still astonished. "It looks like Tarzan's house on top of the trees."

"Only very special friends have ever seen it," he said, "no girls or grown-ups can come up here," he added in a proud tone.

"We light the fire on cold days making it very comfortable and warm, even in the winter," one of the other boys said.

Niels rummaged in the bureau drawers, pulling out four bottles of lemonade which he handed around as we sat down on the pillows.

"Johan, welcome to our club. We have decided that you can join us if you want to, but you must promise to keep everything that goes on here a secret," Niels said.

"I promise, thanks," I eagerly said.

Chatting away for an hour, the boys told me all about their get together and plans. One of the things in the secret department was smoking, just like Rake and I had been doing in the sand pit. They felt that it was cool to smoke.

Everyone did it. The movies showed us how sophisticated it was to smoke. Why not us? Inside a torn cushion was a hiding place for a pack of cigarettes stolen from someone's father. The pack was passed around, everyone taking a cigarette, including me. How could I say "no" on my first trip up. All of us lit up puffing away, with intermittent coughing. I was very concerned about going home with cigarette breath, and made a comment about it.

"Don't worry, we have a remedy for that," Niels said, pointing to a tube of tooth paste on top of the bureau. "Put some paste in your mouth and gargle with the lemonade. No one can smell anything after that."

It had become dusk as I washed my mouth, slightly dizzy, and spit into a bucket like everyone else and worked my way down the ladder. I had to hold on harder and move slower because my balance was not very good. No more smoking, I told myself after reaching the ground. I walked home at a leisurely pace, hoping to clear my foggy head and let the smell of smoke dissipate.

Kerstin met me at the gate where she had been waiting for me for a long time. She told me of being sad that I had not come right home to play with her. I promised to come straight home the next day, but now I would have to rush in the house, being much later than I had promised Mor. She was waiting for me. She scolded me, wanting to know how come I was so late, to which I explained that I was not able to leave my friends the first day in the tree house. I did apologize and promised not to do it again.

At the dinner table I discovered how Mrs. Anderson seemed to appear always at the right moment to serve more food or clear the dishes. I noticed Mor's foot extend under the table and press a hidden button covered by the carpet, at the same time a subdued sound of a bell ringing in the kitchen. It never failed. The grumpy lady entered the dining room. I didn't think it was my fault, but she seemed to give me a dirty look always. Oh well— that was her problem, I decided.

Someday I will push the button when I'm alone in the house with the "grump" I will sit at the end of the table. When she shuffles in with fire in her eyes, I will calmly order a glass of soda and crackers with Lingonberries. She will hate me for sure after that.

13

"JOHAN, HURRY UP!" MOR HOLLERED.

Today was Thursday, the night of the dreaded Salvation Army meeting. I had tried on the dark blue uniform a couple of times thinking that I looked like a hotel bell boy. The uniform was bad, but not as dreadful as the hat with gold lettering and red rim. No matter which way I set it on my head, straight, on an angle or on the back of the head it looked appalling. The leather strap under the chin irritated the skin and if it was too loose, the hat fell off. I wanted to jump on it with both feet and pulverize it. Everyone would laugh at me tonight. I knew it. What in the world would my friends say if they saw me bicycling in that stupid uniform? I would never live it down.

After an early dinner, it was time to go. Mor and I, dressed in our crispy blue uniforms and got on the bikes and headed down the hill. Far never went to these meetings. As we left him, I could detect a sly smile on his lips. Thanks a lot, I thought. We left. Mor was leading the way. We had to stop once to get my pants cuff loose from the chain sprocket where it was caught. Now I had a greasy cuff, which did not bother me, but perturbed Mor but there was nothing we could do about it. The hat was flying in the wind, hanging around my neck by the strap. Mor, in her uniform, was totally proper and composed, pedaling upright. The colorful wicker basket full of cookies and her hymnal that was attached on the handle bars was breaking the wind.

In the hall, uniformed ladies came over to tell me how cute I looked. I blushed.

"Oh- look! Isn't he sweet, he is blushing!" someone commented and I blushed even more. I could feel my face burning. I was surrounded by blue women. Not a place in sight to hide!

Some brushed my shoulder for unknown dust, others fooled with the hat at different angles. Finally we sat down to sing some hymns, Mor at the organ. I held the book in front of me, but could not make out the words, just moved my lips, pretending to sing. The pastor conducted a short sermon, after which we sang again. I was sitting next to a large lady who kept rubbing my knee, whispering in my ear. I could smell Swedish meatballs on her breath and some awful perfume, which even rubbed off on me. I don't know what she was saying. A lengthy meeting about fund raising ensued. I was squirming in my seat. Finally we sang again, after which the pastor said a prayer and, Amen. The meeting was over. I thanked God silently, asking him to tell Mor not to bring me along next time, but He did not listen because I became a permanent fixture here, every second Thursday evening.

The best part began now. The ladies had baked all types of cakes and cookies. No wonder these ladies and the couple of men, were fat. The table contained two high chocolate cakes, cookies in different colors and sizes. It was overloaded with sweets. Mor had brought a cake loaf, which she called a Swiss roll up. There was coffee, tea and milk and some soda bottles. No wonder these people like to come here every Thursday night. I had squeezed between the chairs and the women, grabbed a plate and piled an assortment of sweets on it. After selecting a bottle of soda, I strolled to the far corner of the room to enjoy the goodies and hopefully in peace from everyone. It did not last long until a lady came up to me depositing two more pieces of cake on my plate, telling me that I must try them. Someone else did the same thing making the plate grow in front of my eyes. I would be sick if I ate everything. After eating over half on the plate, I got up and without anyone noticing, and dumped the rest in a trash can.

Stomach bulging, I went to find Mor, who was talking to a group, explaining some ideas of fund raising, this fall and upcoming Christmas. She was suggesting a cake sale, but some of the women opposed to the idea. They were not getting anywhere. I had to pull on her skirt before she noticed me, saying that we would leave soon. I wanted to leave now, but she kept talking for seemingly long time, until finally coming over to tell me it was time to go.

It had turned dark outside. The bicycles were equipped with lights, helping us see the road. I was tired with an achy stomach, as we pedaled home, pushing the bikes the last stretch. Far greeted us upstairs, asking me how the meeting went, still with the silly smile. Throwing myself on the couch I told him that it was very boring and I was exhausted and my stomach hurt. "After a while you will probably enjoy it," he said in a hesitant tone, with a twinkle in his eyes.

On Sunday mornings, the three of us formed a bicycle caravan for church services. We were dressed in our Sunday best, which was not much different from any other day. Mor had clamped a wooden laundry clip to my pants cuff, remembering the previous problem. Far led the way. Mor followed and I, as always last. Why always last? The thought of migrating birds flying in formation, one breaking the wind, made me feel better. Far was the wind breaker and I had an easier ride.

Inside the Lutheran church every seat was taken except for room for three people in the fifth row, almost under the pew. These seats were reserved for us. As we walked the center aisle, past the people already seated, nods and smiles came from both sides. Far and Mor acknowledged with a perpetual broad smile and an unnoticeable hand wave. I felt like a flower boy, which I had been at some friend's wedding in Oulu.

The church was absolutely beautiful with its stained glass windows, high ceiling and several large chandeliers. The altar had been built with shiny granite stone, with etched scroll and a large cross in the center. On top sat a golden linen runner and two candelabras with an open Bible in between the back wall shone with spotlights focused on a painting of Jesus on the cross.

The murmured conversation stopped. The pastor, my Uncle Hjelmer, approached behind the altar, dressed in a black robe with a brilliant white collar bib. He bid the congregation, "Good Morning," in a robust tone, which echoed through the church, after which the services were opened by singing a hymn. Far and Mor's voice carried above all others. The pastor asked everyone to join in a prayer, then reading some verses from the Bible. More singing followed. The sermon was conducted from the pew above us. He had entered it by climbing a spiral staircase up. We sat so close that I had to crank my neck in order to see him. My neck was stiff every Sunday afternoon.

His sermons were very powerful his voice reverberated forcefully to the point. Except it appeared as if he was looking directly at me, when preaching about godliness. When he elaborated about being good, he looked at me. Talking about sin and naughty things, again he looked at me. I always thought of myself as a rather good boy. Sure, I smoked, knew a few cuss words and fibbed once in a while, but how did he know this? It bothered me. God knows everything, but he was not God. I will try to be better this week, I told myself.

I did not know much about God. I remember from the terrible burn at Rantala, when Mother came to stay by my bedside. She prayed aloud for Him to look after me. She told me that God would do this, holding my hand. She tried to explain where God was, but I could not understand any of it. To me, however, God sounded like a nice helpful being. But where was He? Now with the Westholms, my Uncle Hjelmer and the dreaded Salvation Army, I was slowly learning more. Maybe Uncle Hjelmer had inside information of God? I still remained puzzled. Far had taught me a short prayer which I should say every night before falling asleep. Some nights I forgot to do so, but God must understand.

After the church services, we always convened at my aunt's. These were the days when I had a chance to be with their sons. I had found the older boy, Erick, to be very interesting. His hobby was astronomy. In his room he had a long shiny telescope standing on a tripod, next to a large night-sky globe, with stars and constellations outlined. He could spend hours explaining about them. I would sit quietly fascinated, listening to him. The younger son, Alex, having heard all this from his older brother over and over, occupied himself otherwise. Erick told me of wanting to become an astronomer, but his father had insisted he should study for the clergy. Somewhere along the line he was hoping to change his father's thinking.

Upon leaving this day, he lent me an illustrated book of stars, which I could not wait to dig into. Maybe I would study astronomy? It seemed so interesting.

Aunt Elsa called me down to the living room where they had gathered. My grandparents were gone over one month by now. Before sitting down, I grabbed some cookies and a glass of juice. Actually, I would like to have a cup of coffee, but knew it would be a wrong thing to ask.

"Inga will be coming to live with us in November," she said in a sweet tone, watching my face of surprise. "You must be happy to hear this?" she continued, with a tender smile.

I hesitated for a moment from the shock, "Oh- that is terrific. I am so happy to hear this news. I miss her," I said. It came out a bit too loud and too quickly. A tear was running down my cheek. I pulled out my handkerchief, pretending to blow my nose, but wiped the tear instead. Hopefully no one noticed.

"When that day arrives, you can come with us to Mora to meet her."

"I can't wait. Thank you, it will be so nice to have her around. I'll come often to play with her and she can come and visit me at Far and Mor's."

I was already thinking of all the things I would show her. I can't take her to the tree house. Maybe they will bend the rules? Kerstin and her are about the same age. I will get them together. Kerstin seems to be so lonely all the time, waiting for me. Maybe she likes me? I will ask the teacher if Inga can come and visit the class some time. I am very proud of my sister and want everyone to meet her.

After my nightly bath, I was laying in bed trying to read the astronomy book. I recognized the Big Dipper and the North Star, also the Small Dipper and the Bear. The book in its self was too hard to read, but the pictures were great. Before falling asleep, my prayer contained a request for Inga's safe travel, and for God to look after my mother and our new brother, Kari.

14

THE DAY HAD ARRIVED WHEN Inga would reach Mora on the same train from Stockholm that had brought me to Orsa a time ago. My aunt, Mor and I took the small early morning electric trolley car to Mora to meet her. The thought of being able to be together after such long time, had uplifted my usually upbeat spirits, even more.

Overnight the first snow had fallen, leaving us with a sparkling white landscape. It was still coming down in intermittent squalls, hitting the small train's windows and giving us a taste of the upcoming winter season. I had become fascinated by the story of "Robinson Crusoe," thinking just now how great it would be to live on a tropical island with palm trees and no snow. I would lay in the sun and swim every day and eat fish and coconuts when I was hungry. My island was waiting for me in the South Pacific. My daydreaming was interrupted abruptly by the loudspeaker crackling, "Mora." That is crazy. They don't need a loudspeaker on this one car trolley car. Mora was the last stop and the only stop.

Inga's train arrived on time. Several people got off it and finally I saw her. A pretty blond girl, dressed in a warm winter coat, holding on to a fluffy teddy bear, climbed down the steps to the platform.

I ran to her, grabbing her in a strong hug. I was her older brother after all. I did not hug many girls, this was different. She had a broad smile, twinkling eyes and bright red rosy cheeks. She hugged me back, uttering just a plain, "Hello." My aunt picked her up, nuzzling her to her cheek, greeting her lovingly. She had met Aunt Elsa in Finland a year earlier, when she had visited her and Mother. At least she was not met by strangers. Mor also welcomed her giving her a colorfully wrapped present. I am sure that it was not "Peppi Longstocking. It looked bigger than my present. The lady who had accompanied Inga, spoke to my aunt briefly and climbed back on the train to continue her journey.

On the little train back to Orsa, I sat next to her wanting to know all the news from home, and especially about our new brother, Kari. We spoke in Swedish, which she knew almost as well as I did. In fact, my Finnish was not nearly as fluent as Swedish, considering I had been such a long time with my grandparents. She told me everything.

Mother was well, but working too hard. After Kari's birth, she had gone back to work as soon as she was able to. He was a healthy plump baby, keeping everyone awake during the night. She described him in detail, his toes, fingers and everything else. Inga had started pre-school, which she liked very much. She would miss her friends. She also mentioned that Finland was already experiencing winter weather, much colder and more snow than here. She could not stop talking including about her trip over. She was nervous, wondering what was to come.

I was finally able to begin telling her about my escapades, and emphasized that I was sure that she would like it with our aunt and Sweden overall. The thing that had bothered me most, I told her, was my dress code, which Westholms insisted on. I had to tell her about the tie and the awful Salvation Army uniform, which I explained in detail. Inga burst out laughing and could not stop. It was a release of pent up emotions. Tears were running down her rosy cheeks. I tried to tell her it was not funny, but she could not stop the hysterical laugh. By now, everyone on the little train was staring at us. I was embarrassed. I took a walk to the bathroom, from where I finally could hear her silly laugh stop. About time, I thought. Back in the seat, we chit chatted rest of the way.

Inga seemed thrilled, with her new home inspecting her own room done up in a feminine touch. Her teddy bear was the first occupant as she placed the fluffy toy on her bed, leaning its head on the pillow. The pastor had not met her before, so when he came up to the room to welcome her he told her how happy he was to have a girl in the house. "Your presence will calm the two boys," he remarked. I thought of them not being rowdy, but then again, what did I know?

Inga would become dizzy from all the stars and constellations, which Erick would corner her with.

Later, Aunt Elsa had arranged the typical visitors' table of goodies. The fireplace had been lit in the living room, where we sat and talked. Our aunt did most of it, directing the conversation towards Inga, who sat in a large overstuffed chair. I sort of felt bad watching her disappear into the soft cushions, answering timidly from her entrapment. She was a brave girl. I knew that she would do fine and adapt to the household quickly. She was not shy by any means. We had grown up in different and diverse settings, which had honed us to be strong and positive. Even Inga, who had endured so much more hardship, had not changed her fortitude which was ingrained into both of us. I was proud of her.

Mor invited Inga to come with us for a short visit, to see where I lived. A taxi was called to whisk us home. The mode of transportation normally was the bicycle, soon it would be the "kick-sled," as the roads froze until spring. A taxi ride was luxury.

At the house she met Far who she told me later, reminded her of Uncle Runar in Oulu. Far always came across at one's first meeting as a distinguished industrialist or bank president, demanding and shrewd, but as you got to know him, he became a down to earth nice man with a warm heart. Far told me to take Inga for a walk around the house and perhaps even see if Kerstin was home.

As we roamed from room to room, Inga's eyes were wide in disbelief of such grandeur. My room with the balcony was especially interesting to her. We stood on the balcony overlooking the fields and Orsa Lake. I told her about the beaches and the swimming in the summer, the carnivals and circus. She told me that all this was like heaven to her, having arrived from war-torn Finland. We stopped at the organ. I sat down and serenaded my little sister with "Chop sticks." On the organ it sounded so different from Fammu's piano, but she clapped and hollered "Bravo!" I was embarrassed and could fell myself blushing. I will play this at the next Salivation Army meeting, I mused.

When reaching the steps going up to the dead daughter's room, I briefly told her the story, mentioning that room was off limits, explaining to her why but Inga still managed a pout. Heading down the back steps to the kitchen, I mentioned—with a grin, that she would be meeting a "wonderful sweet lady" in the kitchen, Mrs. Anderson.

Sure enough, the woman was chopping something, as always, when we entered her domain. She looked up at me and growled something unintelligible, but seeing Inga her tone and expressions changed.

"But who is this pretty girl?" she asked looking down at my sister.

"She is my little sister, Inga," I said, surprised at her kind tone. She had never used this tone towards me. *She must hate me.*

"Oh, come here, darling. Let me get you a piece of cake," she said, in the same kind tone, reaching for a cake on the counter and cutting a piece. "I guess the boy also wants a piece?" she mumbled looking at me.

"Mrs. Anderson, I have told Inga all about you, especially how nice and kind you are," I said veiling a snicker.

"Don't listen to him. I can imagine what awful things he told you about me. I just don't like little smart boys to get too cocky. Sit down, dear," she said and motioned to Inga, turning her head to look at me with a frosty glare

She had not asked me to sit down, but I did anyway. I must get to this woman somehow, I thought, looking at her fussing around my sister.

Later, after the Mrs. Anderson episode, we strolled out. I showed Inga the shed, sauna and the laundry room, after which we proceeded to meet Kerstin. She was home. Instantly her and Inga hit it off. They were same age, same size and equally pretty. Kerstin showed her around their small apartment and her large doll collection. I was so happy to know that Inga already found a friend and I was happy for Kerstin, who seemed to be so lonely most of the time. They talked about who could come where and when to play with each other. Finally I had to pull my sister out, because we already had spent such a long time exploring.

After a short visit with the Westholms, Far called the taxi to take her home. She thanked all of us, and after hugs and kisses, she climbed into the car waving as they drove away. Even Kerstin had come out to see her off, with a happy face, as she waved. "Come back soon," she hollered after the car.

Well, it sure had been an exciting and joyful day for me, from the moment I woke up. I could just picture how much easier my mother's life would be now with only Kari to care for. Both of us had agreed that we missed our mother very much, but understood why sending Inga here was necessary. It was also the safety factor, due to the war. I still argued with my feelings towards my grand-parents about sending me away, but over time had somewhat adjusted to the idea. At least I could say that I was very content in staying with the Westholms, also with the knowledge that it would not last too long. Yet how long, I did not know.

Stranos and my horse were in my thoughts daily. I missed them so much. Rantala with my grandparents had brought such a memorable experience, even the noisy owl by the outhouse found a fleeting moment in my thoughts. The life at Rantala was a dream life of any young boy. I missed Rake and the sand pit, with our treasure box and faraway plans on desert islands. The life here in Swe-den was fine, but too sanitary compared to the farm, where I could run around in worn out fun clothing. Ukki's hunting trip with me was still waiting. I could not wait for that day. I must remember to tell the rat catching story to Inga and Kerstin. The rat was as big as a cat, I will tell them. I will show them the scar on my thumb and scare them.

Inga would adapt quickly to our aunt's home and at least we were somewhat together. Over the years, there had only been short visits between us, but as for my mother, I had not seen her in years. Maybe when leaving Sweden, I could go finally directly home and stay there. I loved my grandparents, but I truly missed home. I hope the war will end soon

The fighting was still going on at the Eastern front. In the news in Sweden, there were newscasts about the fortitude of the Finnish soldiers in their conquest of the Russians. The small country of Finland had proved a major opposition to the larger Russian Army, creating an obstacle which they had not been prepared for. The Russians lost twenty solders to every Finn. Our father must be in the midst of this bad war but knowing him, he was doing well. We all were hoping to hear from him soon, praying that he was well.

15

In the fall, the warmth and sparkling sunshine had once more surrendered to a gray cold winter. Snowfall was an almost a daily occurrence. The birds had flown south, except for the few minor species that stayed year around. Just like at Rantala, there was an owl living in an old tree, close to my room. I could hear it hooting every evening and the first thing in the morning. That sound reminded me so much of the farm. I wondered if my horse missed me. I missed Stranos and our sign language conversations, also his woodworking skills. I thought about him daily.

Directly behind our house ran a deep gully. It had become our—Kerstin's, Inga's and my favorite ski hill. The snow was deep and fluffy. We would ski down the hill on our side and climb up the opposite side. We would repeat this back and forth for hours. Other children and my friends from school joined in with us daily, bringing their skis or sleds. The spot had become the winter playground for all of us. Often, Mor would serve steaming hot fruit juice and cookies for everyone. A couple of times she had sent Mrs. Anderson in her place, but this poor woman was afraid of the large group of children. I was thinking how much fun it would be to deposit her in a sled and send her sliding down the hill, hoping she would roll off of it in the deep snow. I had to chuckle at this thought.

There was a very pretty and friendly girl about my age, who came over to romp in the snow just about every day. She was in my class. I had seen her, but never thought twice about her. Her name was Sophia. She had bright green eyes, rosy cheeks and long blond hair, which flowed from the bulky winter hat. She always had a radiant smile. First I did not pay any attention to her, but finally noticed her around me most of the time. Where I skied, she sledded. If I fell, she fell close to me. Strange- I wondered why she hung around me, not that I minded it.

One day, we were down in the gully with no one else around, she came very close to me and said in a low hesitant voice, blushing at the same time, "Johan, I like you very much," and kissed me on the cheek. I stood still, dumbfounded, not knowing what to say. By the time some clumsy words popped in my mind, she was already half way up the hill.

That was the first time a girl kissed me! I had never kissed one, except old ladies with powder on their cheeks. It was a surprise, but the more I thought about it, it was an enjoyable shock. She was a pretty and peppy girl. Maybe I was missing something? Girls weren't so bad, especially Sophia. Rake used to talk about his girlfriend, but then again, it was not boy stuff to talk about girls, he had said. What happened to me just now had an effect of a small spark. I stopped to think. What did that mean? I must think about it. As we continued playing in the snow, I could not help but keep an eye on Sophia and the longer I gazed at her, the prettier she looked. Was I falling in love? I don't know, but people talked about it so much.

Christmas was just around the corner and I knew this would happen. Two weeks before Christmas Mor told me that it was our turn to ring the bell for the Salvation Army. I tried to wiggle out of it by coughing, or telling her of head-ache and stomach pains, but nothing worked. Early that Saturday morning, I bundled up into woolen "long-johns," a woolen shirt and a pair of thick woolen socks. Next came the dreaded uniform. I could hardly fit into it with all the clothes underneath. Mor placed a tight knitted ski hat over my head. Thank you God, not that ugly 'pot' hat today. That was very short lived. She fussed with the Salvation Army hat and when she was happy about the shape, she placed it on my head, on top of the ski hat. My first thought was 'paska!' in Finnish was, shit! This lady thought of everything. I was mad. Why in the world did I have to go through this torture? I looked into the mirror, and an odd looking sight greeted me. I almost laughed and cried at the same time, seeing this potato head wrapped in a bright yellow ski mask, with a round flat ghastly blue hat sitting on top of it. It could not be me, but it was me.

Being winter, we used the kick sleds to propel ourselves to town. Mor was first as always. I followed her, standing on my left foot on the left runner, kicking with the other foot. The thing moved rather easy and fast on the ice covered road, especially down hill, where I could stand on both runners. By pushing the handle bar in either direction, the whole sled turned. In the front there was a seat for another person or packages. There was also a hand brake in case I went down the hill too fast but I liked to go down the hill at breakneck speed. At times I passed Mor, who hollered for me to slow down. She wanted to lead the way. I was thinking how comical this normally would have looked but today, dressed as I was, I was sure anyone watching would die of laughter.

We stood all day in the corner by the bank, ringing the bell next to the tripod with the pot hanging in the middle. It was cold and embarrassing. I had pulled the yellow hat so that only my nose and eyes were visible, hoping that none of my friends would recognize me. I rang the bell loud and jumped up and down to keep warm. Most people passing by stopped and threw some coins into the pot, wishing us Merry Christmas. Few of the older ladies who knew Mor and I, stopped to chat would invariably adjust my hat, cooing at Mor about how charming I looked. I could kick them in the shin, but it was Christmas, so I behaved.

The small restaurant next door served as our warming spot and bathroom. I had to run into the bathroom many times. The cold did that to me. In the bathroom I had a major problem. The cold had shrunk my instrument and the many layers of clothes, made it almost impossible to take a piss without getting the pants wet. What a day! I did cuss in Finnish, but very quietly. It would be terrible for some refined gentleman to see a Salvation Army boy taking a leak and cussing at the same time.

Throughout the day, I saw several of my friends go by, but luckily no-one recognized me. If Niels, from the tree house, would see me now, I would never live it down. They would probably ban me from the tree house for being a sissy. Mor and I took turns for lunch in the small restaurant. When she was inside, I rang the bell even harder. Many people stopped, throwing money into the pot, commenting how adorable I was. I forced a lopsided grin at them and thanked them for their donation. When it was my turn for lunch, I sat down and ordered a huge pile of Swedish pancakes with Lingonberry jam. I ate slowly, very slowly, enjoying the food, until finally Mor hollered in the doorway for me to come back out. I wanted to sit inside the rest of the afternoon, but no. Finally the bell ringing was over for the day. It had become dusk and much colder by the time we used our kick-sleds to travel our way home. I was tired, cold and hungry. I could not wait to get out of the darn uniform. Far had the same sly smile, just like every other time he saw me dressed this way. Mrs. Anderson even gave me a crooked smile for a change when I trotted through the kitchen. It was a smile of a torturer.

Tomorrow being Sunday, we did not need not to ring the bell. The town closed down and buttoned up tight on Sundays. Next week however, we were scheduled for one evening and Saturday. I just had to come down with chicken-pox or some dreadful disease. As a small conciliation, I tried to focus on the fact that we were helping poor and sick people. Far had told me on the side, knowing how unwelcome these Salvation Army meetings and bell ringing were to me.

Inga came over often to ski and play with Kerstin. They had become good friends by now. Kerstin had slept over at our aunt's a few times. Inga had stayed with us twice. Mor had given her and Kerstin the guest bedroom on those nights. They had giggly fun times together. We played hide-go-seek throughout the whole house. It took long time to find anyone, the house being so large with many good hiding places. One time they could not find me. I had hidden in the most unlikely place, Mrs. Anderson's cupboard. I waited and waited, almost falling asleep, finally walking upstairs, where the two girls were playing with dolls on the bed.

"Why didn't you look for me?" I barked, mad at them.

"We did, all over the house and could not find you, so we gave up," Inga said.

"I'll never play with you again," I snarled and in a huff walked out, slamming the door. If Mrs.Anderson would find out that I had hidden in her kitchen, she would probably spank me. Oh well, she would never know.

When in bed that night, I could not help but think of Sophia. We had become good friends. I had visited her modest house, just up the hill from the school. Her family was friendly and warm towards me. She had two sisters, both younger, and one brother, several years older than her. We spent time doing homework, drawing and talking. I told her the story of Robinson Crusoe, which she had never heard. She wanted to come with me to the island! She promised to do all the cooking. "Fine, you can come. I will catch the fish and climb the trees for coconuts," I said, thinking how terrific that would be, with no grownups around to tell you what to do. Her green eyes sparkled with excitement. All this was becoming a twist in my thinking, my friendship with the boys and everything else. What was happening? Am I experiencing so called "puppy love?" I had heard grownups talk about puppy love, but never understood what it meant. Maybe it had something to do with a fluffy puppy dog?

Niels and the other boys had noticed that I was spending more and more time talking to her. They did not make fun of it, but instead seemed a bit jealous. They all claimed that they liked her, but she had been very standoffish towards them. "How come she likes you?" Niels asked.

"I don't know," I said, which was the truth, but I was happy of her choice. I wanted to stay friends with the boys and also Sophia.

Early one morning, the Inn just down the hill from us had caught on fire. This was a famous old establishment where the King of Sweden had stayed many times when visiting the Dalarna region. We rushed there, hearing the fire trucks and seeing thick black smoke rise. By the time we reached the burning building, it was totally engulfed in roaring yellow and red flames. The roof was ready to collapse. The heavy smoke was shooting skyward. There was nothing the firemen could do, except keep hosing down the surrounding area. It seemed as if the whole town had come to look. The people were ogling the sight, as this famous old landmark was being reduced to cinder. It was too hot to stand close, even at our distance off to the side. I could feel the heat on my cheeks. The firemen told us that everyone from the building had gotten out in time, but two cats were believed to have perished in this holocaust. Late in the afternoon, on the way home from school, I went to see what was left of the Inn. There was nothing but an enormous pile of still smoldering rubble. It had been a sad day for the town to lose this noted institution.

That night it took a long time for me to fall asleep. My mind had traveled back to Rantala and my grandparents. I missed them. I missed Stranos and the times I had spent with him, watching him build things in the shop. I hoped my horse was well. The Kollis came to mind also and I wondered how they were. The last thought was the scary episode with the rat. I rubbed my scar, still feeling its teeth sink into my skin.

16

SCHOOL WENT WELL. I HAD learned to read and had begun to read Tarzan, Huck Finn, Tom Sawyer, Robinson Crusoe and of course Peppi Long-stocking. This was the book which I attribute as my start of avid reading throughout the years. Tarzan and Crusoe were still my favorites. These were stories which contributed to my day dreaming.

During this first school year I noticed in myself a growth of maturity. Most of my friends followed alike. A few others in the class showed no improvement at all. I wonder if they ever would. To me they appeared to be immature hooligans, which was Fammu's favorite word concerning young rowdy boys. Perhaps in my case, the development had much to do with the exposure I had with so many older people and different locales. The turbulence of the war had entered into this picture. Even at that, I had been honed into ultra positive thinking in self growth through people, education and religious affiliation. Up to now the people in my short life were all well versed and kind, without any turbulence in their life. It did not mean at all that I was conceited and selfish. No just the opposite. At my age, I had been fortunate to experience and see much more than anyone else my age. Perhaps it was good, perhaps in many ways bad. There were no permanent roots which I could cling to. Yet it all was exciting and enlightening. One fact which I do admit is that I was spoiled rotten every which way but that was not my fault.

When spring finally arrived and the tree buds began to open into bright young green leaves, everyone's attitude started to change almost rhythmically with the sun's warming rays. It was as if nature and people were waking up from hibernation. More smiles and rosy spirits could be seen and felt. Far and I were busy tilling the garden for plating. Many days were spent raking the previous autumn's yellow leaves. They were piled in strategic locations and burned on a windless day. I enjoyed this outside work immensely and admiring the results of our hard work. Far and I, with his arm around me, stood admiring our daily progress. At times I was so tired, and even a few blisters popped up on my hands, but I still felt happy for having been able to contribute efforts into the work.

The tree house had gotten its spring cleaning. We met there on weekends, fixing what the winter weather damaged and adding a few new features. One of the boys had brought an old radio, which was sat atop the bureau, but we had no electricity for it. At present an oil lamp hung from the ceiling provided light. I brought up few Tarzan books, storing them in a makeshift wooden crate serving as a book case. I wondered if anyone would read them. My friends were great and fun fellows, but I had never seen anyone reading a book. There was a stack of well worn comic books, but I was hoping that my contribution would entice someone to read a 'real' book. I think all avid readers wish for others to share the adventures found only in books

It was late on a Sunday afternoon when all club members had gathered there for the usual meeting of minds. A pack of "Kool" cigarettes was passed around. Where in the world did these American cigarettes come from? They tasted so good and minty. There was a whole carton of them in the drawer. The answer came hesitantly, as we watched Niels doing something totally strange. He was sitting on the couch sandpapering each finger tip. His demeanor was scared and nervous. He inspected each finger tip carefully. The ones he was not satisfied with, he kept sanding more.

"Why are you sanding your fingers?" a boy named Lars asked. He was the second in command, after Niels. All of us were waiting for a reply.

Almost in tears Niels muttered so quietly it was hard to hear him "I stole them from our neighbor. They had gotten a package from America," he whispered, still sanding away. He had been at their house when the package had arrived.

"Why are you sanding your fingers?" Lars asked again. All our eyes were focused on Niels.

"Finger prints!" he blasted out, "I don't want the police to get my finger prints." By now he was nearly crying.

He told us of having climbed into their house when no one was home, looking for the carton of Kools, which he knew were somewhere. It had taken him some fifteen minutes to search in closets and drawers when he finally found them. He ran back out the same window directly to the tree house, hiding the carton in the drawer. Later he had become scared of what he had done, actually regretting it. But it was too late by then.

"Take them back and tell the people that you are sorry. Ask them to forgive you. "Cry a little bit, that will help," someone suggested. We all nodded in agreement.

"Will they call the police?"

"No, if you confess and say that you will never do it again," Lars advised.

"If they don't call the police, they will at least tell my parents. I don't want them to know," he stammered.

"If you sincerely apologize, tell them that you made a terrible mistake and ask them not to call the police or tell your parents, they most likely will not," Lars continued.

We could see Niels thinking about this suggestion. He had stopped sanding the fingers. He was nervous and trembling. He scanned each of us with red watery eyes. All of us nodded, voicing encouraging comments and coaching for him to take care of it right now. He thought about it, finally getting up, going to the bureau for the open carton and grabbing the now partially empty pack and stuffed it in the carton. We had succeeded into giving him courage to return it.

"Wish me luck," he said, putting the carton under his shirt. Still trembling, he turned facing us in a painful grin and began climbing down the rope ladder.

Over the railing, we could see the neighbor's house and Niels slowly, very slowly shuffling towards the kitchen door. He turned and looked at us in a pleading way for a moment, then continuing the plan of a villain. The door opened. He disappeared in.

We were frozen to the railing, trying to guess what would happen. About fifteen minutes later the kitchen door opened again. Niels rambled out. His face was fire red and it looked as if had been crying. In a slow saunter, he reached the tree and climbed back up. It was hard for us to hold back a bombardment of questions, but we waited until he sat down. He was breathing deeply, looking down at his feet, appearing weak as a person who had endured total humiliation. After a while he spoke in a defeated voice.

"Oh man, that was awful. I was scared stiff of what they would do." You could still see on his cheeks where the tears had run. "Everyone was home, but it was the father who scolded and threatened me. First he threatened me with the police and my parents, but later after begging his forgiveness he mellowed telling me to never ever do anything like this again. When I swore I would not, he said that he would forgive me, adding that it took lots of courage to come and admit my wrong doings." With a deep labored breath he continued, "He even shook my hand on the way out."

"Good for you," we almost said in unison. It was a relief to all of us.

"Damn it, I sandpapered my finger tips for nothing," Niels said, with a faint smile.

We still had one of the good mint cigarettes left, which we passed around like a peace pipe. This afternoon had taught all of us a lesson, which would be impossible to forget.

Later that evening I told the Westholms what had happened. They were very much concerned that I was running around with the wrong crowd. Maybe you should not play with them, they said very seriously. After explaining in detail how we had coached Niels and the terrible regret that he had felt, Far and Mor gave in, with my promise not to get involved in any wrong doings. I had not admitted of smoking, considering it a "fib" rather than a lie. It made me feel better to think of it this way.

I was looking forward to the summer, hoping that it would bring more adventures. Hopefully I would continue to stay out of trouble.

17

CIRCUS, CIRCUS, CIRCUS. IT WAS on everyone's mind. The air snapped with electricity. The circus was scheduled to arrive. And then one sunny spring morning a special circus train arrived. Luckily it was a Saturday. The boys and I had biked down to the soccer-field south of town where they would be erecting the huge tent. We were waiting for the caravan of animals, trucks loaded with equipment and the performers. There was a purpose for our wait, a method to our madness, if you will.

It was a bit later when the first trucks arrived, pulling into the center of the field. The animals would be moseying along afterward. As the trucks began unloading, the boys and I inched closer. Midgets, tall people, skinny people, fat people all jumped out from the trucks. Some men even walked like women. This sight was a circus in itself. It did not take long until our plan brought results.

"Hey boys, do you want to help in setting up? You'll get free tickets to the circus!" one of the short fat men called out to us. He seemed to be a foreman and he was yelling and pointing in our direction. We were the only boys around, so there was no mistake. He pointed at us.

"Yes sir!" Niels shouted back.

"You all look strong, so come here and I'll show you what to do," he called, motioning us over.

Each one of us got some type of assignment. My job along with two of my friends was to help stretch out the huge and heavy tent. There must have been some thirty people involved in this project. All of us pulled as hard as we could. Eventually the canvas was stretched tight, laying flat on the ground. Next the men began installing ropes and pegs to hold it in place. This done, the side posts went up and finally three very tall center posts. All of a sudden there was a huge tent. All this had only taken less than one hour. The colorful crew must have done this chore hundreds of times before.

"See that truck full of saw dust? Get the shovels and start spreading it everywhere inside the tent," the fat man hollered.

By now all five of us became involved in this project. The truck had backed up to the center of the tent. Shovels, wheel barrows and rakes appeared from nowhere. We grabbed one of each. A crewman tipped the truck bed and the sawdust filled the wheel barrows in no time. They were light to push. We went back and forth, piling the sawdust everywhere, later to be raked and spread to cover the whole floor. I had helped to spread manure at the farm which was very heavy work. In comparison, this was a breeze.

Two hours flew by, after which we proudly eyed our work. We were exhausted. My body ached from all the raking. I felt like laying down on the soft and dry flooring.

"Thanks boys. Good job. Here are three tickets for tonight's show for each of you," the short fat man announced, holding out a handful of green tickets.

"Thank you, Mr. Boss," I stammered grabbing my share. Everyone else did likewise.

This caper had been Niel's idea. He had heard about it from some older boys, and it sure paid off. I would ask Westholms if they wanted to come with me, which I doubted. If not, I would take Inga and Kerstin to the circus. I knew how happy they would be. One more ticket would have been great. I could take Sophia also. I tried to trade some marbles with the other boys for an extra ticket, but they called me crazy.

Biking home proudly, with the bounty securely in my back pocket, I realized that this was the first time I had earned something by being employed. At the house, I zoomed past Mrs. Anderson to the living room, where Far and Mor were sitting and reading. My excitement echoed through the house when I told them about this fantastic happening. They thanked me for asking them to come tonight, but told me to take the girls instead. "I am sorry that you don't want to go," I said in a disappointing tone, but didn't mean one word of it. The girls and I would have more fun together. Far complimented me for working for something which I wanted, and for the invitation. I was happy as a cat that had caught a canary. When I phoned Inga with the good news, from Kerstin's home, they were elated. I was a hero.

Kerstin got to see her elephants. The show was great, the high wire acts were breathtaking, the clowns hilarious. The tent was jam packed with people who laughed, cried, hollered and sat at times in awestruck silence. All was quiet before a man shot from a cannon flew across the tent, seeming to land in someone's lap. Lions, tigers, horses and other animals performed unbelievable feats. I pointed out to the girls that shoes were resting on my sawdust floor. "Oh Johan, you worked so hard for us," Kerstin said, looking at me with admiration. I thought I took this comment nonchalantly, but felt secretly elated. We all loved every minute of this grand show. Inga and Kerstin said in unison after the performance that it was the most exciting thing they had ever seen.

When the circus was over, the three of us biked to the kiosk in the center of town for some ice cream cones. Mor had given me six kronor and told me to treat the girls to something good. With cones in hand, we followed Inga to our aunt's house, but did not go in due to the late hour. She thanked me again at the door, asking Kerstin to come over the next day if possible. Kerstin and I continued home. I would never forget my first circus. The fun of working with them, earning the tickets and then seeing the exciting show, had made this day into a memory keep-sake.

The next day I wrote two long letters, at least it took me a long time to write them, one to my mother and the other one to Ukki and Fammu, telling them of our great day.

Even at this late hour, it was still dusk and rather warm. The sun had just set over the tree tops, coloring the sky in bright red vista. It would be a beautiful day tomorrow.

18

THE SUMMER VACATION HAD BEGUN, with the last day being celebrated by a picnic in the grassy field behind the school house. Wild flowers were in bloom, decorating the open ground into a colorful meadow. Each student received a small picnic basket containing a ham and cheese sandwich, an apple, cookies and a soft drink. Eating and frolicking in the sunny afternoon on the soft new grass was the best day of school. After lunch and games, we sat in a circle around Mrs. Sundholm, who gave a short speech and handed each one their report card for the year with a note attached.

It was with much excitement that I opened the folded card with the grades. To my astonishment, she had given me a bold A for every subject. The note attached was very complimentary as to my progress and behavior, including a comment concerning quick adaptation to a new school. I knew that I was doing well, but all A's surprised me. There had been times when my day dreaming trips had whisked me off to faraway places and it was so hard to concentrate. The report card made me very happy, and I am sure that Far and Mor would feel the same way.

Before the day was over, the teacher had each one of us recite a few short comments of our favorite subject. When it came to my turn, I stood up announcing that Geography was my favorite subject. I mentioned especially of liking everything I had heard about the Pacific Ocean islands, like the one where Robinson Crusoe had been shipwrecked. Niels commented that he liked the lunch time best. Everyone burst out laughing, knowing from his pudgy size that he was telling the truth. It seemed as if everyone had gotten good grades, at least all my close friends, because all faces were beaming happiness. The upcoming long summer vacation probably contributed to most of the smiles.

The Westholms were so pleased when they read my report card. Even Mrs. Anderson treated me to a thicker piece of cake than normal. Far and Mor had encouraged me throughout the year, stating their confidence in my abilities and this report proved them correct. Both Far and Mor were very strict and resolute, but at the same time, loving and understanding grown-ups. They reminded me so much of my grandparents except for the fact that it was much harder for me to get away with anything with them. My grandparents were softer in this respect, perhaps intentionally letting me get by with some silly pranks and doings. I had grown to like my new family very much and the life here in Sweden.

I had a few sleepless nights. I was nervous. The day of my first date ever was approaching fast, too fast. "The Midsummer Festival" was only two days away. What is going on with me? I wondered if it was normal for a boy of my age to ask a girl out. It did please me very much that she agreed. I would have been devastated had she said no. It would be her first date also. It wasn't as if we would be alone, because her parents and the Westholms would also be attending this yearly affair, with thousands of other people.

It had happened three days ago, when I had run into Sophia in the little store. She was buying milk and I was buying candy. Outside the store, we sat side by side on the curb. I offered some candy to her which she accepted with a sweet smile. My mind was racing a mile a minute. I was tongue tied. I was sweating. I wanted to ask Sophia to be my date at the festival. How do I do it? Where was Rake? I was dizzy, but finally stammered a few words, which I had practiced for many days.

"Sophia," I tripped over my tongue, looking at a distant birch tree. "I would like for you to be my date at the festival," I finally was able to say, but almost fainting. Huh...I had done it.

"Johan, that is so sweet of you. I had secretly been hoping that you would ask me. Yes, I am happy to be your date." She was looking at me with a glowing smile. She was so cool and collective, where as I was a total nervous wreck.

"I'm so glad. See you at the festival," I was able to say, somewhat more in control of my composure. We shared a chocolate bar and headed home. Wiping the sweat off my brow I mentally thrust my chest out I was so proud of myself for accomplishing one of the hardest things in my life.

The day of the celebration had arrived. It was a warm summer afternoon, with the sun shining high, when the Westholms and I walked to the village of "Old Orsa." The celebration would last until next morning. Mor had dressed up in a colorful Dalarna folk dress. She looked very pretty. I was wearing a white shirt and brown shorts, with comfortable sandals. No tie for a change. Far was dressed very casually, in a sport jacket and gray pants. The village was located about one kilometer away from our house, on top of a neighboring hill. I would meet Sophia there. A solid caravan of people was walking towards the fair grounds. Many of the women were dressed similar to Mor. The atmosphere was festive with few of the people singing old Swedish folk songs.

The village had been enclosed off with a massive high log fence, which encircled the whole complex. As we entered through the solid gates into the courtyard, the first thing I noticed was a giant log May pole in the center of the yard. It had been clad in birch-leaves and decorated with multitude of flowers. Many people, young and old were dancing around the pole and would continue doing so into the night. A band sat on the balcony of an old log cabin playing regional folk music. Many violins and accordions composed the group of weather beaten and bearded musicians who seemed to blend in nicely with the aged thick log cabins circling the court yard. The sounds emanating from the balcony must have sounded the same eons ago. The buildings had stood for hundreds of years and would probably for many hundreds of years to come. They were gray from age, some covered in green moss. I could see mushrooms poking out through the thick logs. The music and the mood were ageless and transformed us back in time to King Olaf's era, where the crops were the treasures and guarded by the "Goddess of the Earth." As the sun began its descent towards the horizon, they looked forward to an abundant harvest. This, tonight, was our celebration. Tradition states that if you pick seven different wildflowers, you will dream of your future love. I had not picked any flowers and would not dare to do so.

I saw her. She was standing in a group with her friends, but I only noticed her, dressed in a vividly colorful folk costume. Her face was as radiant as sunshine. As I approached, her green eyes glittered with happiness. Her friends began to giggle when she left them to meet me. She looked beautiful. Sophia was probably the only girl in her group who had been invited by a boy to this celebration.

"Hei, Johan," she called out waving, running to meet me. "I have never seen so many people here before," she said, grabbing my hand. "Let's dance."

I glanced at the solid group of people, in a long chain, holding hands and dancing around the cross.

"I don't know how to dance," I stammered, staring at her smiling face. "You look so pretty in that dress," I was able to compliment her. My face felt hot, from a blush. I stood proud next to her, still holding hands. Holding hands with a girl was a first for me.

She pulled me towards the dancing multitude, hollering over the sounds, "I will show you what to do."

There was nothing I could say, but to follow her. When we reached the chain of people, she beckoned to break in and was immediately grabbed by an extended hand. She dragged me behind her. In the same instant my free hand had been captured, making us part of the chain. I was moving fast.

"Johan, do what I do. It is so easy," she shouted.

I watched her and the other people hopping in the chain around the pole by turning back and forth towards the person holding your hand, at the same time following the beat from the band, by throwing your alternate leg in the air. The multitude of rainbow colors from the women's folk costumes fluttered, like kaleidoscopes in motion. If you call this dancing, there sure was not much to it, I thought, catching on quickly. Round and round we went. I only got to see Sophia every second turn, the other turn I was facing an older heavy set lady, who gave me a broad smile each time. I grinned back. Dancing is fun, I decided, lifting my leg as high as it would go. We danced in this fashion for many full circles around the decorated pole. The longer we stayed in it, the faster it seemed to move. Finally I began to feel dizzy with all the hopping, turning and leg throwing, let alone the loud music. I shouted to Sophia, one of the times we faced each other, "I want to stop soon,"

"Ok, we'll go around couple of more times," she yelled back, pulling me along.

I nearly didn't make it, by the time we finally let ourselves loose from the hold, which locked up immediately after us, continuing round and round. I was dizzy. I led her to the closest cabin, sat on the ground leaning against the log wall. My head was spinning. She sat next to me, still holding my hand. I could sense sweat running down my face. I almost threw up. I was weak and feeling embarrassed for the state I was in. She could see it.

"Johan, I am sorry I kept you so long for the first time. You get used to it," she said in a tender tone, looking at me with a sorrowful face. "Let me run and get you some water. It should make you feel better," she said, getting up and running off.

What a date I turned out to be, I was musing feeling sorry for myself. I almost passed out on our first date. I closed my eyes and plugged my ears. Just the few minutes sitting still, was making me feel a little better. Sophia was back soon with a container of water, which I drank to the last drop.

"Sophia, I feel like a jerk for spoiling your fun," I told her in a humble voice, looking at those vivid green eyes, her head slightly tilted. She was the first person I had ever seen with these emerald eyes. I was fascinated. "I feel better already. Thanks for the water." The dizziness had subsided and the short rest had invigorated me back to almost normal. Extra energy was transmitted from Sophia's closeness.

During rest of the afternoon and evening, we walked all around the old village, visiting many cabins. We had seen Sophia's parents and the Westholms and all our friends. Entering one of the cabins I wondered how the people could live under such primitive conditions. Life must have been a daily struggle in every respect. While in the cabin, someone was nudging me. Turning around I was facing Inga and Kerstin, who jokingly commented something about "love birds," meaning Sophia and I. They had been at the festival also for many hours, dancing over and over without getting sick, Inga said after hearing about me almost passing out.

"I'm hungry," I said and the girls agreed to this statement. "Let's all head to the food stand for some old fashioned folk food," I said, tugging Sophia's arm. The girls followed, as we pushed through the milling crowd.

I had always heard about the Dalarna potato pancakes, which I had wanted to try for a long time, but Mrs. Anderson refused to make them, calling them "poor farmers belly fill." Now I sat in front of a stack of large crispy potato pancakes. Sophia told me to use butter and blueberry syrup with a sprinkle of cinnamon. I did, enjoying each bite, syrup running down my chin. The Swedish food was good as a rule, but this topped it all. Even the chunks of potatoes were delicious. This feast was washed down with a glass of cold buttermilk recommended by the lady behind the counter. Each one of us had something different enjoying everything immensely.

Later that night after dancing some more, we watched the lighting of the gigantic bonfire, Sophia and I, hand in hand, left. It was past midnight by now. The sky turned into a crimson dusk as we walked slowly home. Our faces were glowing with happiness from the long day's fun and our togetherness. At Sophia's quiet house, everyone must have been sleeping except the mother, whose outline we could see through the kitchen curtain. We stopped on her front porch. I gave Sophia a nervous hug and she threw me a kiss. I was afraid that the mother would be charging out to scold me for keeping her daughter out so late, but yet this fright was overshadowed by "love." I had never felt like this. It was as floating on a puffy, soft cloud from Sophia's tenderness. I guessed that she must have felt the same way. Her eyes were sparkling, ever so much greener, even in the dim light. She quietly opened the door, giving me a quick wave and disappeared.

My walk home was accomplished in a fog of disbelief, yet not knowing what it really meant, but thinking that this must be it. It must be love. At home, everyone was asleep as I tip-toed to my room, laid down on the bed with all my clothes on. Thinking about the evening, reliving it over and over, I fell asleep, waking up late, still tired from the long day. Mrs. Anderson sized me up and down with a critical smile on her lips while serving my breakfast. She did not say a word, but I could sense her disapproval of my late arrival. Perhaps she had heard me pass her room? Later Far and Mor asked if I had fun, stating that they were not worried about my late night. "It's only once a year. Remember that, Johan," Far said, with a wink.

19

SUMMER FLOATED BY VERY SLOWLY. The days were long, filled with activities from morning to evening. The weather was pleasant and delightful in July and August. It rarely rained. Day after day we enjoyed a bright blue sky with fluffy white clouds. At the beach, Far had arranged for me to get swimming lessons at the adjacent swimming pool for one hour a day over one week. During that time I learned to swim with the help of a young instructor and continued practicing in the lake, making me rather proficient by fall. Most of my friends knew how to swim and the ones who didn't were taught by us. Niels, Lars, and I bicycled to the beach just about every day. At the beach, we spent most of the time soaking in the pleasantly temperate clear water. We laid on the sand and played soccer, off and on, and just contemplated everything.

My friends did not have much temperament for girls, tormenting them every chance they could. No, this was the boy's summer. No one tormented Inga, Kerstin or Sophia. My friends were envious of Sophia's and my friendship and knew better not to make me mad with any stupid comments. The Midsummer Festival had bonded us together. Sophia had also become a good friend with Inga. If I was not involved with the boys, I was swimming and biking with the girls.

There was always some type of traveling carnival close by where we found ourselves having fun and raising mischief. These carnivals invariably came along with many rides, galleries and tents with side shows. The rides and shooting galleries were thrilling. Once I scored big by throwing tennis balls at bottles. Somehow I was able to knock them all down, winning the biggest prize, which was an ugly stuffed brown gorilla.

Carrying the gorilla around the fair ground on my shoulders, my friends snickered at me, not wanting to walk close by. They claimed to be embarrassed. But I thought they were jealous. The fake fur tickled my nose. Finally I handed the gorilla to a little girl. She got scared and started to cry. Her mother began to scold me, shaking her finger in front of my face, throwing the gorilla back to me. We rushed away. I passed it to Niels who deposited the ugly stuffed animal on the first park bench he saw. We were sick and tired of it. Later, looking around, I said, "I wonder who will be the lucky person to take the creature home."

The tents advertised unusual people or animals, such as: the smallest person in the world, hairy women, ape man, two headed monster etc. One show which caught our interest on this day, was being promoted by a giant dark skinned man standing on a platform with microphone in hand, hollering loudly. "Come and see the most terrifying show in the world......*The Fakir of The Orient*"

We were standing in the front of the platform, eating puffy white cotton candy. As the giant man kept ranting about the show we studied tall posters of a thin man swallowing swords and sticking long nails through his tongue in addition to nailing his hand to a table.

NO CHILDREN ALLOWED the sign stated. This was a must see show for us.

"Guys, let's look around and scan if we can find a way to get into this tent? This show sure sounds like it is meant for us," Niels said.

The way we proceeded to see many of these shows, including this one, was to take turns in crawling under the side of a tent. Sometimes we got caught, but the worst that came of it was loud shouting and being chased away with threats.

We found a likely spot on one of the sides where to sneak into this tent. It was shielded by an old red truck and some wooden boxes. No one could see us there. The tent bottom was slightly loose at this point. The spot was perfect. I had been selected to go first with my two buddies to clamber in after. I dug the soft sand with my hands creating a shallow ditch under the tent's side. It was a very tight squeeze, but pulling myself on my back under the stiff canvas, I made it. My friends would follow.

Lars, who was the fattest boy in the group, tried to come through next, but could not fit. There was no way he could pull his stomach in. His head and upper chest were inside, but the rest refused to follow. He fought hard trying to wiggle himself back out. He was stuck, half inside, the rest outside of the tent.

I was kneeling inside the tent, under the raised bleachers, when I heard Lars groaning. He was looking up at me with pleading eyes, ready to cry.

"Hurry up and help me. I can't move!" he gasped.

I crawled closer to him. We were nose to nose. He grabbed my arms pulling as hard as he could. Under the canvas he could see Niels on the outside pushing the kicking legs. Nothing happened. Lars was stuck.

All of a sudden, I felt a hand on my shoulder. I nearly screamed from the shock. Turning my head to look at the person, I nearly screamed again.

There stood the skinniest ugliest man I had ever seen. He looked like something from a scary movie I had once watched. The man stooped down, pushing me aside. He smelled of smoke and garlic.

"Your friend stuck. I help..." he muttered, grabbing hold of Lars arms, pulling him in. Lars looked frightened

"You very quiet....no let big man see you," he said in broken English, slithering away, disappearing to the back of the tent. The air still smelled of the man.

We were inside, standing under the bleachers, staring at the empty stage between legs of adults sitting above. I had found a spot up front under the second row. I was kneeling on the ground as quiet as a mouse. My eyes were focused on the stage between a pair of legs, waiting anxiously for something to happen. Glancing around I saw my friends close by.

"And now, here comes the famous Indian sword swallower, Mr.SAMIR. Give him a big hand!" the announcer shouted. Loud clapping ensued even before he finished his spiel.

The lights dimmed. Red and yellow spotlights lit the stage, with a rotating mirror ball, producing dancing dots throughout the tent. Finally a tall skinny oriental looking man emerged from behind a glistening curtain.

I could not believe my eyes. It was the same man, Mr. Samir who had just helped us. Was he the "sword man? He must be. Why did he not chase us away? I was dumb struck. Squatting, eyes wide open I studied the man.

The man walked with a limp, actually dragging his right leg. His head was bald. The bright spotlight shined off it, casting a ghostly shadow against the curtain. His eyes were small oblong slits, black dots piercing through. From his chin a straggly gray beard hung down to his chest. He only wore some type of loin cloth. His legs were a pair of thin white bony poles. In each hand he was carrying a long, slightly curved sword. Golden tassels hung from the grips.

He set one of them on a table which contained many other items. The dirty worn tablecloth was blood red. Mumbling something, which I am sure no-one in the tent understood, he stretched his neck, turned his head back, looking up at the tent ceiling. He stood in this position a long time. Eventually, very slowly, his mouth opened wide. His brown teeth were irregular. There was a raspy cough. You could hear a pin drop. I was hypnotized. The long sword slowly slid down his throat with only the handle sticking out of his mouth. How could he do that? I wondered, totally amazed.. He must be crazy. Next he reached for the second sword, which also very slowly inched its way down his throat. Now he was standing in the spotlights with two sword handles protruding from his mouth. The gold tassels were intertwined with his straggly beard. Finally the audience broke the silence by clapping and hollering at the same time. I joined with the audience. The man pulled both swords out simultaneously stabbing them into the wood platform, where they stood quivering. He took a bow loudly babbling something.

Next he reached for a long shiny nail. He held it up high in the air for us to see. He extended one of his fingers against the sharp point, grimacing at the touch. Now he stuck out his long, almost black tongue grabbing it with bony thin fingers in his left hand, seemingly yanking it out as far as possible. There was a subdued hush in the audience, as everyone stared at the man. With an exaggerated gesture he brought his right hand holding the sharp nail to his tongue. Extending the tongue still further out, with some spittle running down his arm, he brought the sharp nail slowly to it, at the same time seemingly shoving at it with much effort. Blood oozed out dripping down his beard, sliding down in droplets to the floor as the nail was piercing the tongue. Women screamed. More blood, more effort and suddenly the nail went through sticking out through the bottom of the outstretched tongue. He proceeded to slide it up and down. His beady eyes were closed. He let go of the nail, which remained hanging at an odd angle.

A sound of agony filled the tent, not by the man, but by the audience.

An empty soda can flew down from the bleachers hitting me in the head.

I had covered my eyes with my hands when the man began pushing the nail through. I peeked with one eye between my fingers. All I could see was the long shiny nail and the black bloody tongue, everything else being just a blur. Now the skinny man was reaching for the second nail. I almost fainted, almost threw up and felt like screaming.

I could not stand staying there any longer. Quickly, in a flash, I stood up, and sprinted under the bleachers towards the front entrance. I fell, scraping my knees. I had to get out. I ran, not worrying about my friends, scooting between the huge dark skinned door man and the ticket seller. They in turn began chasing me to stop, yelling that no children were allowed in this tent. They did not catch me. I was still sick to my stomach and in a shock. This was the most horrible thing I had ever seen.

I ran as fast as I could and mixed in with the crowds milling around the rides until I was panting, out of breath. Walking around, far away from the tent I later inched back to see if could find my friends. A soda helped to settle my stomach.

Guessing on the time and feeling a little better, I carefully walked towards the Oriental's tent. Hiding behind an ice cream stand, I was able to keep an eye at the tent's entrance. Hearing the commotion inside, I knew that the show was still on. They must be showing the ape man by now. I missed it, but did not care. My friends were most likely still inside. *Wonder what my friends think of the show?* I mused.

Ten minutes went by when I noticed the huge doorman step outside to hold the side flap of the entrance open. People began streaming out. I saw Lars glued to a heavy-set man walking in tandem with him. The doorman was on the opposite side and was not able to detect the boy.

I stepped away from the stand and called out waving, "Lars! over here!"

Lars trotted across the walkway exclaiming even before reaching me, "What a show. I can't believe what I just saw. Where is Niels?"

"Let's wait he should be out any minute."

"That show was fake...fake...fake," Niels burst out when he reached us.

"What are you saying? It was not," I shouted, angry at him for thinking such stupid thoughts. I had been sick from it. It could not be phony, but now in the back of my mind I was wondering if it had been.

"I'll prove it to you guys. Let's go and find the Oriental," Niels challenged.

"You are crazy...the man will not talk to us," I said.

"Lars, what do you think?" he asked looking at him.

"Let's try," Lars muttered doubtfully, starting to walk.

"I don't know. It sure looked awful real to me," Lars was mumbling.

We skirted the tent past some flower beds and hedges and once out of the sight of the doorman, trotted to the back of the tent hoping to find Mr. Samir.

We lucked out. The man was sitting on a wooden box smoking, seemingly in deep thought. He looked startled when he heard us next to him. We could not see any blood on him, but otherwise he appeared to be as dissolved as before. He was covered in some type of brown tunic. His bald head glistered in the sunshine. A big cloud of smoke hung around him. The man began coughing and could not stop. His tangled beard jumped with the attack. Finally, clearing his throat he spit a heavy glob between his bare feet.

"We saw your show," I commented looking at the man.

"Yeh!" he answered.

"It was a trick. It was not real," Lars burst out.

"You kids," he stammered in his broken English. "You fat boy....didn't I help you get in? Now you say my show is a con," he continued eyeing Lars up and down.

"Tell us how you put the nail through your tongue," Niels said. We were not about to let the man off the hook, one way or the other.

"Go home to your mammies," he coughed again, continuing, "I come from India and my father was a snake charmer. I don't like snakes, so I swallow swords and stick nails in me. My father called me stupid. So what, leave me alone....go!"

"Your show was fantastic," I said, "we all think it was the most exciting thing we ever saw," I stated, giving the man a big smile.

His small eyes lit up. The statement hit home. It was probably very seldom that anyone complimented him. Perhaps he would talk now?

"Did it look fake?" he spurted out with his crooked yellow teeth showing when he grinned.

"You can't pierce your tongue over and over. Tell us what the trick is....," Lars pleaded.

"OK...I will tell you and show you something but then you go... and promise not to tell anybody," he rasped, motioning the boys closer.

"Big secret..."he mumbled glancing around carefully.

Next thing we knew, the man stuck his blackish tongue far out, pointing with his bony finger at the center. What we saw, was hard to believe? In the middle of his tongue there was a dime size permanent hole. All eyes were zeroed in, close up, at an ugly black tongue with a big hole.

"Happy now kids?" he asked after sliding the tongue back in his mouth. The smell of smoke and garlic hung in the air.

"No," I said, "what about all that blood?"

"You kids, bothering a working man...I tell you....you. GO!" the man said taking several drags from the cigarette, coughing some more.

"It's like this...." reaching into his pocket he pulled out something very carefully, continuing, see this?" He was holding up a small balloon with red liquid. "I hide it in my hand like so." He closed the balloon in his hand. "When I stick my tongue I squirt some at the same time. If I really want to scare the audience, I squirt a lot....but sometimes the women faint. My boss tells me....only a little."

"What did I tell you," Niels burst out. "Ha-ha, I was right, I told you it was all a fake."

We gave Mr. Samir a wave. He nodded.

20

THIS WAS MY FIRST NIGHT at home, since I was one and a half years old. I had left Sweden four months ago when Ukki and Fammu came to get me. After thanking the Westholms for taking such a good care of me for several years, we traveled back to Oulu where Fammu enrolled me into a Finnish elementary school for a few months in the fall. My Finnish was so rusty by now that I had a terrible time understanding anything, after speaking Swedish for such a long time. I hated every day and the class mates made fun of me. I did not want to go to this school. After Christmas the decision was made for me to finally go home, back to Mother

Was I having a nightmare?

No.

I woke up to screaming and a loud argument, through the cardboard thin wall along with an occasional crash. The argument sounded violent.

"You louse, drunken bastard! Some night I will kill you!" a raspy woman's scream bellowed, with the sound of dishes breaking. "Get out of the house!" she continued.

"If you don't shut up, I'll throw you out RIGHT now!" a drunken slurred man's voice shouted.

The hollering finally came to an abrupt stop. Thank God, I thought.

I was totally confused. Where was I? It took me some time to realize that I was home in Hameenlinna with my mother, sister and brother.

This was my first night at home, finally. What a shock it was. I had been so used to my own room with a warm comfortable bed and much pampering. I had been spoiled rotten, never having envisioned how my mother, sister and brother lived. Father had told me how Finland had suffered from the war with people living in poverty and hardship. Now I was to experience it myself.

Our apartment was on the second floor of an old wooden building with four apartments. It was dingy. It consisted of a small mud room and one closet with several wooden pegs on the wall with winter clothes hanging. A sizable pile of firewood was stacked in the corner. Two very small rooms and a sparse kitchenette with an old wood cooking stove occupied the rest of the apartment. Each room was heated with a tall tile stove reaching to the ceiling, which radiated warmth day and night. It needed to be stoked all day and later in the evening. When nothing but red hot embers remained, the flue was shut for the night. This method kept the rooms semi warm until early morning. A single bathroom with a cold water tap was located in the basement, to be shared with the other tenants in the building. Running down the steps to the bathroom, I kept my finger crossed that it would not be occupied. On the way back up, I brought a bucket of water for cooking and dishes. What a miserable chore this was. There were no shower facilities nor a bathtub, but a sauna was located in the other end of the building. Our scheduled sauna evening was every Thursday evening, which I was looking forward to.

I was scared and cold, wrapping myself in the worn out woolen blanket. The hollering started again on the neighbor's side. The paper sheets being used after the war crunched as I sat up. All linen sheets, cottons and other items had been donated or confiscated for the war efforts. Paper sheets were all that was available now. The wood stove had disbursed almost all its heat by now. Inga and Kari and I slept in the same room. They must be cold also. Still wrapped in the blanket I sat up to check on them. They had not woken up from all the commotion. They were curled up together in a single bed, sound asleep. I had my own narrow bed. The clock on the wall showed it to be past midnight. My mother should be home soon from work. She had a small bed in the other room which served as the living room, dining room and her bedroom. I could not help thinking of my own room at Fammu's and in Sweden. They were almost as big as this small apartment. How could we live in such cramped quarters?

Early that same morning, Mother, Inga and Kari had met me at the railroad station. Fammu and Ukki had put me on the night train to Hameenlinna in the south. The train left late in the evening. They had reserved a second class sleeper compartment which I shared with an old man, smelling of liquor and tobacco. He was on his way to Helsinki. I told him that I was going to Hameenlinna which was about fifty miles north of his destination. This was the extent of our conversation.

I laid down on the upper bunk, tossing and turning in my thinking about the next morning's meeting. The sound of the train clicking on the tracks finally put me to sleep. That morning I woke up early with great anticipation for getting back home after so many years wondering how life would be here. The old man was still snoring when I gathered my belongings and left the compartment. It would still take at least take one more hour before I would reach home. I stood in the cold hallway staring out at the dark, frigid landscape rolling by. The sky was crystal clear with millions of stars twinkling.

The train arrived to Hameenlinna. Mother, Inga and Kari were waiting by the wall of the gray weather beaten station building, with a light snow falling and big clouds of steam was spuming from the locomotive. I could barely see through the steam. I recognized Inga, not Mother nor Kari. It had been so many years ago when I saw Mother last in Oulu, but I had never met Kari, my brother before They were all bundled up against the frigid weather, each one wearing some type of fur hat. Their clothing looked warm but old and worn. Kari was bundled up in a puffy outfit.

It was a tearful happy meeting. As I stepped off the train, they ran over, arms open for a bear hug. Kari clanged to Mother's leg his rosy cheeks puffed out in puzzlement. What a cute pudgy little fellow he was. By now he was two years old. Standing, Mother was hugging me and telling me how much she had missed me, tears running down her cheeks, yet a big smile at the same time. Inga had grown taller but thinner since I had seen her in Sweden. A couple of tears ran down her rosy cheeks as she hugged me, uttering, "Juha, you finally came home. We all are so happy now." The snow was gathering on our shoulders.

"Juha, you are such a big grown up handsome boy now. Last time I saw you were just a baby and now you are eight years old. I have been looking forward to having you back home for such a long time," Mother said, in a tired smile.

To me, she looked beautiful. From under the fur hat, curly blond hair fell on her shoulders. I could see the tiredness on her drawn face from the long war and its hardships but it did not take away her beauty. I stooped down and picked Kari up giving him a kiss on his cheek, telling him that I was his big brother. His blue eyes just registered wonderment as he looked at me.

We stood there shivering from the biting cold. The train started off belching smoke and steam. Finally we walked hand in hand into the station building, close to a wood stove to warm up. There were only a couple of other people escaping the cold, just like us. It would be some twenty minutes before the bus to Hotel Aulanko would arrive. Our stop would be the last one before the hotel, Mother explained. I could hardly believe that I had arrived home.

When the bus finally came, after we had stood outside at the bus stop, freezing and jumping around to keep warm, I could not believe what I saw. A big blue bus pulled over with Aulanko written above the windshield, carrying a huge wood stove and a stack of wood, on a rack, outside, on the back of the bus.

"What is that?" I asked Mother pointing at the strange contraption.

She laughed, realizing that I had never seen anything so strange. "They call it a "wood gas generator" which gives the bus its power and cars use them also. The gasoline is under strict regulation and this is the only way much of the transportation moves," she said.

Sure enough, once we got aboard the bus took off. It was even nice and warm inside. I was curious so I decided to walk to the back window to see what was going on. Smoke was billowing behind the bus from the stove's chimney leaving a long smoke trail, slowly rising in the cold air. I still could not believe what I was seeing. It was like a big stove on wheels. Wow!

Later at home, Mother told me about the only job she had been able to find, while the hotel was closed. She said, "Juha, can you believe, but I am a prison guard in an awful old castle, which had been built by the Swedes around 1200. It is a huge dreary and cold dungeon. In the morning, you can see it from our window. It is directly across the lake. I hate this job, but somehow we manage with the living expenses. My old job as the food controller at Hotel Aulanko should be available again when they open up in a couple of months. I can't wait for it to happen and then we can move back to our old house on the hotel premises."

"I am sorry to hear about this," I said looking at her drawn face and sad eyes. "I will help out as much as I can," I promised.

A faint smile appeared on her face and reached out to ruffle my hair. "Thank you," she said, "you are a big boy by now and we sure need the help."

After waking up to the awful argument next door I decided to wait for mother to come home. It was midnight. I lit the fire in the kitchen stove, putting a pot of hot water to boil for coffee.

The window was half frosted as I sat by it looking into the moon lit wintry bright snow covered lake. Across the train tracks, the Vanaja Lake extended in a white blanket to the far shore where I could make out the outline of a majestic castle, which sat on its banks. The castle had been turned into a prison complex in the past few years. In the moon light, it looked dark and scary. The inmates were mostly Russian war prisoners including a few Finns, men and women. This was where our mother worked as a prison guard, The Hotel Aulanko where they had lived previously had been closed until the war's end for a war hospital and some renovations. Our mother had to move from the house on the hotel grounds in order to accommodate the workmen. She had been fortunate to locate this small apartment just a few miles away. Work was almost impossible to find, but she was thankful in finding this dreadful job as a prison guard.

In staring through the window, my eyes focused on a path on the moonlit snow covered lake when I saw a lonely person trekking slowly, stooped and bundled heavy against the fierce cold. That must be Mother on her way home. Her steps seemed laborious and guarded on the iced path. Before reaching to cross the railroad tracks she looked up, seeing my face in the window, she gave me a wave. I could not see it, but knew that there was a tired smile on her face. I waved back, eager to have her walk through the door.

I heard her climbing up the stairwell and reaching for the door which I had unlocked. She walked in looking frozen and worn out. The work alone must be tiresome and the walk across the lake, gruesome, in the fierce cold.

"I am so happy to be home and more so in seeing you here," she said while peeling off the heavy long coat and felt lined boots. She was wearing an ugly, rough, ill fitting, black uniform with the prison's logo sewn on the right arm.

"Sometimes I feel like collapsing on the ice," she said in a tone of hopelessness, her cheeks ripe apple red from the long cold walk across the lake. "There are no busses this time of the night. Once it snowed so heavy that I could not even see the path and had to turn around and stay the night in the prison employee's cafeteria, worrying about Inga and Kari. That was awful. Our neighbor helps with the children when I am at work but I don't like to be away from them so long," she said with a sigh.

"I have water boiling. Show me how you make coffee which will warm you up," I said walking towards the stove.

Mother followed me to the kitchenette, still shivering from the cold, stopping next to the warm stove, rubbing her hands over the heat. After a short while she reached for the coffee pot with boiling water. She lifted the lid to see how much water it contained, emptying some into a nearby pot. "I normally put a tablespoon of coffee for two cups and it looks like we have enough water for four cups, so two tablespoons should do it," she said spooning the ground coffee into the boiling water setting the pot on the side of the stove. "Now we wait a short while for the grounds to settle," adding, "this is called 'poor farmer's coffee. Some people add egg shells for the grounds to settle faster but I don't like to do it."

We sat at the small dining table, the only table, waiting for the coffee to settle. The fighting had stopped in the next door apartment, but some hushed words could be heard through the thin wall. We talked quietly, almost in whisper, in the light of one small table lamp casting shadowy light. It was still cool but the kitchen stove had radiated some welcoming warmth.

Mother was telling me about the hard and scary times during the war. She had seen Father only three times during that time for only two days at each visit. There had not been any bombing in Hameenlinna which everyone was grateful for. He had seemed in very good shape and had moved up in the ranks to become a captain of his regiment. Soon he would be able to leave the cavalry as the war was almost over. She also told me in a sad tone that their marriage was not going well. "I don't know what will happen to our relationship when he is out from the service," she said with a slow, tired smile. "I am so unhappy to tell you such news on your first day back, but you need to know." She laid her trembling cold and rough hands on mine, across the table and I could see how emotional she was. It showed in her sad and tired eyes and her shaky voice.

This unexpected news was a shock to me. I had always thought them to be a happy couple. "What happens to all of us, if you two separate?" I asked her, still holding hands.

"Juha, I don't know except that you and your sister and brother will stay with me. I am sure that Father has some other plans. I don't know what? But he indicated something in that direction." She wiped a tear from her cheek. "I always loved him and I thought it to be mutual. We will not know anything until he gets in touch with me. I don't know when?"

"Don't worry, we will do just fine," I said but still could not understand how.

The coffee was ready and Mother poured two cups with milk and sugar. The aroma of the coffee filled the small room. I don't think that my coffee had more than a drop of coffee, the rest being milk. I was still sitting dumb founded at the table. My mind was scrambled with this news. How could our father do such a thing? I wondered if Ukki and Fammu, his parents, knew about that.

I was so tired from the long trip and day. The coffee tasted good. I had not had any since Far, in Sweden. I think Mother had added extra milk and sugar in mine. I would probably stay up all night worrying and the coffee would not help.

We heard Inga cry out in the other room. Both of us ran to see what the problem was, but found Kari and her sound asleep. "She must have had a bad dream?" Mother said and adjusted their blanket. The room was still slightly warm from the stove.

"It is time for you to go to bed. I hope you are happy to be home, even so it is very modest compared to where you have lived but nothing will stop us.

I crawled in bed, Mother sitting next to me saying her evening prayer in a hushed tone, leaning over to kiss my cheek. "Good night. Sleep well."

I did have trouble falling asleep thinking about what Mother had told me about her and Father. It was just a terrible thought that they would separate and something which I found so hard to understand. I loved both of them. I was so sad. The sheets crunched beneath my weight as I restlessly battled for sleep.

21

THE FOLLOWING WEEKS WERE SPENT exploring the new environment. Inga was home from school on winter break for one week. She introduced me to her many friends who lived in our small compound of five similar buildings, each with four apartments like ours. We took a daily trip to the local food store, a half mile away, to shop for milk and other necessities for daily meals. Without refrigeration at home, we needed to shop daily. The store carried a charge account which Mother paid monthly leaving her hardly any money left except for the rent.

Most days our meals consisted of oatmeal, rye porridge, pea soup with perhaps few small pieces of ham, cheese and black bread. A special treat was cabbage rolls with ground beef. When Mother could afford to buy a small piece of beef, she would make a beef stew with potatoes and vegetables. That was delicious. Herring casserole was something that none of us children liked, but ate it anyway to quell the hunger. Milk was always available. "Silver tea," which was just boiling water, milk and sugar was a simple hot drink. With a limited budget and diet we got by.

The only candy we had to earn was by collecting five pound bundles of paper for recycling which awarded us one small lollypop. What a treat that was. I was thinking back to Sweden where the store's shelves were full of candy and chewing gum. Not here. Here we chewed on a piece of hardened tar chunk as a substitute for chewing gum. It did not taste good but served its purpose.

Once in a while, a package arrived from my grandparents with gifts of mainly clothing and some canned or dried food items. These gifts helped a lot and were much appreciated. My uncle also sent some hand-me-down clothing for me from Rake and his sister, Anna Lisa for Inga. Mother had taught me how to mend woolen socks. Holding a wooden mushroom inside the sock, I would sew the hole. I became good at it and wound up mending everyone's socks in the family. The socks were as good as new after my handiwork.

My daily chore became wood chopping and carrying it up into the mud room where they created a small puddle as they thawed out. Many times I was so close to chopping off a finger. The wood pile sat outside covered by snow which had to be cleared off the frozen logs. I was disgusted. The pile never seemed to get smaller.

Kari and a couple of youngsters about his age played in the snow building igloos and sledding at a nearby hill. It was a chore to get him in for lunch or dinner. The freezing cold weather did not seem to bother him. His cheeks were bright red with a line of snot running down from his nose.

The daylight was very short. On a clear day, we could see the sun low on the horizon for some four hours emanating a dim light before becoming dusk in the early afternoon. With the bright white snow, it never really got very dark. On the nights when the moon and the star lit the sky it was shining so bright you could read outside. It snowed nearly every day. With the sky overcast, sometimes only for a few hours, a fresh cover of new snowflakes would fall silently and envelope the earth in a new, soft, white blanket.

On top of the hill close to our apartment sat a long white building, partially covered in pine trees. Mother had told us to stay away from it because it was a tuberculosis sanitarium. One day I snuck close to it and saw a long deck facing our house. It contained a group of lounge chairs with a few of them occupied by patients covered in thick quilts enjoying the cold clear air. I was scared. Did I come too close to them? Quickly I ran down the hill not wanting to catch what they had.

"Juha, let's ski to Aulanko, it is so close," Inga said one day.

"Ok, let's go. I want to see what they have done there to our house which was waiting for us," I answered excitedly.

If we would get back after Mother had to leave for work, the neighbor would keep Kari until we got home.

I had met a boy named, Mikko who was about my age and lived in the apartment below us. He let me borrow his skis. After buckling up, Inga and I took off for the hotel. Cross country skiing is so invigorating and peaceful and quiet. For me this sport falls into the best category. Inga was dressed in a warm white parka with a fur hood. I was wearing my old bright yellow ski jacket and a warm knitted hat. The snow was soft and fluffy. We stayed on some previous trails yet mostly making our own. I had done so much skiing at Rantala and in Sweden. I had no problem keeping up with Inga who was leading the way. She was fast and agile. I shushed along.

She followed a trail through some fields, small hillocks and clusters of birch and before long, we reached the hotel property. Even in mid winter it was a gorgeous sight. We passed the outdoor tennis courts and now seeing the hotel itself. The sun was hitting the majestic building which glistered from the millions of small glass beads imbedded in its outer shell. It looked like a huge diamond sitting on bed of snow. The large outside patio was snow covered reaching up to the dining room windows.

Other buildings surrounded the hotel. Some served as extra accommodations for visitors and others as the employee's homes. Aulanko, with its first class accommodations and parks, was a famous landmark in Finland. Tourists from all around the world visited here when in Finland. Father had been the Dining Room Manager of the large dining room, seating up to five hundred people at any time. The war began and he was called to service. After I was born, I also lived on the premises my first year before being sent to my grandparents and later just Mother and Inga also Kari when he was born.

It appeared that most of the work had been done, as there was very little activity going on and just a few workmen about. "I hope we can move back here soon," I said to Inga as we were leaning on our ski poles.

We skied down a slope past many buildings, towards the laundry and the employee's accommodations. Our cabin was about ten minutes away from here. "In the next day or two, we'll come back and I will take you to it," Inga said. "Now I want you to see something different," she continued. By the lake side to the left a large white stable sat next to the caretaker's house. Riding in the summer time was big business. Inga had ridden many of the horses and had become quite good in even steeple jumping. It would be fun to see her this summer taking part in competitions.

"Let's ski to the stable, before it gets dark, so you can meet some of the horses. They are beautiful," Inga said.

"Ok, great, I love horses," I said, already heading in that direction.

The caretaker had seen us coming, waiting by the door to the stalls.

"Hi, Inga. Who is this young boy with you?" he asked looking me up and down.

"He is my brother Juha. Is it all right for us to come in and see the horses?" she asked as she introduced me to the old man.

"Sure....come on in," he said opening the door.

We unbuckled the skis in a hurry and followed the man in. He was a short stocky man with ruddy weather beaten face partially hidden in a scraggly, irregular beard, large chapped hands, wearing a heavy parka and thick felt boots reaching up to his knees. Even before entering the stables, I could smell strong odors of horse and manure on his clothing. It was a smell which I always loved. It was inspirational to me.

Inside there were twelve stalls with a horse in each one.

"Follow me," Inga said, pulling me by my arm past most of the stalls to almost the last one, where she stopped.

"Isn't he beautiful?" she said walking up to a magnificent stallion. "His name is Simonen." She stroked his forehead. "This is my horse every time I ride. He is very gentle but also very sporty in jumping steeples. I am just learning how to jump over low jumps. It's so exciting. We have become good friends."

I had to agree, the horse was a beauty. He was light brown, so shiny from grooming and possessed a long mane. He was a tall large horse. How could my little sister ever ride such large animal let alone jump? I was wondering. I thought about my horse at the farm which was more of a work horse, whereas Simonen was truly a riding horse.

Inga walked over to a sack of oats grabbing a handful to feed the horse. As he ate from her hand it seemed as if his big brown eyes smiled at the treat. "See you later," Inga said giving the horse a kiss on his nose. Walking back we stopped at each stall. Every horse in the stable looked to be of champion quality.

We thanked the old man. "Come back any time," he said as he led us out. "Your sister has become a very good rider. You must come and watch her ride, when the weather gets good," he added, giving me a big grin.

By now it had become dusk as the sun had dipped beyond the tree tops. "We must leave now before it gets dark," Inga said.

"Let's get going. Thank you for taking over to meet your horse. He is a beauty. I don't think my horse could ever even jump over a thick branch, but I like him very much," I said while buckling up to the skis. "He is mainly a work horse, big and strong but clumsy. He is also a 'scary cat'. Once in the woods we were trotting along, when suddenly a hare ran across the path. He reared up. Lucky for me, I was able to grab hold of his mane which kept me from falling off him," I told Inga laughingly.

We skied in semi dark. The moon was waning. The millions of stars lit our way in the bright white snow. I pointed out the North star to Inga. It was almost above us. The temperature had dropped noticeably from earlier, yet as our track continued we stayed warm from the exercise. It was so quiet and peaceful the only sound coming from the rhythmic movement of our skis over the snow.

It took us over half an hour to reach home. Mother had left for work already and Kari was at the neighbors. We picked him up and climbed to our apartment. It was cool inside. I proceeded to stoke both fireplaces and the kitchen for Inga to heat up some leftovers, which happened to be pea soup - again. But we were hungry after the ski trip, making it taste better. Even Kari ate a healthy serving. For dessert we shared one orange which Mother had been able to find some-where. Fruits and fresh vegetables were almost impossible to find in any store.

That night I slept deeply, dreaming about horses.

22

MANY THINGS HAVE BEEN ON my mind for the last week. The most disturbing was the possible separation of Mother and Father once he got done with the service. The second unpleasant idea was going back to a new school. Sure, I had fun getting used to the new life here and I was making friends. Our neighbor Mikko and I got along so well. But school? I didn't know if I was ready for that.

Now Mikko was another story. He lived with his mother and grandmother directly below our apartment. His mother was a sweet lady who worked in the customs department in Hameenlinna and the grandmother was an old, frail and blind lady. Compared to me, he seemed stronger and was a bit taller, with bushy, curly blond hair and bright blue eyes. He was a mischievous fellow, taking me by my arm and leading me in to all types of trouble. A few months later, the police came to talk to our mothers and threatened to haul us to the police station. We were petrified. The police car was parked outside the apartment door. The burly police officer told us that several complaints had been received from passing automobiles which had been snowballed, almost causing accidents by the startled drivers. Someone had seen us doing this and reported us. The officer gave us a severe scolding telling us we would be going to jail if we did it again. Both Mikko and I swore up and down that we would never do it again. "We are sorry!" came out in unison. This was the first time I saw my friend trembling. Mother was furious. I was grounded for one week. "Juha, I'm disappointed in you," she snarled. She had warned me about Mikko but I went along with him anyway. I needed a friend. He was a tough fellow around my age, so different from me, yet we got along fine. He was the "bully" in our complex and ready to fight anyone. One day he got mad at me and punched me in the nose. With blood seeping from my nose, I ran home where Mother put a cold compress on it and told me to lay still, scolding me for playing with him. A couple of days later we were friends again. Maybe I should learn to fight, but I did not like the idea.

The day arrived when Mother and I took the smoky contraption bus to Hameenlinna. It was a short twenty minute trip but to me it was too quick. I was wearing my best school clothes from Oulu. A pair of warm pants, a knitted woolen sweater with colorful birds, boots from my uncle's leather factory, and a stuffed parka. I was over dressed but Mother did not agree. She was taking me to the elementary school to be registered. I had tried to talk her out of it, but to no avail. This was the same school were Inga went. She was in the second grade. She had told me about the school and how much she liked it. Girls always like school, I was thinking.

Getting off the bus in the center of the city, next to a beautiful white Lutheran church very much like pastor Gunnar's in Sweden, we walked four blocks to the school. A light snow was falling. The sidewalks had been shoveled, except for a thin coating of today's snow. I tried to walk, slow not wanting to get there too fast but Mother was coaching me along to hurry up. Eventually we reached the school building which was much larger than any previous school I had attended. Before we even reached the front door, I was trembling and scared to enter the building. Tall glass doors led to a long hallway, painted bright white, only interrupted by student's artwork. The floor was an ugly gray linoleum. I could hear classes in session as we passed several class rooms. No one else was in the hallway as we walked towards a sign, half way down stating OFFICE.

We entered through an open door into a good size room with two large windows overlooking the snowy landscape. The air was smoky. The walls were painted bright yellow. Several tall book cases packed full of books covered three walls, a few large photographs hanging on one wall, reminded me of the library in Sweden. There were two desks. One large one was stacked with books, papers and folders. To the left, at a smaller desk, an old gray-haired lady sat behind a stack of papers. Her hair was in a tight bun, her face was wrinkled with a pair of huge Coke bottle glasses, making her eyes seem almost as large as Inga's horse. Her gray sweater had seen better days. She was smoking with the smoke lingering above her head. What a strange sight in a school, I thought.

"What can I do for you?" she asked in a raspy voice. "My name is Mrs. Aalto. I am the school secretary," she said, taking another puff of the cigarette.

"I came to register my son, who just moved home from Oulu," Mother said. "He is eight years old."

"Fill out these papers," she said, handing Mother several sheets. "You can sit in that chair," she said pointing to a worn leather chair opposite of her desk.

Mother sat and started to fill out the paper work while the gray haired old secretary glared at me. I stood next to mother. I was not happy and tried to avoid her stare. She did not look friendly.

Finally she spoke to me in a somewhat forced smile and harsh voice. "What is your name, young man?"

I stammered, "Juha," looking down at my boots.

"Juha -heh, are you a good student?"

"Yes," I said, still eyeing the boots.

"Look at me when I talk to you," she barked, "you are going to like our school and your teacher will be Mr. Kallela who is the principal of this school. He has been with the school over twenty years. He is very strict but if you behave, you won't have any problems. You will be in the third grade."

This did not sit well with me at all. Perhaps Rake was correct when he was explaining school being like a prison. My previous teachers had been friendly and kind, but now I was facing a strict teacher and a man of all things. The old lady's tone and looks did not help the situation.

Mother had finished all the paper work, handing it to her, she asked,

"When does Juha start school?"

"In the next fifteen minutes, when the class stops for a break." she stated staring at me with a devilish smile, blowing out more smoke, watching my horrified face. "Sit down on that chair," she said pointing at an uncomfortable, straight back wooden chair next to a tall pile of school books. The chair was wobbly.

I had hoped she would say something like next week, but fifteen minutes? That was horrifying.

I was actually shaking. I was scared to face a new teacher and all the new pupils. I mulled over why life had to be so complicated and mean as I sat on the uncomfortable chair. I felt like crying and throwing up.

Mother walked over to me, noticing my miserable appearance. She patted my head lightly and spoke in a kind voice. "Juha, don't worry, you will be fine. The first day is always scary. At least now you don't have to sit at home worrying for several days." She reached into her purse and handed me some coins. "Inga will be getting out the same time as you. She will show you where the bus station is. The money is for the bus ride," she continued and kissed my cheek. "Have a good day," she said and walked out from the room. I felt like running after her, but did not dare. The secretary's glare had me glued to the chair.

Now I was facing the torture alone. I was gazing at the ceiling where the gray smoke was dancing around. I had been thrown to the wolves.

I almost jumped when the school bell suddenly rang. It must be the signal for my torture to begin. The woman reminded me of a wrinkled prune on two legs, when she walked over to me, and commanded, "Follow me."

Few children were milling around the hallway when Mrs. Aalto stopped in front of a class room, leading me in. There was only one person in the room. The pupils were outside for the fifteen minute break, which came every forty five minutes.

"Mr. Kallela, we have a new student by the name of Juha. I have assigned him to your class," Mrs. Aalto said as we entered the room.

Mr. Kallela, stood on the upraised platform next to the blackboard and looked down at me. I could see that he was stern, just from his gaze. He was dressed in a black suit, a bit crumbled with shiny elbows. His tie, brick red, was knotted into a large knot,

His shoes were brown, which even I knew should not be worn with a black suit. He had a full set of dark hair. He wore black rimmed glasses below bushy eye brows. The eyes were bright blue. His clean shaven face had slightly depressed cheeks. He was tall, at least six foot, but on the platform he appeared to be seven foot and in good shape. By the looks of him, I was thinking that the secretary's comments about his toughness are probably correct. Yet somehow he seemed welcoming and friendly.

"Juha- nice to meet you. Let me shake your hand." He stooped down to reach me. His shake was firm, holding my hand for extended time, saying, "I am a very strict teacher which everyone knows, but as long as you follow the rules, study and learn, I will mold you into a scholar," he said releasing my hand. "The class is on their break. We have twenty six students now, you included. When they come back in I will introduce you. The desk in the third row by the window will be yours," he finished pointing to my desk.

I did not know what to say. I was still scared, but not as much as in the gray woman's office. I could still smell the cigarette on her, as she stood by me.

The break was over and the students piled in. I sat stiff at my desk all of them staring at me. There were more boys than girls. I must have blushed and did not know how to hold my hands and where to look. A boy, about my age, with blond curly hair and rosy cheeks, sat at the desk next to me and said, "Hi, I am Allan. What is your name?"

Before I had a chance to answer him, Mr. Kallela announced, "We have a new student in the class, his name is Juha. Please stand up. Give him a welcome greeting."

I stood up looking at my boots again, then the class clapped, saying in unison, "Welcome." My cheeks were red hot. It was embarrassing having the class clap at me. I sat down where I slowly started to relax looking around at the other students. I looked out the window. It was still snowing lightly. It would be so much fun to be skiing in the woods, instead of sitting in this classroom. Suddenly my thoughts and gazing were interrupted by a young girl laying a book on my desk and whispering, "This is our daily geography session. Here is your book," she said and walked back to her desk.

We were studying the country of India, which I found to be very interesting. Geography was my favorite subject. I was fascinated in learning about other countries and lifestyles. Mr. Kallela talked about India colorfully explaining in detail about the British ruling for centuries. I was impressed the way he made the subject sound interesting. For homework, he gave us reading from the book.

The bell sounded, meaning that the fifteen minute break before the next class would start. I had been so intrigued that the time just flew by. We ran out from the classroom, collected our warm coats and went out to play. Allan stood by me, explaining that this was a period to "wake" everyone up. The cold air with twirling snow fall did that very quickly. It was turmoil of children in snow ball fights, with others just hanging out. When the bell rang again it was a stampede back to our classroom.

Now the subject was Math. I was very good in Math. It was so easy. I did not realize that Mr. Kallela was the teacher for all subjects in our class. One more book was handed to me and more homework.

When the bell sounded next time, Allan told me this was lunch time. "Follow me. I hope lunch is good, which it seldom is," he continued, as we walked down steps to the basement into a large room where long banquet tables with benches were set up. The room was filling up fast with hundreds of students. I sat down next to Allan.

Suddenly a bowl of food appeared in front of me, delivered by a lady in a white uniform and black hairnet. I looked at the food. Pea soup! Not again. This was rather runny and lighter green than Mother's. I was sick of pea soup. It even smelled different. When I finally tasted it, it was awful.

Allan was snickering next to me seeing my face. "I told you. Wait until tomorrow when we get oatmeal. You can use it as glue for wallpaper," he said laughing.

After lunch was over we ran outside again. I was hungry and tired from the days ordeal and it was not yet even over.

The afternoon classes of Finnish, Social Studies, Art, went by quickly. Mr. Kallela appeared to me to be a very good teacher, if you could call a teacher good. The pupils behaved, knowing what would happen otherwise. Allan had told me that Kallela would run over to some student when they were misbehaving, lifting that student up from their desk by his or her ears, scolding the poor youngster severely. They had learned their lesson. I would never want this to happen to me.

The final bell rang. I met Inga outside and we walked to the bus terminal, her inquiring me about my first day. It was still snowing lightly and the temperature had dropped into a biting chill.

"How was your day?" Inga inquired with a grin..

"It was fine. So far I like the teacher. I made a friend, his name is Allan. Lunch was the worst I ever had -yac." I told her, making her break into a loud laugh. "We are studying about India which is interesting," I said.

"What is India?" she asked.

I could not believe, she did not know what India is. "You dummy. It is a large country in Asia. Don't you ask me what Asia is," I growled at her.

Inga's face turned to a pout. "Don't call me a dummy. You are older than I, so I have not learned about all the things you have -DUMMY!" she barked.

At the bus station several busses were lined up for various destinations. I could not help marveling these "fireplaces" on wheels. Smoke was billowing from the each stack. It almost obliterated the meager daylight left. The snow on the ground had turned into an ugly gray color from so much soot. Our bus was stationed in the middle of the lot. As we clambered in finding some empty seats, I could smell the smoke from the idling bus.

At home, mother greeted us with a wonderful smell of some type of beef stew cooking on the stove, "I see you survived your first day at school. Tell me all about it."

"I'm starved," I started and continued to tell her about the day.

The beef stew was delicious.

23

IT WAS BEGINNING OF APRIL. The days had grown longer. On the south side, where warm rays from the sun reached, the snow had began to melt. Small rivulets of water ran down on the hillside. The ground was still frozen solid. It was dark in the mornings when we left for school and the sun was setting late afternoon, on the way home. All around, even on the bus, people seemed happier, as if waking up from a long hibernation. Spring was in the air. Pussy willows will be budding soon.

School went well, to my surprise I even began to like it. The lunch was as bad as always, but gave us some energy. Mr. Kallela hollered at me once, when he caught me chewing gum, which had arrived in a package from Sweden. He stormed over to my desk. He petrified me. I was shaking. His eyes were piercing and his mouth was contorted. He was fuming. He did not lift me up by my ears, but slapped me hard on my head and told me to swallow it, which I did. "Never chew gum in my class," he shrieked. The class was chuckling until Kallela turned his head. Dead silence fell.

Mother had visited Helsinki twice by now, meeting with Father and lawyers. Father insisted on divorce, but we never found out why. Mother did not want it, but finally had to give in and the divorce was granted in rapid order. Father was to send support payments for us, the children, but that he never did, making it harder for Mother to support us. He disappeared, no one knowing where. It took another ten years before we found out that he had moved to Norway, where he signed up with The Norwegian American Steamship Line, as the steward on one of their cruise ships. We, Kari, Inga and I met her at the railroad station, when she arrived back from the last trip. The train had stopped on the furthest tracks, making her clamber over two sets of railroad tracks. She stopped, looking left and right, to make sure no other trains were coming. Her face was swollen and sad. She had been crying. She hugged us when she reached the station. After boarding the bus home, we sat huddled together -all of us crying. Even Kari cried, but probably did not understand what was going on. It was so sad. We all loved our father. How could he do this to us? It took a long time to get over this tragedy.

Mother's life had been tragic from birth. Her recollection of her early childhood was very hazy. She was born in Viipuri in 1918. Shortly after her birth, the Russians invaded the city. Her parents were killed and they became orphans, she and her brother who was one year older. They were sent to a orphanage in Karelia, close to the Russian border, in southeast Finland. The orphanage was a ramshackle barn, totally filled with small babies and young children. They froze in the winter with only rags on their back The mainstay food was bread baked from pine bark. Somewhere along this time, she and her brother were separated. She does not know what happened to him. Eventually she was moved to a foster home, close to Hameenlinna. Father and she got married, which changed her life for the first time, to a loving and happy family life. I was born and Inga was born one year later. Two years later her life changed back to hard times again, when Father was called to service. Kari was born during the war, four years later. Now again, mother was experiencing heartbreak yet again with the divorce.

One day in April happy news arrived. We would be moving to Aulanko shortly. The old log cabin on the hotel premises was waiting for us, rent free. Mother would start work at her old job in the hotel, in one week. She was so happy to be able to leave the miserable job as a prison guard and this cramped small apartment. It was not only miserable with thin walls, where you could hear the neighbor's conversations and arguments, but it was a fire trap also. With wood stoves and paper sheets, a careless spark would ignite this flimsy wooden building into an inferno. Mother had taught us exit strategy for such an event. Now she was excited and happy, giddier and smiling more. She had been so concerned about getting home from the prison at midnight, since the spring thaw would make the nightly lake crossing impossible. At our cabin, it was only ten minute walk for her to the hotel and she loved Aulanko Hotel.

Inga and I had skied a month ago to the cabin. She wanted to show it to me. It was a beautiful sunny day with the snow conditions perfect for cross country skiing. We passed the gleaming majestic hotel, in a short time, reaching a group of buildings amongst birch trees and pine. Snow hare tracks led into the woods.

"There is our cabin," Inga said, pointing with her ski pole. "Isn't it beautiful and peaceful here?" she continued in a big grin on her rosy cheeks, leaning onto her ski poles.

We stopped outside the cabin which was surrounded by clusters of birch trees with several tall pine trees in the background. It had been built solid with heavy hewn logs, which had aged over the years into a gray-brown color. Spotty green moss grew between the logs. The door was painted in barn red color, with noticeable fading. Deep drifts of snow covered the steps and lower part of the door. Two small windows faced the front yard, and two more at the end of the cabin. They were framed same color as the door with window planters sprouting wilted plants from last summer. The roof was supporting a thick cover of snow, with two chimneys jutting out. There were no footprints or shoveled paths. The cabin was empty. It was an idyllic picture perfect sight. I loved it!

"See that small building on the far side of the cabin? That is the wood shed and the yak...outhouse," she said with a smirk which became a laugh.

"I am so used to outhouses at the farm. I must be crazy, but somehow I like them." adding, "but not so much in dead winter."

"You are crazy!"

I was wondering and asked her. "Why didn't you stay here, instead of the stinky little apartment?"

"Because, as we told you, the hotel was closed for renovations and various workmen were housed in these buildings, last summer still. Not only that but Mother did not have any work here and it would have been impossible for her to travel back and forth to the awful prison from here," she belted out, as if I should have known.

"Let's ski around and look at some of the other buildings and the lake," Inga suggested.

Off we went. There were several more cabins in the woods. Some were in good shape, showing occupancy with shoveled paths and smoke arising from the chimneys. Few were just skeletons, with collapsed roofs and logs jutting in a tangled pile. We passed one large two story building, close to our cabin, when Inga, who was still involved with the thoughts of the outhouse, stopped to make a comment: "We sometimes run over here to use the bathroom. It is like a big rooming house for waiters and waitresses. They don't mind if we use their bathroom."

We continued our trek to the lake, where she wanted to show me two small man made islands connected with bridges from the mainland. Each island sported a large grouping of silver willow trees, now barren of leaves, their branches drooping, waiting for spring. These were the hotel's beaches in the summer. The islands were encircled with wide sand beaches, now snow covered, but still showing some bare spots of golden sand. On one of the islands stood a small snack stand, painted light blue, with a wooden patio for tables and chairs. Large colorful Coca Cola signs hung on the outside wall. Next to it a hand painted menu with prices, hung lopsided. One chair had been left behind on the patio, now snow covered, appearing as a soft white cushion. I could just imagine how beautiful this place was in the summer.

Aulanko has long traditions. A prehistoric castle was discovered on the Aulanko Hill, dating back to 1250 in the pagan times. In early 1800, a large estate, by the shores of Vanaja lake, became known as The Karlberg Manor. A resplendent time for Aulanko began when Hugo Standertskjold bought the existing estate, with vast grounds, including the future park at Aulanko Hill. He had made his fortune as an arms manufacturer in Russia, in the early part of 1900. The main building was rebuilt into a French Manor house. Greenhouses were erected, housing palms, cacti and multitude of flowers, with several grand water fountains. The shore line was reconditioned with granite walling and lined with silver willow trees over a stretch of three kilometers. Admirers arrived from as far away as the South of Europe. Aulanko became famous as the "gentlemen's" holiday paradise. This was where wealthy business men and politicians came to get away to an opulent resort. All amenities were available to them. Many spent their time gambling, accompanied with lovely ladies. There was no wish, which was not handled with utmost attention for these gentlemen.

Standertskjold had new driveways, wide walks and paths built on Aulanko Hill, in the forest. He created it into an English style park. The woods were thinned, two large ponds were dredged and named Forrest Lake and Swan lake. They became home to water birds, even to the rare black swans. The shores of the lakes were surrounded with fifty six species of trees. Further up on the top of the granite "mountain" a tall, five story, solid, lookout tower of local stone was erected. It had been constructed of "Inca" size cut granite rock. From the top of the tower, one could see the beautiful Finnish vista of meadows, lakes and forest. On a clear day, the sight was endless. A large Finnish flag, flew atop most, from a high flagpole. Aulanko Lake, with its crystal clear water, sat below the granite "mountain," The lake was known for delicious crayfish during August crayfish festivities. Beneath the tower, a bear statue cave was carved into the solid rock. The park was also dotted with intricate pavilions.

The estate was bought by the town of Hameenlinna in 1926. The manor house was taken over by the Finnish Tourist Association. Unfortunately the manor was destroyed by fire in 1928. The present Aulanko Hotel was built in 1938, becoming a flagship for tourism, throughout Finland and rest of the world. In the course of history, Aulanko attracted heads of states, other dignitaries, movie directors and stars. The beauty of Aulanko also inspired Jean Sibelius, the world known composer, who was born in Hameenlinna. A number of Finnish film classics were also shot there.

"What do you think of our "homestead?" Inga asked, looking at me with her bright blue eyes. Her fresh face radiated a glow of happiness.

"I cannot wait for the moving day." We are going to be so happy here, especially Mother. "Let's start for home but this time skirt the shoreline."

For the next hour, we skied without rushing, admiring the beautiful surroundings next to the frozen lake. There wasn't need for us to cut our own trail. A well traveled ski trail skirted the shore. I followed Inga whose strokes were long and even, her blonde ponytail swinging from side to side. We passed the hotel to our left. Its large dining room picture windows, cast reflected sun beams at us. To our right, a long dock for the summer cruise boats extended far into the lake. The silver willow trees lined the length of shore.

We had reached a small intricate pagoda.

"Let' stop here and take a short break," I called out to Inga.

"Yes, I can use a break," she answered, starting to unbuckle her skis. I did likewise, standing them into a snow bank.

We swooshed the snow off the bench and sat down. My legs were starting to feel like lead. Inga dug into the pocket of her parka, coming out with a welcomed chocolate bar. "Where did you get that from?" I asked, already drooling for the sweet.

"I saved it from the package from Sweden, for a special occasion, which is now," she said, with a wry grin. Inga unwrapped the bar of chocolate, and broke it into exactly same size pieces, handing me one.

The sun was still shining above the tree line across the frozen lake. It was warm. I let the chocolate melt in my mouth slowly, enjoying it immensely. I watched Inga's content expression, as she took pleasure in chewing her piece and running her tongue across her teeth, making sure she didn't miss anything. Neither of us spoke. The only shushing sound came from a light breeze blowing through the willow trees. It was so peaceful. After resting for a short time longer, we continued unhurried home.

This international famous complex was our home. To think that our family was a intricate part of this hotel and its success was gratifying. All loyal employees were well cared for, with housing like us, meals in the employee's dining room and fair wages. Father had been the dining room manager until he was called to fight the Russians. Mother had worked in the kitchen as the food checker, until the war started and the hotel was turned into a temporary war hospital and at the same time being remodeled. Inga and I had lived at the premises since birth. I had been sent up north to Oulu when I was one and a half years old. Mother and Inga moved to the small apartment, just as the war had started. Kari was born there later.

We would be moving home to Aulanko soon.

24

"**T**RUCK- TRUCK! IT'S HERE," INGA hollered excitedly, looking out the window.

We all could hear the rumbling engine. The building was vibrating early on a Saturday morning. We had been notified by the hotel prior in the week that they would send the truck to pick up our meager belongings and help us move into our cabin. I ran down to the front door, meeting two men next to the noisy idling truck, with Aulanko painted on the door. One of the men was older and heavy set. The other was tall and skinny, looking to be in the early twenties. The truck was discharging diesel smoke. How can they get diesel fuel? I was wondering. The busses were still running with the wood burning stove.

Both men were dressed in tan colored coveralls. The older man had a cigarette hanging from his mouth, when he turned towards me, asking, "Are we in the right place for the move?" he mumbled the words, so not to drop the dangling cigarette. I could hardly understand him, but knew that this was our moving truck. The younger man just stood leaning on the truck's door. He looked tired and bored and ran his hand through his greasy blond hair. His complexion appeared yellowish and sick.

"Yes, follow me," I said, coaching them to up the steps to our apartment where several boxes with our goods, stood stacked in the mudroom. Once inside they walked around, eyeing what needed to be carried into the truck. The younger man sat down on the kitchen chair, with his face in his hands, but jumped up when the older man howled, "Erkki! You lazy bum, get your ass up and start to carry the boxes into the truck." Looking at Mother, he said, "He is worthless....stays up all night drinking and now suffers from a hangover. I'm going to kick his ass out the door." Still facing Mother, looking a bit embarrassed he said, "Sorry madam." Mother just laughed.

Slowly but surely with all of us pitching in and with extra energy from this happy day, the furniture, boxes and clothes were on the truck. A group of onlookers had gathered around the truck. Many people wished us good luck others said that they were sorry to see us leave. Mikko came up to me, pulling me aside and said, "Don't forget me. We had lots of good and crazy times together. Maybe I can come and visit you at the hotel?"

"After we get settled, I will get in touch with you," I said, thinking -no way, because it seems that we created one problem after another. Some were just innocent pranks, but not all.

The scariest episode on the list happened a few months back. Very often we hung around the railroad tracks, laying coins or other small objects on the tracks, and waiting for the train to run over them and inspect them after the train had passed. They were very flat. One day there was a work crew of two men inspecting the tracks. They had arrived in a small two man 'handcar' lifting it off the tracks. It had four small wheels, like train wheels and two seesaw like handles, in the middle of the small platform. By the time we arrived, the men were several hundred yards away from the cart. We walked over to the cart, lifting it to see how heavy it was. Straining, we were able to lift it. The men did not seem to notice us. The railroad tracks were straight as far as we could see with no trains in sight. Mikko nodded and I agreed. We lifted the cart onto the tracks, jumped aboard and immediately started to hand-pump with all our might. We pumped the handles up and down, finally gaining traction. We were moving. The harder we pumped, the faster the contraption moved over the tracks. The men had noticed what was going on. They began to scream and run after us, but the distance from them and us grew. The cart was too fast for them to catch us. We pumped hard. Keeping a sharp eye we did not see any train coming. By the time we were at least a half mile away from the men, we slowed the cart to a stop, by using the foot brake system it had. We climbed off it and strained lifting it to side of the tracks, far enough so a train would not hit it. The men were still running, slowly by now, far away from us. Now we ran as fast as we could into the nearby woods, disappearing far into the forest. When safe, we stopped sitting down on a fallen log and laughing without being able to stop. Sweat was running down our faces and our breaths were laborious after all the excitement. We never got caught for this episode. Thinking about Mikko's urging to stay in touch, I decided against it. I better turn a "new leaf "in my life.

The truck was ready to leave. The older man asked mother if we need a ride to the hotel to which she said, "Yes please."

"Ok, you ride in the cab with me. Your children and my worthless helper can ride in the back. It is not too cold and the ride is short. They will be all right in the back and hopefully the air will clear the bum's head."

The truck's gears ground. We were moving, leaving behind us a cloud of diesel fuel smoke. All of us were waving to the friends being left behind. I was so cheerful for leaving making me wave more than anyone else. Mikko looked sad. I did not care. Through the small window into the cab of the truck, I noticed the happy glow on Mother's face.

Inga, Kari and I had made ourselves comfortably on the open truck bed. Inga found one of the beds and actually was lying down. Kari snuggled against me between a stack of boxes. Erkki looked surly and sat on the hard truck bed, all the way in the rear. During the ride, his greasy blond hair did not move at all. It was glued to his skull. The morning sun had risen a short while earlier, shining on our travel. The road was clear of any snow and ice. Spring thaw had arrived. The driver kept the speed slow, probably thinking of us on the open back. It was warm.

Twenty minutes later, we passed the hotel to our left. The large parking lot was clear of snow, with only a few cars parked on it. The sun shone directly at the hotel, creating a mirror effect from the glass chips plastered walls. A group of international flags fluttered in the light breeze, above the front entrance with a handsome large sign of AULANKO.

A few minutes later, we reached the cabin. The driveway had been plowed of the remaining snow. The entrance way had been shoveled from the deep drifts, which we had seen just a few months ago. Smoke was rising from the two chimneys. Our home was welcoming us. The truck backed up to the entrance, leaving the engine rumbling and smoking.

Mother climbed out from the cab, stopping by the steps to admire the sight. There was a peaceful, happy smile on her lips. We jumped down from the truck, joining her. No one said anything. The mood was exhilarating. Finally we walked up the three steps to the cabin's front door. I reached out to open it. There was a screech from the rusty hinges. It opened to a small mudroom. To the right, I opened the second door. A greeting of warmth and smell of pine welcomed us as we entered the kitchen. The wood stove was lit, with a pot of water boiling. It had a rustic and idyllic country kitchen feeling. Someone had cleaned the cabin and started the fires in the kitchen and living room before our arrival. I had only seen the cabin from outside, up until now. The first impression was great. The kitchen was large, just like the one at Rantala. Rustic cupboards lined the walls, with an ice box. I opened the door to it, where two large blocks of ice sat. It was cold. Great, now we did not need to go to a store every day. A large rough wooden table sat by the window surrounded by long benches. A beam of sunshine shone through the window, lighting the room in yellow glow. On the table sat a shallow glass dish, with four oranges and a note. Mother reached for the note, reading out loud.

"Symppe" which was my mother's nick name, "welcome home signed, Sophia." She hesitated for a moment. We could see a tear running down her cheek. "Sophia is my best friend. We have known each other for many years. She works in the hotel kitchen, as a cook. She lives behind us, just a short walk away. How sweet of her," she said, placing the note back on the dish.

The movers were impatient. They wanted to know where everything went. Mother told them to start bringing the stuff in and she would direct them. Now it was time for me to walk to the next rooms and inspect. Inga grabbed my hand leading us to the living room. Kari moseyed along. It was a modest cozy room with two small windows, framed in light green drapery, overlooking the thickets of birch trees. The tall stove emitted warmth. The walls were covered in light wood planking. The next two small rooms were the bedrooms. Inga explained that Kari and her would share one room, Mother the other. "Where do I sleep?" I asked her, in a puzzled look.

"Your bed will be placed on the back wall of the living room. It is still tight quarters here, but much bigger than the apartment, cozier and quiet. No neighbors fighting next door. I love it here and you will also, I'm sure," she said, with a joyful grin.

That sounded fine to me. I was happy to be here and especially for Mother's job at the hotel. She would have collapsed as a prison guard soon. This was such cheerful time for her again, with her feelings and pride of her position and the hotel overall. We would be taking the bus back and forth to school, right from the front door of Aulanko Hotel.

The movers were done and ready to leave. Mother thanked them slipping some money to the driver. I am sure it was not much, but at least it was a token gratuity. Now the unpleasant chore of unpacking the boxes began. The smell of diesel had almost dissipated.

Few hours later, our new home had a comfortable feel to it. A flexible reading lamp sat on a small night table at the head of my bed. I was happy about this set up, now being able to read in bed. I had graduated from Tarzan books to Mark Twain's books. I had begun reading Tom Sawyer, which was hard to put down. I laid it on top of Huckleberry Finn, next to my lamp. One thing I had liked about the apartment complex, was that there were lots of youngsters who liked reading. We borrowed books from each other and traded back and forth. Mark Twain's books had cost me two Tarzans. It was a fair trade. My bed would serve as a couch during the day.

The old, small kitchen table was placed under the two windows. Mother had covered it with a yellow tablecloth, setting a clay vase in the center that sprouted naked birch branches. Three chairs sat by the table and the fourth one in her bedroom. An oval woven multi color rag mat sat on the floor, partially covering its wide planking. The two bedrooms were ready with the beds and throw rugs. Mother said that she would try to find a small bed for Kari but at least the first night, Inga or she had to share their bed with Kari.

I carried all the cardboard boxes into the wood shed. There was ample stack of split wood and kindling for the rest of the winter. I also walked next door to the outhouse. The door had swollen from the melting snow, making it very hard to open. It was a two setter. How strange, I chuckled, thinking how interesting it would be to invite a friend along for a potty meeting. I did initiate the outhouse before walking back to the cabin.

We all loved our new home. Now it smelled of fish. I was surprised. As I walked in, she was busy at the stove grilling four perch, which she had bought the day before. She had kept them in the hallway of the apartment, which stayed just above freezing through winter. This would be our first fish dinner in a long time. I was looking forward to it. Fish always reminded me of Rantala. We

would be eating most of our dinners at the hotel's employee dining room, starting tomorrow. I had been told that normally the food was very good, but not
always. Probably it was leftovers from the daily lunch buffet in the main dining
room.

Inga had been occupied by putting away all our clothing. She had thrown
mine on my bed, into a pile.

"Why didn't you put my clothes away?" I snapped at her.

"I'm not your maid. You take care of your own things. I don't know where
to put them," she growled back.

Looking around, I saw that she was correct. I had no drawers or shelving
where to put them. Just inside the kitchen door there were hooks for coats, where
I hung the jackets. The rest of my clothes wound up on the floor at the foot
end of the bed, in a semi neat pile. Maybe someday I would have a bureau with
drawers?

There was a soft knock on the door. Mother called out, "Come in!"

"Sophia....it is so nice to see you again," Mother called out, dropping the
fish and running to greet her friend. "I know that all the cleaning and the heat
is your doing," she called out as she grabbed Sophia into a bear hug. "It has been
so long since we saw each other. I am so happy now. Thank you," she continued,
leading her friend to the kitchen bench.

Sophia was a short pudgy lady, shorter than Mother. Her face reminded me
of a full moon, with a twinkle in her eyes and a broad smile. Her blonde hair
was in a tight bun. She did not use any makeup and her cheeks were naturally
rosy. She seemed full of energy. Her dress was a simple, perhaps homemade, in a
woolen country style. She reminded me of Kolli's wife, at Rantala.

We all sat around the kitchen table. Mother put a coffee pot on the stove and
brought a tin can with homemade cookies, setting them close to Sophia. Inga
and Kari grabbed one each, munching them slowly. Sophia was telling Mother
that everyone in the hotel was waiting for her return. It was not the same without her. Now that the war was over, it had brought brisk business back. People
wanted to celebrate. Mother told her friend about their divorce. Sophia was
startled. Her face showed a sad disbelief in hearing this terrible news. She hesitated, looking at Mother speechless, but finally uttering, "I am so sorry to hear
this, at least you will be amongst many friends now."

The coffee was ready. I even got a diluted cup. Inga and Kari were served
milk. The conversation continued for long time. The cookie jar was emptied. At

one point, Mother mentioned needing a small bed for Kari, wanting to know if Sophia knew anyone who was willing to part with one. "Of course," she said." Go to the hotel's employee rooming house, next door to you, there are stacks of all size beds. Help yourself, they will not mind if you borrow one."

"Great," Mother said. "Later Juha and I will do that and get one. Thanks for the information," Mother said, looking at Kari with a smile. "Now you will get your own bed." Inga had a relieved grin on her face. My first thought was, maybe we could find a small bureau also for me? After all the news had been dispersed, Sophia bid farewell. "See you tomorrow at work." She hugged everyone, giving us a peck on the cheek and with a wave, she left.

Shortly thereafter, Mother and I walked through a couple of thawing snow drifts to the rooming house. It was a two story building, much newer than our cabin. Long hallways ran on each floor, with many doorways to private rooms. No one was around as we searched for a storage room, at last finding it at the end of the downstairs hallway. It was a rather large room, crammed with beds, bureaus, chairs and few tables. "This is a treasure trove," I said, looking around for our needs. We found a small bed with a mattress which was perfect for Kari. In the corner, I saw a bureau for myself. It took us two trips to carry the furniture home. The bed was no problem, but the bureau was heavy. We had to stop a couple of times, in order to catch our breaths, but it was well worth the effort. At home we set up Kari's bed in Inga's bedroom and my bureau against the wall at the foot of my bed. Now I had three drawers. Two were used for clothing and the bottom one, served as a junk drawer. Everyone was happy. Our cozy, solid as a brick cabin had turned into a comfortable home.

That evening, after enjoying a delicious fish dinner, everyone was tired from the day's work and excitement. It was time for bed. After Mother's evening prayers with us, we retired into our beds. Kari was so happy not having to sleep with Inga, and she was glad not have to sleep with him. I laid in bed, with my reading lamp on, continuing Tom Sawyer, but falling asleep somewhere along the evening, with the light on and the book on my stomach.

25

"**Y**OUNG MAN, ARE YOU THE shoeshine boy?" the well dressed man called out, looking at me. He was tall, on the heavy side, wearing a light top coat and a black felt hat.

"Yes sir," I answered, in a business-like tone, looking down at his shoes. They were brown and in desperate need of polish. "I am your man. Please sit up on the stool," I said pointing at my shoe shine station. The stool was padded and comfortable, with a step up. Under the step, in a drawer, the supplies of my trade were stored. The location of my operation was positioned in a large vestibule, between the outside and inside door of Hotel Aulanko.

It was early summer and school would be over in two weeks. On Saturday evenings and on Sundays, I had manned this station for over one month. The hotel had provided me with a blue uniform, with Aulanko sewn on the left shoulder. No hat, like the ugly Salvation Army thing. Thank God. I was always so excited to come to work. The tips on busy days or evenings were very good. It seemed as if most men, before entering the hotel, were in need of shoe shine. Yes, I was their man. If I was not polishing, I would open the front door and greet the people. On their way out I bid them farewell, with most of the time receiving a small tip. Wow, what a job. Just by opening the door, money would come my way.

The tall man, sat rigid in the chair, drumming his fingers on the arm rest, placing his feet on the two shoe stands. I began the cleaning and polishing, wondering when he had his last shoe shine. He was wearing bright red socks. How odd. I had discovered by making a big fuss and show with the polishing, the tips grew. So I did my 'song and dance' with this customer, finishing off with a spit shine, when he was not looking. His shoes shined, looking almost brand new. I tapped his leg, looking up at him. "All finished, enjoy your day," I said, with a broad grin. It never failed, but these small comments also added to the tip. He had become fidgety, kind of distracted and impatient.

"Thank you. They look like new," he said, looking at the shoes with a satisfied glance, and opening his wallet, giving me a good size tip. I thanked him, running to the inside door, holding it open, for him, to the hotel lobby. Another satisfied customer and a good tip. Great!

Several weeks had gone by. We had become very comfortable in our home. All the snow had disappeared and some spring lilies were blooming on the sunny side of the cabin. The birch trees sprouted small early leaves. The warm temperature was welcomed after the long winter. The days had become longer. The warmth and sunshine shone on everyone's face.

The long dark winters had a negative effect in the peoples' lives, making the population gloomy and tired. Alcoholism rose every winter. Amongst the drunken men, knife fights were common. Suicides increased. There were more divorces during the winter than in the summer. All types of studies had been conducted about this seasonal change, and it was concluded that the long darkness and lack of sunshine was the reason, for the population's behavior. There was nothing that could be done about it. This was part of living in Finland. Years later, special home lighting had been invented to cheer up the mood during the long winter, and apparently they had proven to help.

Mother was happy being back to work, which she loved. Her sunken cheeks from the prison guard time had disappeared. She looked healthy with a rosy outlook. Inga, Kari and I were doing fine. Kari was taken care of by one of Mother's friends while she was at work and we were in school. School for both Inga and I was going well and we came home with good report cards. The last two weeks were a drag, going by very slowly.

Our dinners took place in the hotel's employee cafeteria, except when Mother had her day off, once a week, when she cooked at home. The room below the hotel's main kitchen was set up with tables for four and a few banquet tables with seating for eight. The employee's food was good and nourishing. It was served buffet style from a long steam table. Swedish meatballs mmm… with mashed potatoes and cabbage, were served at least once a week. Other choices consisted of pot roast, hearty meat and potato soup, and fish dishes at occasion. I especially liked the days when stuffed cabbage rolls were served. We could eat as much as we wanted, from the buffet line, which changed every day. There was also a meager salad table which did not look very appetizing, and a beverage station. My favorite was the dessert table, which contained day old cakes and other goodies. All of us had gained some weight, looking healthy and feeling well.

Inga began riding again. Often Kari and I went to watch her at the corral, where she was riding proudly on the big horse. She even practiced some low jumps, looking as a beginner equestrian rider. I was proud of my sister. She was wearing a pair of brown riding boots, and riding pants, and tan colored jacket. The pants, slightly too large for her, and the boots, were a gift to her from the stable master, having belonged to some youngster who had outgrown them. She sat ramrod straight on the horse, with the reins loose and relaxed. There was a hint of determined smile on her face. Her blond ponytail peeked from under her riding cap, dancing rhythmically with the horse's trot. After the session was over, she led the horse inside the stable, unsaddling it, wiping the sweat off it and giving the horse a good brushing before leading it into its stall. As a small thank you token, she fed it a handful of oats and gave it a little kiss on its forehead. As we walked home, I told her how proud I was of her. She brushed it off, by saying, "Oh, it's nothing. I want to learn to ride well and take part in competitions," she said.

School was finally over. The last, day our teacher Kallela had arranged a small party, with cookies and soft drinks. He made a long speech, emphasizing how important it was to take school seriously. He complimented our class, mentioning that we all had done well, hoping to see us again this fall. He was jovial and friendly, not stiff and scary like he was in the class room. The report cards were handed out. Mine was above average, making me happy that my efforts had not been in vain. We shook hands with him before leaving to go home. Inga's report card was as good as mine. On the bus to Aulanko we sat side by side, mentally celebrating the upcoming summer freedom.

"I am looking so much forward to this summer. I will ride every day," Inga uttered, as the bus was nearing our previous home. "Yak…I'm glad that we don't still live in that apartment," she said, pointing out the window, as we passed the residence.

"So am I," I said yet thinking about the summer and hopefully more work at the hotel. "You ride and I work," I said with a sneer.

"Juha, when I get older, I want to work at the hotel's souvenir counter."

"That would be a perfect job for you. You speak Swedish and few years from now, you will speak some English also. Mother and I have an in with the hotel, and I am sure they would consider you."

"Thanks," Inga said with a big smile.

After picking Kari up from Mother's friend, we showed our report cards to Kari. Mother was at work. Kari had no idea what he was looking at, wanting to draw some pictures on them with his crayons. "No-no," Inga and I said in unison. Kari took a fit, throwing the crayons to the floor, sitting down next to them, pouting.

It was the men's sauna day today. Tomorrow would be the women's day. The hotel had two saunas. One beautifully tiled sauna in the building's basement was for the guests. The second sauna was designated for employee's use, on the shore of the lake, directly below the hill of the greenhouse. At times it had been reserved for guests of the hotel, who preferred the lake sauna. It was an old, well used wooden building, probably dating back to the estate days, painted barn red. It sat on the shore just some fifty feet, with a wide dock jutting out over the water. The water was still very cold from the thaw from the winter ice.

Kari and I left just before four o'clock for the sauna. The sun was still high in the sky. It was warm. A gentle whiff of early summer breeze blew over the lake. From our home, it was about one mile walk. I was happy about the walk, knowing the treat waiting for us. Kari complained that he was tired. In the winter, it was another story. Our hair was a frozen chunk by the time we reached the warmth of the house. It was still worth it.

Stepping into the sauna, the familiar smell of smoke, birch and soap greeted us. Not only that, but the 'matron' of the sauna. She was a woman, a woman of a fighter's proportion. It was very common to have an attendant in public saunas. Their duties consisted of keeping the sauna clean and heated properly. Not only that, but they also served as washing person. First class service, if you will. If you looked close, you could notice some stubble of beard and other long facial hairs. She always frightened Kari, and I must admit she frightened me also. She was dressed in a full length white doctor's coat, which was wet and glued to her ample body. Her face did not attribute any kindness, and her voice was a garbled bark. There were two dressing rooms, and seeing us walk in, she barked, pointing to one of the rooms, "That's your room!" Timidly Kari and I walked into our room. We got undressed, grabbed a towel and walked into the hot sauna room. She was not there. The steam room was empty except for us. Kari liked to throw water on the hot stones, but sit on the lower level. I sat on the upper level, where the steam smacked me viciously, having me bend down with the head between my legs. It felt good but very, very hot. After about fifteen minutes of the heat, and drenching in sweat, we ran naked to the dock. I stuck my foot into the water which felt like ice water. Later in the season when the water was warmer, we would jump in and swim around. Kari even knew how to doggy paddle by now. We went back into the steam room, where we contemplated the torture waiting for us in the washroom.

Hesitantly we emerged into 'HER' washing room….the torture chamber. There were two long wooden benches. When we walked in, she barked: "Little boy, lay down there, pointing at one of them, you bigger little boy, you lay down here."

Scanning for her tools of torture, she grabbed a rough looking brush, lathering it with an ugly soap, shaped like a brick. Then she filled a bucket of warm water and attacked Kari, who was stretched out on his stomach squirming on the bench, knowing what was coming. "Ouch-Ouch" he was moaning, as the woman was scrubbing his back.

"Turn around," she commanded and scrubbed his front and lathered his head. Finally she rinsed my brother off with two buckets of warm water. Kari was gleaming of red color.

I was next. Being older than Kari, she decided to grab a scarier looking brush for me and the same ugly soap. It smelled of sulfur. It was yellow ugly rotten egg smelling stuff. She scrubbed probably two layers of skin off my back and without asking me to turn, just flipped me over in a quick motion. Some sweat droplets of her face, were dripping on me. Revolting! The front of my body received the same treatment. Mrs. Anderson in Sweden could be this woman's sister, I was thinking. "You were playing with matches. What are these scars on your stomach? Hot water, right?" she asked. Without answering, I just groaned from her rough handling. Finally she poured two rinse buckets of warm water over me. I was gleaming. I was red like Kari. Well, this was nothing new we got the same torture once a week. Later I learned that this woman had been the "the sauna matron" for many years. I wondered what the tourists thought about this treatment. It would be conversation at their dinner tables back home.

Wow…that was a brutal handling we had received. It was time to go for dinner at the hotel. Our stomachs were growling. Sauna always made you hungry and relaxed. We took our time, walking very slowly. The weather was warm and fresh. Kari was complaining about his shirt rubbing against his tender back.

In the evening I read for a while, but my mind was focused at the upcoming summer vacation. Perhaps I could do something else besides shoe shine? I must talk to the manager, Mr. Hellstrom, with whom I got along well. He treated our family with respect. New escapades were in store over the next years.

26

THREE YEARS FLEW BY. SCHOOL went well and I only got hollered at a few times. I had a very high opinion of Mr. Kallela. He was a stern teacher but very good. He demanded much of us, yet he made even the grammar of the Finnish language sound interesting, which it was not. Yet, Kallela was the best teacher I ever had. Years later, while I was attending Temple University in Philadelphia, I wrote a long letter to him to express my feelings about him and his disciplined teaching.

I kept shining shoes for the couple of years. My trade became first class. I should open a stall in Paris or London. I would become 'The Finn of Polish' unless the competition would get rid of me. One duty which I did not like was shoe shining early in the morning. I had to walk each hallway, where shoes were left outside of the occupants room to be shined. This task took often a couple of hours, without any tips. Besides shining shoes, I also helped out as a bell boy which I liked better. I had met people from all over the world. I loved this. It was so exciting to show these people to their room. By that time I spoke a bit of English, my favorite saying was "How are you? And "Take it easy." My outburst normally took place in the elevator on the way up to the customer's floor. This always brought chuckles from them. Some of the luggage was so heavy, that I could hardly carry them. When I huffed and puffed, it seemed to help the tip amount. The tips from the American tourists were always the best. Every so often, I got a one dollar bill from an American tourist and this was gold. The black market was waiting to buy it from me. I was very astute to the monetary exchange. I made sure the rate was excellent. My tips were so good, that instead of eating in the employee's cafeteria, I often ordered from the hotel's menu, pork chop cutlet being my favorite. There was a back room behind the front desk, where I devoured my delicious pork chop 'gourmet' dinner, with trimmings.

In the same room was the telephone switchboard with a board full of lines. When the operator needed a break, I was the one to take over. It was fun to plug a proper line to the proper recipient. Don't get the lines crossed, I had been warned over and over and yet very rarely, did I make a mistake. When I got the lines crossed, I got chewed out. Well, that was one part of working in the hotel

Midsummer Festival arrived this year on June twenty fourth. The hotel provided spectacular fireworks, with a gala of food and drink, and a German orchestra playing until early morning. At midnight, a huge bonfire was lit, close to the hotel, by the lake shore. The bonfires were a yearly Finnish tradition. They would be burning throughout the country, people partying until early morning. This was an annual festival, celebrated from the heart, to welcome the summer. It was to rejoice the summer solstice, the longest day of the year. It would be twilight only for couple of hours, with the sun rising again.

That night, I had been picked as the "balloon sales boy" of the hotel. The dining room was packed with some six hundred people, all in party mood. Balloons were blown up in the back room. They were red, blue, white and multi colored. I was to squeeze through the throng of diners and sell these colorful balloons. The price I was to charge was fifty marks each. With my huge bouquet of balloons I walked through the tightly packed people, dining and drinking, enticing everyone to buy one. Most every table bought several, to add to the festivities. It took many refills to cover the whole crowd. I was happy, very happy, because I sold them for seventy five marks, making a good profit on each sale. At the end of the night after several hundred sales, I paid the hotel their price of fifty marks, and the rest was mine. Everyone, including the party goers and the hotel, were content. I was ecstatic with the profits I had made. On top of the price of the balloons, I also received tips. My profit came to more than I made in one week, tips included.

The next day I told Mother about my fortune. She was astonished, happy and mad at the same time. We sat at the kitchen table. Her fingers were nervously tapping the tabletop. A cup of coffee sat in front of her. She was shocked. She was speechless, but finally saying, in a gruff tone.

"Juha, what you did was cheating," she said, scolding me, looking somewhat mad, and her brow giving me the impression of being disappointed in me.

"I did not cheat anyone," I said in defense. "The hotel got every penny they had told me to get for the balloons. What I did was entrepreneurship from my part. No one complained and the customers even tipped me on top of it. Your son is a.....salesman." I chuckled, not feeling guilty.

Mother looked straight at me, hesitating if as thinking how to proceed, "I don't know what to say. It was not stealing, but still, what you did was not quite right,"

"Think of it this way, it will make you feel better. I bought the balloons from the hotel, then sold them to the customers at a marked up price." I justified my actions. "The hotel made profit and I made profit. Everyone is happy."

From the looks of it, Mother still wasn't pleased, pondering the issue.

Over the next few days, I made up my indiscretion, by buying Mother a nice new summer dress. Inga received a new shiny pair of riding boots and Kari got a small bicycle with training wheels. This action closed the issue of the expensive balloons, and I still had some money left for myself.

The summer flew by too fast. I worked all kinds of crazy hours at the hotel. On the days off, if the weather was nice, Inga, Kari and I spent the day on one of the islands, swimming and enjoying the sunshine. The willow trees were in full bloom, with their leaves creating soothing background music in the gentle breeze. We laid on the warm sand and swam in the moderately warm water. We ate lunch at the small coffee shop on the island, sitting at one of the small round tables on the patio Our favorite lunches were from an assortment of open face sandwiches, washing them down with Coca Cola. Kari learned to swim, and did not want to get out of the water. When it was time to leave, he would have a fit. The three of us slowly became tanned. We looked and felt healthy. The winter pale of our bodies was replaced by a golden brown hue.

Inga had been riding three times a week. She modeled her new boots with a big grin. She had gained a little weight and the riding pants fit her better. She and her horse had become a team. They understood each other, and rode in an synchronized harmony. The steeple jumps had grown a little taller and more demanding. She navigated them without any problem, proudly smiling to her audience, Kari and myself. The ride master was also pleased of her progress, but did not wish to rush her challenges. It would still take some time before Inga would be ready for competition, which was her goal.

Mother was happy with our life and with her work. Her schedule varied and she often worked late into the night. I kept reading. The library in Hameen-linna possessed a rather good collection of various authors, which I enjoyed. A Scottish author by the name of A.J. Cronin, became my new admired author. It seemed as if I had graduated from the earlier writings, except for Mark Twain to some new notorious authors. Cronin was one of them. He was a Scottish doctor who became an author. The library had six books by him, translated into Finnish. I read each one with pleasure. Especially his novel titled, Adventures in Two Worlds which became my favorite before reading his other novels. Over time I had become a very regular visitor to the library.

My mind traveled in memories from Rantala and Sweden. Sophia and I had corresponded with each other a few times. I would never forget this beautiful girl, with sparkling green eyes. A letter had arrived from the Westholms, telling me that Mor had given birth to a healthy baby boy. This surprised me because of their age but what a wonderful event it was. I wrote to congratulate them of this happy news and thanked them for their kindness while I had stayed with them. I also mentioned that I was so happy to be home, finally.

27

LIFE WAS GREAT. I HAD finally come home. I did miss Rantala and my horse. Over time, Fammu had sent several letters telling me what was going on. Stranos had been pardoned a year earlier and shipped back home to Russia. They all missed him at Rantala. He had become part of the family. He would remain in my memory forever, as the most kind and thankful man. The violins he had made became heirlooms. My truck and the small boat remained at Rantala, waiting to greet me on my visits there. I was sorry to hear this, but happy in knowing that he was back home with his family. Ukki and Fammu were well and so joyful that the war was over. Oulu had begun rebuilding the city from the bombing. Rake was ready to start college in the fall. He must have changed his feelings about school, now that he was continuing in the college. In length in one of her letters, she talked about our father. He had left the service with high honors from the President of Finland and the Field Marshall Mannerheim. Years later, he gave me all the letters of honors and a collection of his various medals. Fammu was sad that he and mother had divorced. It had been a shock to her. Her sadness continued because they had not heard from him since the end of the war. All she knew was that he had moved to Norway and become involved with a cruise line. There had not been any calls or letters from him. I could not help thinking about the way he deserted us and now his parents. What a bum, I thought, but I still loved him as my father.

Our father died a lonely, broke old man in Helsinki, in 2009 at the age of ninety five. He had three failed marriages over time that we know of. I don't know how many half sisters and brothers I have. Our father was known as the ladies' man. Three months after Father's death, my family and I met a lovely lady from Vasa, Finland, who was my half sister at our home in Charleston, South Carolina. She was a beautiful woman, with a constant big smile and a joyful personality. Everyone commented that she and I resembled each other. She knew about me, but I had never heard about her. Lena and her husband Christer visited with us for several days. During that time, we became family. Her family had experienced the same desertion as we had with our father. It appears that Father had come back to Finland from Norway and married Lena's mother. After a certain time, he did the disappearing act with her, just like he had done with us. It was sad for them, we understood this feeling. I was so happy to meet Lena and for her to meet my wife and children, and three grandchildren. We all fell in love with each other. The grandchildren enjoyed Christer's joviality very much. He was the life of the party. Father had never told me about my half sister Lena, but had left information with the doctors to contact her in any serious event he might experience. It was her and my niece and nephew who contacted me about his death. Finally we met over the phone. Lena organized Father's funeral and even met Kari for the first time. It was a simple family funeral with Father's ashes buried in a funeral park in Helsinki. I did not attend the service.

Over the years, we had met him in New York a couple of times when the cruise liner pulled to port. He visited our home south of Boston and met the children. He was still the fine gentleman as I recalled from childhood. Father had moved back to Finland and lived in a government provided apartment building in the center of Helsinki. His small living quarters consisted of one room, with a closet size kitchenette and a tiny bathroom with a shower. He was physically broken, but mentally alert. He had no friends, nor any relatives keeping in touch with him. I visited him in Helsinki, the year before his death, feeling so good of having provided him with few days of company. He looked shorter and much thinner than I remembered. His cheeks were sunken, pale, but without any wrinkles. His eyes were clear, light blue. His hair was long gone, claiming that it was during the war from wearing the helmet. We sat and talked for many hours on his old worn couch. I had brought a bottle of red wine, which we shared. I had also brought with me a stack of photographs of our family. He took his time with each photo, making complimentary comments about Paula, my wife, and our three children and his great grand children. His speech sounded just as it did over fifty years earlier. He had always been a gentleman. Today he was dressed in a dark pin stripe suit, as always, with a white shirt, but today he was not wearing a tie. He looked refined, even though the clothes were long worn. His sparsely furnished room was dreary. It smelled old. There was the couch and one chair with a small wooden coffee table, with a glass top. Against the wall, a single bed sat made in military fashion. A television on a corner table showed fussy color program of a soccer game in England, the sound was turned to mute. The only picture on one wall was the picture of my family. He had proudly told the care takers that we, my wife and I and our children were his family, never mentioning anyone else. The apartment was hot in the summer and cold in the winter. It was midsummer and one of the hottest summers in Finland's history. I excused myself and ran to a store around the corner and bought him a window fan, setting it up in the single window. It brought some relief from the heat, but not much.

I had rented an automobile and took him for a ride to Aulanko Hotel, about one hour ride north of Helsinki. It was an unusually hot day. The air conditioner kept us comfortable. We passed the beautiful country side of southern Finland. Several lakes, shimmered in the sunshine. Open fields with grazing cattle were abundant. Barn red houses and farms were dotted by the lakes and the fields. T

"Where did you travel with the cruise line?" I interrupted the quiet.

He thought for a moment, answering, "Just about everywhere in the world. Much of our time was spent in the Mediterranean, especially around Naples and the island of Capri in Italy."

"We have been there, staying in Sorrento on the Amalfi coast. It is beautiful."

"The last four years I was the Chief Steward for the whole cruise line. I flew around the world, to different ports, to inspect the ships and its crew. Once I tried to figure out how many times I had traveled around the world....and came up with an approximate number of one hundred times. I was tired of traveling so much, from Hong Kong to New York and all countries, in between," he answered, with a sigh.

"That sounds exciting. I love to travel, but maybe not that much," I said, looking at him. Just the thinking of his answer had made him tired.

Rest of the trip, we enjoyed the vista, looking forward for our destination, Hotel Aulanko. We were dressed appropriately for the occasion. Father in his usual suit and I was wearing a dark blazer with tan colored khakis.

Father was so excited to go back to his old stomping grounds. He had not visited it in over fifty years. At the hotel, we had a unhurried, delicious cold salmon with dill sauce and asparagus lunch in the same elegant large dining room where he had worked so long ago. The sparkling white linen table cloths and napkins were immaculately ironed. The service was perfect and unhurried. Father reminisced about the many celebrities he had met and the importance of his position as dining room manager. His voice was shaking and his eyes were tearing. He was deeply moved by his memories. His mind had traveled back in time.

After lunch, we moved into the hotel lobby, where we enjoyed a glass of wine and a cigarette, on comfortable leather chairs. Soft classical music was playing in the background. He appeared very content in this plush setting, which he was used to, but having been away from it for so many years. The aura and smell of the large lobby was the same as I could remember. The theme had changed from art deco, to a more conservative modern look. The same polished granite floor remained. Tall, potted Fichus trees had been strategically placed throughout, under tract lighting. The hotel had been modernized and large addition had been added from my time, it but still felt like home. Below the lobby floor, an ultra modern sizeable night club and a small casino had been built. I met couple of old time employees, who still remembered me, who were still working there, after all these years. It was like homecoming for me and probably for my father. It was a memorable meeting of father and son.

I told him about all the different jobs that I had held at the hotel. He laughed out loud, about my balloon 'caper.' Later we drove around the Aulanko Park and the lookout tower. He was too weak to walk around, but I stopped the car at all the significant spots. On the way back, to Helsinki, he dozed off most of the way. It had been along and exhilarating day for him. When we reached the city, I helped him up to his apartment where he hugged and thanked me, saying that this day was the best he had experienced in many years. I could not help feeling sorry for him. As far as I was concerned, I had forgiven him for deserting us. I still think of him as a gentleman, and my father. I returned to my hotel, happy to have been able to extend some enjoyment into his gloomy life. After the several days visit with two dinners at couple of his favorite restaurants, which he had not visited during the last ten years, I returned home, to South Carolina. It was during this trip that he gave me his mementos.

He died that winter, a few months after my visit with him. Even though he had caused much hardship to our family, I am proud to have had him as our father. Only the pleasant memories of him were conscious in my mind. As my brother spoke at Father's eulogy he said, we can thank him of us being here.

28

FINLAND WAS ELECTRIC WITH EXCITEMENT. It was 1952. Helsinki had been in a building boom of new hotels and the main structure, the Olympic stadium. The building had begun four years earlier and now in 1952, the country was ready for the Summer Olympics. Finland would receive a worldwide influx of athletes and visitors. Even at Aulanko Hotel, three new multi room buildings close to the hotel had been erected. There was tension in the air, which affected the planners down to everyday people. I was excited just like everyone else, knowing that the hotel would be packed with international visitors. Aulanko was close enough to Helsinki. A caravan of shuttle buses had been organized. Many of the Olympic events were taking place in other cities besides Helsinki.

In Hameenlinna, a state of the art swimming stadium had been constructed. All the swim and diving events would be held here. A second memorable honor for Finland came in June, one month before the Olympics. The world's first Miss Universe Pageant had been held in California, and the first Miss Universe ever chosen, was from Finland. Her name was Miss Armi Kuusela. The year1952 put Finland on the map, with two grand events. The world learned of the small country of Finland.

By now I had become a full time bell boy during the summer and part time during school in the winter. The previous summer had been interesting. I had been employed on the hotel's daily sightseeing cruise ship m/s *Roine* as one of the mates. The ship carried some one hundred and twenty passengers of all nationalities and a crew of seven, on a long trip through interconnected lakes north to Harjula. The captain of the ship was a tall, middle aged, high seas captain, with years of experience. He was dressed in a crisp white uniform, with a smart captain's hat. Being on the lakes for him was different but just as demanding. His temperament was even, but rigid. He sported a hint of a smile on his lips at all times. The ship left the hotel at nine a.m., traveling north, reaching Harjula in the early afternoon. Some passengers disembarked, new passengers came aboard for the ride to Aulanko. After a one hour layover for lunch and sightseeing, it departed homeward, docking back at the hotel at seven p.m.

The ship had inside and on deck seating and a small dining room set with crisp white linen tablecloths and napkins. The menu listed a limited array of fine meals, partially prepared in the hotel's main kitchen. The galley, in the bow of the ship, was small and cramped with two chefs. One waiter, dressed in a white shirt and bow tie, white long apron and black slacks, hovered over the diners. There was seating for only twenty two persons at any given time. The waiter also acted as the bartender.

The trip took the ship through post card picturesque lakes. Idyllic small islands dotted the whole trip. Many of the islands contained small rustic and colorful summer cottages, each with a sauna on the lake shore. The ship navigated so close to some islands, that you could throw a stone and hit it. At other times when traversing the lake system we threaded inlets f so narrow that it took the captain's expert steering in order not to hit the shore. We passed the two locks at Valkeakoski, lifting the ship to the next lake level where we continued to our destination. It is claimed that Finland has close to two hundred thousand lakes.

My main duties consisted of attending a complex music system and collection of tapes from a tourist director. The timing of inserting the correct tape describing the sights and history of certain areas was critical. It was a demanding job and interesting at the same time.

Before leaving the dock in the morning, I had been issued an inventory of various cigarettes, assortments of chocolate and other wrapped candies and six expensive cigars.

The mode of selling these items, was to walk throughout the ship, carrying a "Las Vegas" type half moon shaped tray hanging from leather straps behind my neck. It was quite heavy. Once per hour I took my sales trip, calling out, "Cigarettes, cigars and chocolates!" The sales were brisk throughout the day. I inflated few of the prices, and the tips were good. It was a dream job. I enjoyed beautiful scenery and good tips to top it off. September first was the last trip for the season.

Now it was summer Olympic time. The opening day was July 19. Finland was chosen over six other bidders, several years earlier to hold the 1952 games. The country was proud and would do everything in its power to make it an unforgettable event for the athletes and visitors. Aulanko played a big part of this grand event. The day of the opening ceremonies of lighting the Olympic torch in Helsinki and continuing with elaborate shows, had gone flawlessly. The weather had been rainy the day before, but on the ceremonial day, the weather cooperated. It was sunny and warm. The southern part of Finland, enjoyed a gorgeous day. Aulanko was fully booked, months earlier. I was excited. I would be working from morning to late evening, just like Mother, and even Inga became a helper behind the souvenir counter. Kari would be staying with an elderly family friend until life would turn back to normal.

Busloads of visitors arrived daily. Others arrived by train or car. At times it was bedlam. I was ready to faint from the loads of luggage, which I had to sort out and deliver to the correct rooms in the main building. For the distant buildings, I had been provided with a three wheel bike, similar to a rickshaw, with a large luggage platform in the front. By the time I had peddled the half mile to the new additions, I was huffing and puffing with sweat running down my face. I did not mind it, because the tips were good.

A doctor from Sweden and his wife, who I escorted to their room on the fourth floor, in the main building, asked me in the elevator, "Aren't you too young to be handling this luggage?"

"No sir," I said feigning a more robust voice, "I have been doing this for some time by now, and have grown stronger by the day."

After reaching their room, I carried their luggage in, carefully setting the pieces on the luggage stands. Then I opened the curtains, exposing the view of the lake and turning the lights on in the bathroom. After this I asked, "Is there anything else I can do for you? If not, have a pleasant stay with us," I said, turning around to exit.

163

"Just one minute," the doctor said, reaching for his wallet, giving me a nice tip.

"Thank you. Call me any time if you need something. My name is Juha," I said, closing the door behind me. Wow, another satisfied customer. I was tired, but the day was not over.

Some new guests arrived each evening at seven, when the *Roine* pulled up to the dock. I would be on the dock, sitting atop my "rickshaw" waiting to greet them and escort them to the hotel with their luggage. I wish the 'tricycle' would have a small engine, because it was all uphill from the dock to the main entrance. I had to push the thing, loaded with luggage. That was not fun.

Throughout the Olympics, it was a daily hassle and bustle. By night, both Mother and I were beat. Inga was fine she only worked a few hours per day, without any craziness in her department. The Olympics came and finally they were over. Finland had done very well in the competitions. Of the sixty nine nations taking part in the games, our country came in seventh, with twenty two medals. It was a proud demonstration of our fortitude. The multitude of guests and parties subsided to normal summer business. It became peaceful. Once again we had time to go swimming and enjoy the beautiful days.

About a week after the Olympics, Mother came home one night and told us some interesting, but puzzling news. The hotel had asked her to take over the restaurant and the daily operation of the lookout tower in Aulanko Park, for the rest of the summer and thereafter, every summer. The manager, a middle aged woman, who had run the restaurant for two years, suddenly took ill, having to leave immediately. The thought scared her and she wanted to talk it over with us. We were excited. It sounded as a great job for her and we could work there with her. I would remain at my position at the hotel, but would help out at the tower on my free time. The place was busy with tourists and yet it would be her operation, which she could handle with proper help. Mother would have to start the next day. With mixed emotions, she wanted our opinion on the matter. We urged her to accept the offer, because she would not be under the often hectic pressure of the hotel. Later that evening, she agreed to accept it. She would still work at the hotel over the winter months. It sounded good to us and the more she thought about it, she finally smiled in agreement.

This sounded great to me. I would still work at my job and also help Mother at the tower. There were living quarters in the restaurant, where we could stay, or at our home by the hotel. It was about one and a half mile walk, uphill to the tower. The restaurant was located at the foot of the granite giant lookout tower. The menu was more of a coffee shop, with a simple selection of foods, beverages and lots of souvenirs.

Her crew consisted of a ticket seller for the tower and three to four young girls in the restaurant in addition to Inga, as waitresses and kitchen help. She inherited this crew from the previous manager. The girls had worked there from the beginning of the season, which did calm Mother's nerves of not being thrown in totally green to the job at hand.

In a way, now we had turned a new leaf in our life.

29

WE WOKE UP EARLY THE following morning. Mother had stopped over to the hotel to pick up the keys for the restaurant and fill out some paper work. All four of us began the twenty minute trek to the tower. It was a beautiful sunny morning. We were excited and only stopped for few minutes at Swan Lake to feed the three black swans. Inga was carrying a bag with some stale bread. Kari became carried away with these striking jet black birds, getting too close to one. The bird became angry and ran snorting after him, latching its beak on his behind. Kari screamed. Finally the bird let go and Kari ran to Mother, crying. "That hurt," he sobbed holding his behind. Tears were running down his cheeks. We laughed, telling him not to provoke them. He had learned his lesson.

After a short walk from the lake, we reached the steep hill below the restaurant and the tall gray granite tower rising towards the bright blue sky. We were high up on the granite mountain. The air was crisp and calm with the smell of pine. Small birds of were singing in the trees. The walkway was covered in a thin layer of pine needles.

Aulanko Lake shimmered far below. It was calm as a mirror, in a golden hue reflecting a blue green contrast. Across the lake rose another dark gray granite peak against a forest background.

The large oblong restaurant building was to our right. It had been painted red with white trimming. It had a large open covered terrace with a wooden railing surrounding it. Long wood window boxes ran the length of the railing. Colorful summer flowers were in full bloom. Their sweet scent filled the air. At least a dozen tables with chairs covered the deck. The tables were adorned with blue table cloths with a white runner, in the Finnish colors. A long counter ran across the deck, separating it from the kitchen. The wall behind the counter was enclosed with built in cabinetry. As we walked to the other end of the building, we arrived at the kitchen door. The door was white, with a small square window. Mother took out the key, unlocked the door and we walked into the kitchen. A huge wood stove faced us, next to a long worktable with a sink. A large heavy wood table with a matching bench sat against one wall. To our left was a doorway to the downstairs bedroom, with two beds and a bureau. On the right of the kitchen, a wide open doorway led to the store room and makeshift office. The room was brightened by the light of two windows. One was facing the tower the other one overlooked a ravine behind the building.

A pair of double French doors led to the outside deck, behind the long counter. There was a crude stairwell leading up to the attic from the storeroom. Mother stayed below as the three of us climbed up to see what was there. It contained two small bedrooms, each one with just a mattress on the floor. The pitch of the roof was so steep, we had to stoop down in order to get into the rooms. It was hot, stuffy and uncomfortable and we only a few minutes there. These rooms and the larger one downstairs were available for any employee to stay overnight, instead of walking to Aulanko and take the late bus to Hameenlinna. The next morning they would have to repeat the trip early for work.

"Juha, please start the fire in the stove. It won't be long until some tourist will come in for coffee," Mother ordered me. She was busy trying to orient herself and figure out what to do next. "Inga," she said her tone tense, "go and see that all the tables are clean and in proper order and open the cabinets behind the counter. There was so much for her to do.

Just then a nice looking middle aged lady walked into the kitchen. Her hair was dark brown, set into a tight bun. Her face was round, with a pug nose. She was huffing from the long walk to the tower. She introduced herself as Maija, telling Mother that she was the ticket seller for the lookout tower.

"Hi, Maija. Nice to meet you, I'm Sylvi and these are my children." She introduced us, continuing," I don't know what to do and where everything is.

Show me the tickets you need and you probably must go to the booth. It is already nine and there are tourists milling around."

Maija walked over to the desk, picking up a roll of ticket, giving Mother the beginning number. "This is all I need," she said, grabbed the tickets and a small change box, and went to her station. Over her shoulder she said, "One more thing, could you have Juha walk up the tower and raise the flag?"

"Ok," Mother said, becoming dizzier by the minute. She had been sent up without any training or orientation. The first few days would be touch and go for her. There were boxes and boxes of items in the store room. What was in them? Her face looked turbulent.

"Mother," Inga called from the patio. "There are customers here for coffee and cakes. What do I do?" she called, apprehensive.

"Juha, put some water to boil for coffee," Mother hollered. "Where are the coffee cakes?" she shrieked, totally losing her composure. "Inga, tell them to wait," she hollered, looking like she would hide under the desk. I had never seen her like this. She was so customer conscious, and having this thrown into her lap, was like being thrown to the dogs.

"Juha, go and raise the flag in the tower, *now!*" she commanded.

I grabbed the key to the tower, by the kitchen door. The key was large and heavy, reminding me of the Monte Cristo novel. I ran up to the steps to the first landing of the massive tower. This was the base for the tower, two stories up. There was a huge solid wooden door waiting. Wow, this is old I thought. The key fit in the large key hole, and I pushed the heavy door open on rusted hinges. Now I stood inside the second level, looking up to the top of the tower looming in the darkness, four stories high. There were a few windows casting the sun's rays into the tall granite structure. On this level, there were two tables and four chairs, built from tangled tree limbs. They had been varnished into a dark tile red shade. A thick guest book sat on one table. The steps were thick stone and hugging the wall, with a solid hand rail. It was a long climb to the top, and a metal door. It just had a latch inside. I pushed the door open and was immediately greeted with the most beautiful panorama I had ever seen. I could see endlessly in the bright sunshine. The lake below, the restaurant next to the tower, seemed so small. The pine trees seemed like Japanese Bonsai. I was on top of the world. I raised the large Finnish flag on a tall flag pole where it began undulate in a gentle breeze. On the way down, I already encountered tourists walking up.

Several of the people were huffing and puffing. At the foot of the tower, Maija was busy selling tickets.

It was my day off from the hotel, so I would stay here all day and help out as much as possible. Mother was still running around in circles, issuing orders. Two young pretty girls had arrived to work while I was at the tower. Mother introduced them as Lisa and Annukka. My senses perked up. Lisa was tall and thin, with a short cut blond curly hair. She looked about sixteen. Wow, same age as I. In a couple of months I would be seventeen. She was very pretty, with freckles on her face and a big smile. Annukka was also pretty, shorter than Lisa, with a nice tan and light green eyes. Her green eyes reminded me of Sophia, but they were not as deep as hers. She was perhaps a couple of years older than Lisa. They told me that they had worked in the restaurant since first part of June. Mother interjected, "I am so happy that these girls showed up. At least they have an idea what goes on here." There was a hint of a smile on her lips, for the first time of the day. Inga was behind the counter selling coffee, sweets and souvenirs. It seemed that she was doing a good job. Annukka joined Inga and Lisa stayed with Mother, showing her where everything was and more or less told her the daily schedule, as she knew. Kari was helping to open boxes. Many contained dry goods, others souvenirs of the tower, Aulanko Hotel and the shimmering lake.

In the back of the building, directly under the kitchen, was the wood shed. There was quite a pile of chopped wood for the stove. I decided to stay there and chop some more wood. It was more peaceful down here away from the confusion upstairs. So far I liked everything about this place, and of course Lisa and Annukka. I had gotten to the point that beautiful and friendly girls interested me very much. I wondered how Rake handled these situations. I had not talked to him in couple of years. I had planned a trip to Oulu at the latter part of the fall. I would see him and everyone else then.

There was commotion outside, close to the kitchen door. I ran up to see what was going on. To my surprise, the first sight was an old haggard looking horse, with a wagon hooked to its harness. Next to the wagon stood an old man in coveralls, appearing as haggard as the horse. He was wearing a worn straw hat, with some fish hooks hanging off the rim. His lower lip protruded of a big wad of chewing tobacco. He spit next to the wagon wheel. Some brown drool lingered on the corner of his mouth.

Mother came out to find out what was going on. "Hello. I am Sylvi and just started here today. Who are you?" she asked looking intently at the man with the horse. She also told the man, that she was taking over the running of the restaurant and tower, explaining the sudden illness of the previous manager.

The old man stared at her, also in a questionable look finally speaking, in a croaky voice, "Hi Sylvi, I am your delivery man. My name is Hannu and my horse's name is Twenty One." He coughed, taking a deep breath and continued, "We come and visit you twice a week with supplies you had requested from the hotel, and water which you always need."

"Oh...no one had told me about this. I didn't even realize yet, that we don't have running water here. I have been here less than one hour. It's all new to me. Welcome Hannu," she said, extending her hand to him.

On the wagon sat a large round metal drum and several boxes of different size. Hannu got busy hooking up a hose to his drum and the other end to a large drum, by the kitchen door. He used a pump lever getting the water to flow into our drum. Lisa had come outside also and between all of us, we began unloading the boxes, carrying them into the store room.

Hannu stood next to the wagon, keeping an eye on the water flow. "Sylvi, I come every Monday and Thursday morning. If you have an order sheet ready, I will deliver it to the hotel, if not, you can drop it off, and I will deliver everything on the next trip, which will be Thursday.

"I have no idea what we need at this point. Someone will drop a list at the hotel. These supplies must have been ordered by the previous lady. Thank you. How can Twenty One make it up this steep hill?" Mother asked.

"We have been doing these trips for many years. The load is heavy, especially the water. Sometimes I have to help the horse, by pushing the wagon. This last hill, up from the parking lot, is murder. I don't know how long he will be able to do this," he said, patting the horse's rump.

"Why does your horse have such a weird name?" I asked, petting the horse.

"Well, he is that old now. Next year I will change the name to Twenty Two," he said, snickering. "Strange -huh."

When everything had been unloaded and the water drum filled, Hannu asked for a cup of coffee for the trip back to the hotel. The horse drank a half bucket of water. They left, with Hannu calling out, "See you on Thursday. Good luck!"

"Juha," Mother called. "Come and help in the kitchen to make some sandwiches with Lisa. It's almost lunch time and there are lots of people milling around," adding in a pleading tone, "please!"

With Lisa. Sure! I ran into the kitchen, where she already had various cold cuts and a collection of sliced fresh cucumbers, tomatoes, radishes and greens lined up, with assortments of breads on the large table. I had no idea what to do, but she told me how to do them. She showed me. My favorites were the thinly slices black bread, with ham and cheese, twirled atop, with sliced radishes and tomatoes. Lisa made artful smoked salmon sandwiches, with cucumbers and dill. Other sandwiches were, chicken, roast beef and Swiss cheese. We had fun doing our creations and in no time, there were six artistic platters, which we carried into a glass enclosed display case onto the counter. Mother was surprised, and had a big proud grin. "Thanks, you two make a mean culinary team," she said. During the hurried sandwich making, we could not help bumping into each other. That felt so good, I would do this every day. We laughed and admired our fabrications. Customers were already waiting for them. Inga and Annukka were busy behind the counter. Kari had been designated to be the busboy and dishwasher. He was not happy about that, but when Mother promised that he would get paid for his work, he pepped up with gusto.

The day flew by so fast. The sun was still shining low on the horizon. It had been a very busy day, with tourists milling around until late evening. We closed up at nine. Maija came down from her ticket booth and reconciled her sales with Mother. She left calling out to all of us, "See you tomorrow."

I climbed up the tower to lower the flag for the night and lock up the entrance. Mother was sitting at the kitchen table, with a cup of coffee, looking totally exhausted. Inga and the girls sat at a table on the terrace, enjoying Coca Cola and cookies. They seemed as worn out as Mother. I poured a cup of coffee for myself, sitting next to Mother.

"Juha, this was the craziest day I ever had. I am so tired. Everything went well even though it was chaotic. Thanks to everyone, especially Lisa and Annukka. You and Inga and Kari were super help also. I...well, almost lost it."

I took a big swig of coffee, laying my hand on her shoulder and said, "Tomorrow will be a much better day. Now we have an idea what to do. Why don't we stay here overnight instead of walking home? There is enough room for everyone. Let's ask the girls if they also want to stay." I didn't have to be at the hotel until noon tomorrow.

"Tomorrow I must make out some type of schedule. There is no way any one of us can work from morning to evening. We would collapse soon. Your idea of staying here sounds good. Go and ask the girls," she said in a weary tone, staring at me.

I walked out to the terrace where the girls were still sitting, but loud giggling filled the otherwise open room. Kari was sitting with them also. When they saw me coming, the giggle stopped.

"What was so funny?" I asked, looking at them.

"We were laughing at Lisa's description of your first sandwiches. She told us that they looked like someone had stepped on them, but after she showed you how to roll the meats and decorate them with the assortments of fresh vegetables and herbs they gave the impression of being appetizing and edible. Juha, you did fine. Now you are a pro almost," Lisa said with a smile.

"Thanks, Lisa. You are a sweet teacher," I said, feeling heat on my face.

"It is late and everyone is beat, if anyone wants to stay overnight here, you can."

Both Lisa and Annukka thought it would be a good idea. In the past they had stayed overnight and their parents had given them permission to do so, at their choice.

"There is a closet in the downstairs bedroom, with extra blankets and sheets from the hotel, enough for all beds. Pillows also," Annukka informed.

"Ok, let's go and get the rooms ready," I said, walking in. The girls followed.

We told Mother of the decision. "I am glad to hear it. Everyone is too tired to go home and it is late already. Inga and I will stay downstairs, the two girls in one of the upstairs rooms and Juha and Kari in the other room. We all agreed and proceeded to the closet for the bedding.

It was still hot and stuffy in the attic. Kari opened the window, which immediately helped. It was still twilight. The temperature had dropped to a comfortable coolness. Together we made the bed. The mattress turned out to be lumpy, but at this point we did not care. We said good night to the girls. Kari slept on the wall side, with me next to him. During the night, I woke up from being devoured by hungry mosquitoes. They were entering through the open window, which I closed, but too late. They were buzzing all around us. Kari was covered totally under the sheets. I followed suit which kept them from attacking me. Finally I fell asleep again. My last thoughts were about Rantala and my horse. I would never call him Twenty One, or two, or three.

30

THE SUN WAS TICKLING MY nose when I woke up. The rays were filtering through the window. The old dry smell of the attic hit me, after a night of tossing and turning. Kari was still curled up, covered totally with the sheet. I slid off the mattress and opened the window, letting in a cool breeze with the smell of night dew into the small room the chirp of the morning birds. I could still feel the bumps from the mattress. I got dressed leaving the room quietly, to see if anyone else was up. I walked to the girl's room, peeking in through the partially open door. They were still asleep. Very silently I made my way to their window, opening it half way. They appeared so peaceful and comfortable. Their faces shone of mellow rest.

I had not noticed earlier that each step squeaked as I made my way downstairs. There were some sounds coming from the kitchen, it must be Mother, I assumed. Sure enough, it was her. She was busy lighting the stove, the coffee pot sitting ready.

I had come in so quietly that she jumped, when I greeted her, "Good morning."

She turned around, angry, spouting, "You scared me. Next time make a little noise. Good morning to you! Did you and Kari sleep well?"

"We did, except for the miserable mosquitoes. What about you and Inga?"

"It took me a while to fall asleep because my mind was so rattled from the day, but when I finally fell asleep, I slept like a rock. Your sister is still in her bed. Coffee will be ready soon."

"You know, I am so surprised that we don't have running water here or electricity or telephone. Then the outhouses? Two for women and two for men. I can just see the Japanese tourists using them. They must be pissed?" I said, chuckling.

"Juha. You should be ashamed. You should not talk like that about our customers. Maybe they understand that we are way out in the woods and running water is not available. If you talk like that again, I'll put you in charge of keeping the outhouses clean. What do you think about that?" she growled at me.

"I'll never use the word piss again," I said laughing.

We sat at the table having a cup of coffee, when Mother looked at me and said," Juha when you go to work later, I will send a list of items which we need. Hannu can bring them on Thursday. Call my friend Helen and tell her to come and see me as soon as possible. She is not doing anything right now, and I want to talk to her about working here the rest of the summer. She is a good hard working and honest person, and with her here, I can make out a new schedule, which will take much pressure off us."

"Ok, I will," I said, sipping the coffee and chewing on a coffee roll.

Lisa and Annukka entered the kitchen, rubbing their eyes. They still appeared half asleep. "Good morning," came out in unison, not much louder than a whisper. They poured a coffee each and came to join us at the table.

"Did you girls sleep well?" Mother asked.

Annukka, who seemed a little more awake than Lisa, said, "I think so, but between Lisa kicking me and the mosquitoes biting, it was a bit turbulent. Next time I want to sleep with Inga," she said, sneering at Lisa.

"You talk in your sleep," Lisa said in defense.

"Juha, it's only seven thirty. You and the girls have plenty of time for a swim at the lake before we open. That will pep you up and it is a beautiful morning," Mother suggested.

It was only ten minutes later, when the girls came back down in their bathing suits. I had changed in the downstairs bedroom. Inga was still asleep, and so was Kari upstairs. We threw towels over our shoulders and headed for the steps down to the bear sculpture at the foot of the steps, which was almost at the Aulanko Lake level. Beside a lookout terrace, the steps began with a sign mounted on a post, stating: Bear grotto stairway 332 steps, with an arrow pointing downward.

The stairs were made with the same granite as the tower, with handrails on both sides with steps wide enough for two people to walk side by side. The descent was pleasant. The stairs circled downward the granite mountain to the left. On two different locations, rest area seating had been constructed, with solid granite benches and a table. The scenery was majestic, with the lake below shimmering in the morning sun and the solid rock rising high, next to us. The climb down was easy, but would be demanding on the way up.

The girls and I reached the last step of three hundred and thirty two, the 'bear cavern' was waiting for us. It was a grotto, hand carved into the rock face. It was about forty foot tall and quite deep with a tall solid stone carving of a bear family. The statue was a mother bear, huddling three cubs. We were looking at a very large beautiful, gray black stone creation, which had stood here for over fifty years. It was life size and life like. It was a master piece. We stood admiring it for a short time.

By now, we were almost at the lake level. It was a couple of hundred yards walk to the lake. Continuing along the shore, we arrived at a large rock sitting off shore about twenty feet. "Let's stop here and swim," I called out to the girls, who were walking behind me.

"Ok," Lisa said, throwing her towel on the shore and began to wade to the rock. "Wow! The water is crystal clear and ice cold." She reached the rock which was large and flat, jutting out of the water a couple of feet. "Come on, you scary cats," she taunted us.

Annukka and I sloshed to the rock. The water was as Lisa had claimed, very cold and clear. This lake was fed by a natural spring, deep in the center of the lake. It was nothing like our lake at Rantala, which became lukewarm late in the summer.

The three of us stood on the rock, looking at the water directly below it. Apparently the rock sat on a ledge, because just beyond the bottom dropped straight down to the depths. Schools of small silvery fish were swimming in formation. We could barely make out the bottom.

The only way to take a dip would be to just jump in. It was too cold to slowly work your way in for a swim. "Who wants to be the first to jump?" I asked. No sooner I got my words out, there was a big splash. Annukka's head emerged from the water, screaming. "My God, it is cold," and she began to swim back to shore.

"Juha is next!" Lisa hollered, pushing me off the rock, laughing.

I splashed in an ugly belly flap into the freezing cold water. It numbed me immediately. I was sinking until my mind told me to swim towards the surface. I felt like I had been underwater forever.

"Don't laugh. Wait until I get hold of you," I hollered, with teeth clattering when my head popped to the surface. It was freezing. A couple of small fish came and nibbled my feet. Quickly, I swam back to the rock, climbing up, with Lisa as my target. I was too late. She jumped in, screaming when her head popped up. "Your mother said that the water would pep us up. She was right. I have never been as peppy as now," she shrieked.

Back on shore, we dried ourselves and jumped up and down, trying to warm up. The sun was bright, extending some warmth. "That was fun. I will get you, Lisa, the next time we come here," I stammered with my teeth still clattering.

The climb back up the steps was incredibly tiresome. The peppiness from the cold swim slowly drained with each step. "Only one hundred and fifty more steps to go. Let's stop at this rest plateau for a short time and catch our breath," I suggested. The girls agreed. Sitting here on a thick granite bench, overlooking the tree tops at the calm lake, shimmering in the sun shine, was so relaxing. Several chicken hawks circled above us, gliding and circling in the minimal breeze. The mountain side was scattered with yellow, blue and red wild flowers. Their sweet scent was almost hypnotic. The sun had warmed the stone bench, which was welcome after the icy water. After a short rest, we continued on up climbing the rest of the steps.

"How was the swim?" Mother asked, in a sly smile, knowing how cold the water was.

"It was great. We woke up in a split second," Lisa said, continuing, "Wow!"

Inga and Kari were milling about, giving the impression of being irate. "Why didn't you wake us up? We would have liked to come along," Inga asked in an unpleasant tone.

"You were sleeping so deep. Next time we will all go. Sorry," I said.

Later that same week, Kari and I went rock climbing on this jagged solid mountain. A gentle breeze was blowing directly at us over the lake. Without taking the steps for a swimming trip, we decided to try climbing down the mountain. There were outcroppings, and large boulders on the steep incline.

In the crevices, moss, with juniper bushes and small cedar trees protruded with beefy stumps from long by gone tall trees. We made slow progress by giving careful attention to our hand and foot holds. Half way down the rocks, Kari fell. All I could hear was his scream. I looked, but could not see him.

I hollered," Kari are you okay. Where are you?"

A whimper came from below. Then louder, "I'm here!"

I looked down below the outcropping where I had seen him last, and there he was Lucky for him, he had fallen down some twelve feet, on his behind, smack on top of an old rotten tree stump. It had crumbled under him, creating a cushion, which saved him from falling on bare rock. Ants were franticly running all over him. He had squashed their nest. They were biting his arms and legs. When I reached him, he was crying and laughing at the same time, trying to slap the ants off. I was shocked, but could not help but to laugh also, seeing his miserable look.

"Ouch, ouch! Shit! These ants are vicious," he hollered with his face contorted in pain. He stood up carefully, not wanting to roll down further.

He was not hurt, but stunned. Maybe we should turn back? After resting for a short time we decided to continue. That had been a frightening moment for both of us, but did not stop our descent. When reaching the bear grotto, we looked up and wondered how we had accomplished this chilling climb.

"Next time we'll take the steps," I said to him. "You were very lucky. Poor ants."

"That was not funny," he grumbled, scratching his welts from the ant bites.

Our episode had become the talk of the girls.

Everyone became busy in opening up the restaurant for the day's business. Mother was much calmer today compared to yesterday. By now, she had a semi good idea of what needed to be done and where most everything was. She checked the ice box, which still contained two large ice blocks and was cold. Hannu would be bringing more ice on Thursday. I carried in chopped wood for the stove, setting it by under the sink. Shortly thereafter Maija showed up and picked up her tickets and change and left for the ticket booth. I moseyed up to the tower to unlock it and climb up top to raise the flag. The routine was falling in place. The girls did their duties and by nine o' clock we were ready.

Mother had thought that this position was for the rest of this summer, but it turned out that she would be taking care of this tourist complex for the next five seasons. As time went by, she grew to love her job, the employees she hired, and the beauty of this place. She loved the trees, the rocks, the birds and most of all the tourists.

Usually a gentle breeze whispered through the trees but on a windy day a chilling groan from the tower could be heard. That was spooky. When the weather was sunny and beautiful, it was heavenly, but when a periodic thunderstorm and heavy rains occurred, it was cold and raw. It appeared that the lightning was attracted to the tall tower, hovering over it for a long time.

One afternoon later in the summer, mother was by the sink. A relentless thunderstorm was roaring above the restaurant, when suddenly a fire ball, as large as a grapefruit, came through the wall next to her. It danced around the kitchen a short while, after which it flew out through the wall in the bedroom. There was no fire, but two large holes in the walls. Mother was in a shock, and as white as a ghost. At another time, late in the evening a severe lightning hit the roof of the restaurant, setting the corner of it on fire. Luckily the heavy rain put the fire out, but only after Kari had biked to the hotel, at break neck speed, for help. By the time help arrived, the fire was out and the next day a repair crew arrived and fixed the damage.

It was time for me to go to work at the hotel. Mother gave me the list and reminded me to call Helen.

"I will probably staying at home tonight, because I have to be back to work early tomorrow morning," I told Mother.

"Ok, we might stay here again, I don't know right now. If we don't see you tonight, come back later tomorrow. Now we have two living quarters. What a difference from the stinky little apartment. I love it up here and our home by the hotel. Have a good night, Juha," she said, giving me a kiss on the cheek.

31

A COUPLE OF YEARS FLEW BY so fast. It was summer of 1954. I had graduated my first year from the Lyseo, which is an advanced high school. I was still two years away for college. This was also Inga's last year in the grade school and Kari's first year. All of us had done well and now we celebrated summer again. Mother was working at the hotel during winters and managing the tower operation in the summer time. Inga worked with her at the restaurant. Mother had a knack of hiring only friendly and beautiful young girls, some a year or two older than me. Each summer I enjoyed a close friendship with one of them, which of course made me very happy. There had been Lisa, the following summer, Anja, then Lena and this summer was still open to be decided. Inga, Kari and I went swimming in the cold lake just about every night. Often one of the girls or all of them came along. Mother had joined twice, but could not believe how cold the water was. She refused to come again.

I still carried luggage and steered the guests to their rooms. I was happy with my job, but had started to think what I wanted to do in the future. I did not want to be a bellboy all my life. The idea of becoming a sea captain rolled around my head most of the time. I wanted to be in charge of a big ship and travel around the world. The aspect of a captain's license was very appealing. I still had time to make up my mind. Kari had taken over the shoe shining, doing his job well. He liked the money very much.

The first week in July on a Sunday, there would be an equestrian competition show at the rink by Aulanko stables. In the rider's circle, this was a well known yearly event. Riders and the audience had arrived as far away as Helsinki. It was a beautiful day with bright sunshine and a mellow breeze. Bleachers had been raised on two sides of the rink. Elegantly dressed women sat in the audience wearing colorful hats, large and small, red and yellow being the prominent color. Men were also present for this event, smartly dressed, some wearing fedoras and Panama hats. There was anticipation in the air. The proud riders were parading in the rink on horses that had been groomed to a shine. The riders were dressed in stylish riding attire. Inga was one of them. She sat ram straight atop of her horse, with a relaxed but determined smile. She would be jumping in the junior class. Dressed in new riding breeches, and a riding helmet she had a personal touch. It was in earth colors, not the basic black. Her pony tail swung with the trot of the horse.

Inga had become a proficient rider. She and her horse navigated many difficult jumps. The instructor as well as her own confidence assured her that she was ready for this competition. She was daring, but not foolhardy. This day had been on her mind for over one month when she had signed up as a junior rider. She had practiced relentlessly and felt comfortable and excited about the challenge.

We were part of the excited audience sitting front row, center. My sister was riding her first competition. I found it hard to believe. My horse at Rantala would be scared of the crowd and the other horses. He would gallop into the woods with me atop and hide, I mused. Inga gave us a wave when she passed us.

The competition started with the first round prize winning competitors. The jumps were high. It was beautiful to watch them fly gracefully over the high jumps. Each rider took two rounds on the course. The second group was the intermediates and the jumps were lowered one notch for them. The juniors were next. The jumps were lowered once again for them. Mother was hugging me and Kari, whispering, "I hope Inga will do well and be safe."

Inga was at the starting line, standing still, waiting for the starting signal. It sounded and she was off. She and the horse followed the course jumping gracefully over each jump. Her first round was flawless. We were so happy for her, hugging each other firmly. She waited for the start signal for her second round. It sounded and she took off. She was jumping with ease and with grace, until she came up to the fifth jump, which was a weathered fence. She had jumped this obstacle many times. They had picked up the speed for this jump. Inga was leaning forward on the horse's neck, in a relaxed posture. They arrived at the jump with perfect speed. Inga was gearing up for it. Something spooked the horse. The horsed stopped abruptly in front of the jump, on its fore legs and lowered its head and upper body. We could not believe what happened next. Inga went flying over the jump like a rag doll head first, landing in a heap on the other side of the fence, lying motionless on the turf. There were screams from the audience. People, including us, ran over to her. Someone yelled."Don't touch her. She might have hurt her spine. CALL AN AMBULANCE!"

Mother was crying. Inga was not moving. She had passed out. Did she have broken bones? No one knew. We kneeled next to her. Mother felt her pulse and told us that she felt it. You could see Inga's chest rising and falling. I took hold of her other hand. It was cold and limp. My God, I hope she will be all right. There was a quiet hush amongst the crowd who encircled us. Some people exchanged whispered words about paralysis. Kari touched Inga's forehead very gently. I could see tears running his white, scared face. Finally, about fifteen minutes later, we could hear the sirens of the ambulance. The paramedics pushed the crowd aside and brought a stretcher where Inga was carefully placed, still unconscious. They allowed only for Mother to ride along. She kissed us before climbing aboard. Some friendly individual with a car told Kari and I that he would give us a ride to the hospital.

By the time we arrived, she was already under doctor's care. We had to wait in the waiting room. Mother was in the middle with me and Kari on each side. We were holding her hands, while she quietly said a prayer. We sat there for what seemed an eternity when the doctor finally came out, telling us that Inga was fine. There were no broken bones, but she would be sore for some time. She had a concussion, which would take about a week to heal, but no neck or spinal injuries. Our sad teary faces lit up. "This is truly a miracle," Mother said looking up to the ceiling, "Thank you God." She hugged us. The doctor told us that Inga would have to stay in the hospital for at least three or four days, in order to medicate her and keep an eye on her progress. He gave us permission to visit her for five minutes. "Thank you, doctor," Mother said smiling at him.

When she saw us enter the room, the first thing she whispered was, "Sorry" with eyes half open and a thin smile on her lips. Her eyes were not focused. She was pale.

Mother touched her cheek tenderly, with a sigh, and said, "Thank God you did not hurt yourself more seriously. We were so worried. You have nothing to be sorry of. You did so well and we are so proud of you. We love you," she murmured, pressing a kiss to her cheek. "You frightened us with your fall. It was such a horrible sight to see you fly head first."

Kari and I held Inga's hands and I said, "We were so scared when we saw you flying and then not responding when you were lying on the ground. Please get well real soon." Both of us had tears in our eyes. Inga appeared so frail.

Inga laid still. Her eyes were still half closed, but a light pink hue had appeared on her cheeks. She just nodded to our comments, without any words. She looked tired and hurt. The medication was making her sleepy and relaxed.

"We will come and visit you tomorrow. The doctor wants to keep you here at least three days. We love you. He only gave us a few minutes to visit you. You are in good hands here. Bye." Waving at her, we departed.

We rode the bus back home, quiet, in our thoughts about this accident. She could have been paralyzed, or worse. We thanked God.

We arrived home, tired, sad and happy all emotions mixed in from the days happenings and noticed there was a large brown envelope hanging from our door handle. It was marked: INGA

Mother took it inside to the kitchen table, where we gathered, puzzled to find out what it contained. Carefully she opened it, pulling out a card and a beautiful green, red and yellow ribbon, with a round medal hanging from it. We admired it. It shone bright silvery in the kitchen light. There was a beautiful horse in the center, outlined with writing around the edge. The card, had a striking painting of a horse, nothing else. Mother opened it with trembling hands. Kari and I moved closer to see what it said. It was from the equestrian committee, wishing Inga a full recovery, and:

Under the sad circumstances, it still gives us pleasure to honor Inga for a well deserved silver medal, in her class for excellent riding. Signed: The committee.

We were dumbfounded. What a kind gesture on their part. Inga was not alone. We were with her and so were all the people who had seen her riding, and especially the judges. Tomorrow we would take her medal and the card to the hospital. That would certainly help her recovery.

Four days later, she was released from the hospital, with the doctor's orders for her to take it very easy for the next month. The concussion still lingered, but day by day it would get better. She was so happy to leave the hospital. "The food was awful", was one of her comments. "It was total blah...It tasted like wet cardboard with some kind of gravy which stuck in my palette. I am starved," she said.

We had ordered a taxi cab for the ride home. Inga wore her medal proudly around her neck. She still looked weak but most of her radiant color had returned. To me she looked like she had lost some weight.

32

KAISA, KAISA, KAISA. SHE WAS after me with every chance she got. When I saw her approach, I did everything in my power to fade away from her proximity. Not that I had anything against her, but I was simply embarrassed to be seen with her. She worked at the hotel as a bus girl in the dining room. She had started her job early that spring. Apparently she preformed her duties well, because she was still there. She had been hired from good recommendations from an old time employee, otherwise she would have been working somewhere else.

I felt sorry for Kaisa, for many reasons. She was a couple of years older than I, perhaps eighteen. Kaisa looked as if she had run into a dump truck. She was short and plump, with big feet and short, chubby legs. Her hands were large, with short rotund fingers. Her finger nails had been bitten down to bare minimum. Her face was flat, hence 'the dump truck' effect. Her eyes were small and piercing, off color blue, below painted black eye brows. Her nose, instead of being pug, was flat, like a prize fighters, who had received too many punches in the face. Her small lips were easy to detect from the bright red lipstick. They were the focal point on her face. Her hair was short and jet black, probably colored from a light brown or blonde. She wore some type of perfume which smelled of lilac and lemon. When she walked, she waddled like the ducks at Aulanko Park. She spoke in a way that was muddled, and hard to understand.

She could not help how she looked, but the unpleasant fact for me was that she was after me. I tried to steer my friend who also worked at the hotel, to connect him with her. "You are crazy, Juha. I don't want anything to do with her. You are the one she is after. She is your problem," he sneered, walking away.

I felt sorry for her for the way she looked and the fact that she had no friends... that I knew of. I was nice to her when I got cornered by her, but that is where I wanted it to end. Poor girl, she was after someone's affection.....but not mine. Please.

Inga had healed back to normal but did not feel like riding any time soon. She was so fortunate of not having broken her neck. Similar accidents had happened around the country and the world with dire results. She was back working with Mother at the tower. My job had been so busy all summer. The hotel was booked solid until late September. There was a practice for visitors who arrived with their own car to leave the car keys with the front desk. In the event of any problem at the parking lot, we would be able to move their car. I had discovered that it was easy to borrow someone's car for a short joy ride, normally up to the tower for a cup of coffee and a quick visit. The road leading through the park of Aulanko, was a beautiful and exciting ride. It was hilly and curvy, and woodsy, past the two lakes and flowering meadows. My driving was very careful, never causing any problems. And luckily, I never was caught for having borrowed them. I don't think that the hotel management would have taken my episodes kindly.

It was a warm sunny afternoon, when Kari and I had gone to the island for a swim. We were laying on a blanket on the warm sand, soaking in the sunshine. I was half asleep, when I heard my name called. I rolled to my stomach to find out who was calling me. I groaned. I could not believe who it was. There was Kaisa standing on Kari's side looking over at me. There was no place to hide, but I was so surprised to see her on the beach. Very nonchalantly, without any emotion in my words, I said, "Hi Kaisa" and turned around onto my back, looking at the few fluffy clouds slide by. Kaisa proceeded to throw a towel on the sand next to me. Now I was trapped.

"Juha and Kari, can I join you?" she asked meekly, looking down at me, casting a shadow over me.

"Yes sure. We are here for a short while," was the only thing I could think to say. Kari was laying with his eyes closed, but listening to see where this would lead.

Kaisa sat down on her towel, too close to me. She was wearing a black bathing suit, surprising me. She did not look too bad in it. She was rather well developed and even her toe nails were painted pink. My eyes studied her for a little longer than I had planned. Her body was white next to the black suit. This must be her first day in the sun, I surmised. Kari stood up and told us that he was going for a soda, and left.

"Juha, can I ask you a question?"

"Sure," I said, curious. Knowing that she had the 'hots' for me, nothing would surprise me.

"Would you take me to see a movie, in town?" she asked hesitantly and timidly.

I gave that question a long thought, thinking that I did not want anyone to see me with her, but then again, now that she did not appear too bad, and I did feel sorry for her, I justified my underlying thoughts. I looked at her... and the bathing suit.

"I'll be happy to take you," I said giving her my out of the blue answer.

"Can we go tonight? I am off from work and so are you. The movie *African Queen* just started today?" she asked without a muddled voice. "Please," she added and inched a little closer to me.

"Okay, we'll leave on the seven thirty bus. I'll meet you at the bus," I told her, still calculating my decision.

"Thanks Juha, See you tonight," she said with a bright smile and ran into the lake.

After swimming for awhile, I told Kaisa that Kari and I had to leave, "I'll see you tonight," I called out to her in the water.

Kari was laughing, after we had walked inland and burst out," Juha, she has you roped now. She has a wild reputation at the hotel. They call it 'loose' whatever that means," he said, still chuckling, with a crooked smile.

"Well, I'm older than you. No one is going to rope me," I said but not believing a word of what I just said.

I arrived at the hotel five minutes before the bus was to leave and climbed aboard. My clothing was casual. I was wearing blue jeans and a white shirt sleeve shirt and brown sandals. I could see Kaisa sitting in the bus in the island seat, next to a grumpy looking woman. The woman was eyeing Kaisa with a disgusted look. No wonder. Kaisa was wearing a colorful array of clothing. She had on a bright red short skirt, green bobby socks with tennis shoes, and a tight off-white shirt with no bra, unbuttoned quite low. The worst sight was an awful pink hat, aligned with multicolor fake flowers. Oh my God... I thought, smacking myself in the forehead for agreeing to this date. I don't want to be seen with this girl. She gave me a big smile as I walked by her. I gave her a subdued wave. A whiff of some lemony perfume emitted from the seat when I passed her walking to the far end of the bus.

When we got off the bus in town, it was a two block walk to the movie theater. The woman who had sat next to her on the bus got off and gave Kaisa a nasty, burning look. Kaisa just smiled, whispering one word, "Bitch."

"Kaisa, take off that ugly hat," I said, still standing next to the bus. "I am sorry if you get hurt from my comment, but I hate hats," I said, thinking back to my Salvation Army days. Her hat was even nastier.

She did not look hurt. "I thought you would like it," she said, taking the hat off and putting it into her purse. She had to double it up before it fit. "Is this better?"

"Yes," I said, wondering whether I should mention something about the buttons on her shirt but decided not to say anything. Truthfully, I enjoyed the view.

We arrived to the theater, after receiving countless stares from people on the sidewalk. The men especially gawked at her. I was embarrassed and tried to walk behind her, to seem disassociated from her. I went to the ticket counter and bought two tickets, handing her one. The lights would be dimmed momentarily. "Kaisa, I have to stop in the bathroom. Why don't you go in and hold me a seat? I'll be right there," I said and headed to the bathroom. Hopefully it will be dark by the time I get done.

I saw her sitting off to the side, with an empty seat next to her. The movie had just started. I sat next to her. The air was perfumed into a blend of lilacs and lemon. She grabbed my hand the minute I sat down and intertwined her fingers with mine. Her hand was warm and soft. Her fingers were chubbier than mine. The movie proceeded and it was great. It was the best movie I had ever seen. Kaisa was so intent that she forgot all about me, except squeezing harder in the frightening scenes. We sat spellbound throughout the show and when it was over, walked to the bus station talking about it. To her it had also been the best movie she had seen. By now the evening had turned into dusk and I was no longer concerned about the stares. On the bus, we sat next to each other. It was almost empty.

When we reached the hotel, we walked slowly, hand in hand towards my home and the employee's dormitory, where Kaisa lived.

"Juha, let's go to the employee's recreation cabin close to your house, there is normally no one in there," she said, squeezing my hand harder.

"Okay, we can play some table tennis," I said, looking at her buttons, planning on some other games.

The cabin was about the size of a large living room. We entered through an unlocked door into the room, with two windows letting in subdued lighting from the evening's dusk. It was furnished with two long couches and three stuffed easy chairs next to a large book case, which was overflowing with well handled books. There sat a floor reading light next to each chair. The center of the room was occupied by a standard size table tennis stand. Some old throw rugs covered the floor. To my surprise... and delight, Kaisa locked the door from the inside.

Before I had a chance to say or do anything, she grabbed hold of my hand, leading me to one of the couches. I could faintly see the excitement in her eyes, when we sat down. Kaisa grabbed my face with both of her hands and planted a sensual kiss on my mouth. I did not resist but contributed my share in return. She proceeded to undo the rest of her shirt buttons, and I was just a young boy on my way to oblivion.

There was no table tennis game that night. I was going to teach her the proper game techniques. Instead, she taught me games which I had heard of, but never experienced before. What I learned that night from Kaisa was much more exciting than table tennis. Both of us were exhausted by the time we left the recreation room. Kaisa walked to the dorm, after a last kiss, and said, "Thank you. I had a great night. Hope you enjoyed it also?"

"Kaisa, I like to learn new things and you sure are a first-rate teacher. Thanks. The movie was great and what happened afterwards was fantastic," I said and walked home in a daze.

33

THE DAY WAS GLOOMY WITH light rain falling. I was working on my regular morning shift with the dozens of shoes left for polishing outside of the guest rooms were finally done. I always wished that someone would slip a tip in the shoe, but it had only happened once. The hotel was full as usual, with some overflow in the buildings from the Olympic days.

Mother's operation at the tower was going very smoothly. Occasionally on my day off, I would work as the ticket seller for the tower. On a slow day, it was a perfect quiet place for reading. Jack London's writings had now become my favorites. The *Call of The Wild* was hard to put down. It was amazing reading and so well written. Today, with the rain, I would have all the time in the world for reading in the small booth, but I was working at the hotel.

Guests arrived throughout the day and others had left in the morning. I saw Kaisa running around in the dining room. We just waved to each other. After the movie night, we had not seen each other, except at work. Perhaps she had some other conquest in sight.

Late that afternoon, a taxi pulled up to the front door. It was my duty to keep an eye on arriving guests, so I ran out to open the car door. "Welcome to Aulanko," I said in Finnish. The lone gentleman passenger, assumed this to be a greeting and answered in English, "Thank you." He appeared to be

American rather than an English gentleman. Over time I had learned to distinguish one from the other. The American dress code was more colorful than the stiff Brits and their demeanor was easy going. Their speech was twanged and casual, which was not the case with the Brits. I was right again. After retrieving his two suitcases from the trunk, I led him in to the front desk He was a tall man, a bit on the heavy side. Well dressed, he wore a green sport jacket and light tan colored slacks and a white polo shirt. He looked friendly, with a perpetual smile. His eyes were dark brown, highlighted by his silvery hair. His demeanor was of someone who was well educated and sure of himself, someone who expected nothing but the best.

He signed in, leaving his passport with the desk attendant. This was a practice for all foreign tourists. The same evening all passports were transported to the local police station for inspection and returned the following morning. I could never understand why this was necessary. It was year 1954, two years since the Olympics. The war was long over and there were no problems. Why this silliness?

Key in hand for his room on the upper floor, we proceeded to the elevator. I carried his suitcases, which were not very heavy.

In the elevator, he asked me. "Do you speak English?" in an American accent.

"Yes but very little. I have studied English in school for four years," I said, trying my best to get the words correct.

"Does it rain much here?"

"No, almost every day is beautiful," I said, still on the right track. We arrived at his floor and I proceeded to show him to his room. I did my normal routine with the bags, turning the lights on and opening the window shades, finishing by saying, "Enjoy your stay."

He was looking out the window at the calm blue green waters of the lake at the foot of the hotel. "What a beautiful sight," he commented, turning to look at me, saying, "Thank you," and handing me a two dollar tip, and adding, "what is your name?"

"Juha in Finnish, John in English. Thank you," I said and closed the door behind me. I was whistling on the way down in the elevator. That was a good tip.

At the front desk, I looked up his reservation. He would be staying with us for one week and his name was Laban Schwab, from Philadelphia, USA. He had signed in as a vice president of a railroad company in Philadelphia. His last name would be easy to remember. As much as possible, we had been instructed to call our customers by their name. Schwab was registered into my memory.

Later in the afternoon, the sun came out and after the gloomy morning, it was a welcome sight. My shift was over at five and I decided to walk up to the tower and visit with Mother and Kari and the girls. When I arrived, they were having dinner and I joined them. Inga had cooked it, which was some type of stew concoction of and it tasted good. "Inga, you outdid yourself," I said and got back in return a happy smile from her.

Our schedules were not quite normal. Sometimes we did not see each other for a couple of days, when they decided to spend the nights on the mountain, and I would stay home alone. It worked out fine. It was silly for them to walk down to the house every evening and back the first thing next day. Later that evening, all of us except Mother took the swimming trip. There was a new girl working in the restaurant. Her name was Lisa. She was very pretty and petite, about my age, with long blond hair and sparkling blue eyes. We became friends immediately, enjoying the climb down and up getting to know each other. It was late, but she decided to go home for the night, not having to be back until noon the next day. I walked to the hotel with her and waited for the bus to arrive. She told me that her dream was to become a doctor and I told her of my dream of becoming a sea captain. "Gross…a sea captain, you would never be home," she said.

"True," I agreed, "but I want to see the world. The bus arrived and we bid each other good night. I like this girl, I was thinking, on the way home. Thank you Mother for hiring such nice girls, I added to my thoughts.

The next morning greeted us with clear skies and warm sunshine. At about eight, I was walking through the lounge, when I spotted Mr. Schwab sitting at one of the small tables, with a coffee cup and a platter of toast, seemingly enjoying a simple breakfast. I approached him, greeting him, "Good morning, Mr. Schwab."

He looked up with a big smile, and said, "Good morning John. You were right about the weather. It is a beautiful day."

"It is a typical Finnish summer morning. I am glad for you," I said.

"I was looking out the window at the lake. What is that big boat, tied down to the dock, right next to the hotel?" he inquired, taking a sip of coffee.

"It is *Ms Aulanko*, a sightseeing ship, which travels on a day trip."

This ship was new, only a few months old. It replaced *M S. Roine* where I had worked one season. It was twice the size of the old one and much more comfortable and plusher. "It leaves in another hour. If you would like to see it, I will take you down to it, after you finish your breakfast," I suggested. My English was somewhat muddled, but he seemed to understand what I had said.

"Yes, that sounds interesting. Give me ten minutes and we'll go."

"Okay, I will be right back," I said walking over to the reception desk to see if I was needed at that point and explaining of taking Mr. Schwab down to the boat.

Shortly after that, we were walking down to the dock, passing the outdoor terrace with its colorful flower beds and two grand water fountains. Two waiters were setting up the tables for lunch. Down a short hill, it took us to the pier where the sleek ship pulled gently at her mooring, swaying in a light breeze.

I called out for the captain, from the foot of the steps, asking him permission to come aboard and show the ship to Mr. Schwab. "Of course, Juha, come aboard," the captain called back. "Walk around. Welcome aboard."

We walked up the five carpeted steps, arriving in a vestibule. To the left a few steps led down to the large inside cabin with huge windows, seeming as if sitting outside. On each side of the center walk, was comfortable seating a in deep burgundy color. It had been arranged for at least ninety to over a hundred people. It smelled of leather and a hint of diesel fuel. Above this salon was the outside seating, almost as large as this area. To the right, was the dining room, with all tables set in crisp linen and silver flat ware. The dining room crew was putting the finishing touches to the set up. Lastly, we would visit the bridge, where the captain and the mate were involved in preparations for the day's trip, leaving in less than an hour. During our walk on the ship, I tried to tell Mr. Schwab, how nice the trips were. My English sure was terrible, but it seemed as if he understood most of my comments.

As we entered the bridge, I said, "Captain Maki, this is Mr. Schwab from America. He is a guest at the hotel and wanted to see your ship," I said. The captain was the same captain from *Roine* but the mate was new. Both of them were dressed in sharp white uniforms. The captain's sported shiny gold epaulettes.

"Nice to meet you," the captain said. The men shook hands.

We admired the well appointed bridge, with teak and polished mahogany. The instrument panel, in shiny chrome, looked impressive with the latest arrays of radios, radars and other instruments. A polished large chrome wheel, sat in the center of the instrument consul. Charts were laid out on a side table.

"Perhaps I will take the trip with you one day. I am staying here for a week. You have a fine vessel, and Juha told me how enjoyable the day trips are," the American said, smiling at the captain.

After we stepped off the ship, we saw several groups of people, young and old, head for the dock, to wait for the day's boarding. A busload of tourists, was being unloaded further up the hill. These boat trips were very popular throughout the summer.

We took a short walk on the shore road. I pointed out the red sauna building sitting at the tip of the peninsula and the multitude of the silver willow trees. Mr. Schwab made a comment, "I have never had a truly real sauna experience. I will take one here one of these days." Back at the hotel, he shook my hand and thanked me for giving him the tour. His handshake was firm and dry, just like mine. "I like your handshake, and absolutely detest a limp one. Good for you," he complimented.

"Perhaps tomorrow, if you have the time, you could show me the Aulanko Park and the lookout tower? I have read much of it in the tourist literature, where they claim that it is beautiful," he said, looking at me, waiting for my answer.

"Sure, I don't have to be to work until three in the afternoon, so we have plenty of time. You will meet my mother, sister and brother. Mother runs the operation there.

"That is great. Why don't we meet around ten a clock. Is that fine with you?"

"See you at ten tomorrow. I will show you everything." I promised him, in assuring tone, adding, "It is quite a walk, so dress comfortable and wear good walking shoes."

We bid farewell. Mr. Schwab took the hotel taxi to Hameenlinna and to other sites. I was excited about our trip tomorrow. I will be proud to introduce this fine man from America to everyone and let him see how beautiful the park is. The day flew by fast with guests coming and going. One family, who had arrived in their own car, asked me if I could escort them in their car through the park. I had to turn down their request, because I was on duty for the day and could not leave.

Later Mr. Schwab arrived back from his sightseeing trip, which he had enjoyed. He specifically was happy to have seen the composer Jean Sibelius's home and birthplace wash was now open as a museum. Also there had been a tour through the old castle, from the 13th century, where Mother had worked. It had been discontinued as a prison and turned into a historical museum. He had done some light shopping and had lunch in a coffee shop. After lunch he visited the historic Hattula church, dating back to circa 1320. It was a Gothic sample of architecture, brick built with several statues and paintings from that era. He was carrying a couple of shopping bags, with the local department's store label. He told me that he was tired by now and was going to his room for a nap. "See you tomorrow," he said and with a wave he took the elevator.

I had not talked with Fammu or Ukki in a long time. We kept writing letters back and forth, but now I decided to call them. Fammu answered after the third ring. She was so happy to hear my voice and I her voice. We talked. She told me that Kolli's family had left to go home to the southeastern part of Finland, because Ukki had decided to quit the large farming operation and sell the cattle. They only kept my horse, but all other animals were gone. Rantala had now turned into a summer home for them. Ukki's tobacco crop was still an important commodity and Fammu's garden, even though at this point it was much smaller than before, was still her joy. I told her about all the happenings here, Inga's accident being the major topic. She was so happy to hear that Inga had totally recuperated. They had not heard from our father in over two years and were very much concerned about him. After a long conversation, we bid farewell to each other. I promised to come for a visit later in August, before school started again. "Please say hello to Rake," was my last comment.

I loved my job. It was so interesting to meet people from around the world. Everyone seemed to be happy and pleased to be in our beautiful hotel and surroundings. I looked forward to every day and each day was a learning experience from the people I met. Then of course the money aspect was great. I was proud to be part of the hotel. I don't know why, but to me being here felt liberating.

34

THE NEXT MORNING I WOKE up to bright sunshine casting its beams through the kitchen window. I lit the kitchen stove, setting the coffee pot to boil. The smell of wood burning always sent a pleasant scent into the room. I ran for a quick shower at the dormitory next door. Looking into the mirror, I was wondering when my first beard stubbles would show. When I looked really close, I could see some peach fuss. I was going to be seventeen years old, so beard should follow soon.

While waiting for it to settle, I made myself two cheese sandwiches on black bread for a quick breakfast. After breakfast, I got dressed. It was a warm sunny day, so I chose to wear my favorite tan shorts with a dark blue shirt and sandals. No socks. I wanted to look casually sharp.

I arrived at the hotel a few minutes before ten. Mr. Schwab was already waiting for me. He was dressed in a green polo golf shirt, with a Titleist logo, and light sand colored linen slacks and brand new white sneakers. He looked ready for the golf course.

"Good morning, John. It looks like a splendid day. That must be your doing?" he said and chuckled. "How do you like my new sneakers that I bought yesterday? You warned me to wear comfortable shoes, and all I had with me were street shoes. These feel so comfortable. I am ready to start our trek, if you are," he said, looking at me.

"Let's go," I said, walking to the outside door and holding it open for him. "It is a tiresome walk, so we will take it easy and rest here and there," I said as we crossed the parking lot, to a set of granite steps leading into the woods. We climbed the steps up to a broad, well groomed walking path. So far he was not winded, but we were closing into a rather long uphill. It was not steep, but a long gradual hill. We walked slowly and conversed about the park and its history, which he was familiar with. Half way up a bench had been placed as a rest spot. We sat there for some five minutes and continued, until reaching the top of the hill. Now it was a short downhill, to the picturesque Swan Lake. The lake shore was nestled in overhanging birch, silver willow and poplar trees. The yellow and red water lilies floated in full bloom, like huge open grapefruits. I had brought some dry bread with me for the swans. No sooner when we stopped by the water edge, they swam over to us. "Be careful, they like to bite," I warned my companion. After feeding the swans, we walked half way around the small lake, on a birch trees lined walkway, to a petite pagoda. It was painted bright white, with a weathered cooper roof and dark blue benches hugging the inside walls. It was time for another rest stop. By now we were half way to the tower. Many sightseers were milling around the lake. Some families sat on blankets, with picnic baskets. Children were reaching in the water, feeding gold fish by hand.

We sat there quietly for a while. Mr. Schwab came up with a pack of Camel cigarettes, lit one and asking me if I wanted one. I declined, as at this point I was not smoking yet. He also reached for his wallet, drawing out an embossed business card and handed it to me. I studied it. It had his name, title of Vice President and the railroad company's name, and several phone numbers. "That is me," he said in a pleasant tone.

He leaned back against the railing. I could see his mind working despite his relaxed eyes and still posture. He did not say anything. I was wondering what he was thinking. Finally he inched a little closer to me, placing his hands in his lap and giving me the impression of having formulated his thoughts. He positioned his head so that we had direct eye contact.

"I have been thinking seriously about something for the last two days and now I am going to ask you something which might come as a shock to you," he said in a warm and even tone.

It might shock me? What in the world could that be? Had I done something that I should not have done? I sat still, looking directly at his eyes, waiting.

Then he asked me a question which did astonish me. "Would you like to come to America?" he asked.

I sat there with my mouth open, probably looking stupefied. A million thoughts rolled around in my brain. Sure I would like to go to America. Everyone was dreaming of going there. There was no way, we could afford for me to travel there. And then what? Where would I stay and what about school? He saw that I was totally flabbergasted. Was this an invitation?

I thought that I was dreaming, when he said, "I will send you tickets for the travel and enroll you in a school in Philadelphia. You can stay in my house, or I will rent you a room, if you wish. After I meet your mother, we'll talk about it with her and get her feelings about this," he said, continuing, "What do you think about this?"

My mouth was glued and unwilling to open, until I was able to utter, "I cannot believe this. I would be so happy to come to America, but I must be dreaming," I said swallowing hard.

"No, you are not dreaming. I am inviting you. I will explain all this to you. I would be very happy if you accept the invitation. I am alone. My wife died four years ago and we never had any children. I am very lonely. If you don't like it there, you are welcome to go back home at any time." He gazed at me, hands clasped, with his eyes as serious as his tone.

As we continued our trek, I just floated along. We walked slowly on the narrow roadway to the tower. I did not want to wake up, but it almost seemed inevitable. After a short while, we could hear horse hooves behind us. We turned around to look and saw Hannu and his horse coming behind us, with his delivery. Sitting high on the carriage, he called out, "Hei, Juha, jump aboard for a ride." He stopped the horse and both Mr. Schwab and I jumped onto the back of the wagon. We sat there, with our feet dangling, when Mr. Schwab commented, in a child like happy voice, "I have not done this in some fifty years, since I was a child at my grandparent's farm. I often dreamt about it. I feel like a little kid. This is fun," he whispered, almost in a giggle. "The railroad board of directors should see me now. They would die," he said laughing.

Finally we reached the tower and restaurant. We even helped to push Hannu's wagon up the last steep hill. The restaurant had few people sitting at the tables. A young baby was crying at one of them. One of the tables was occupied by six Japanese tourists, with cameras hanging around their necks. We walked up to the counter, where Inga was attending it. "Hi Inga, this is my American friend, Mr. Schwab," I said, introducing them. "Is Mother around?"

"Hi, let me get her," she said and disappeared into the back room.

"While we waited, Mr. Schwab commented, "Your sister is a very pretty girl."

Mother came out, wearing a white frock, looking surprised in seeing me with my friend. I introduced them to each other. Mother came out, from behind the counter, onto the terrace and suggested for us to sit at a table and order whatever we wished. After we placed the order with Lisa, who was the waitress today, I began telling Mother the unbelievable offer. Mother sat with her jaw agape, eyes in rounded surprise, looking at me and Mr. Schwab, back and forth, hands folded on the table. Finally, when I was done talking, she uttered, "This can't be true?" looking at Mr. Schwab, who was sitting still, not understanding what was said until I translated it to him, in my broken English.

Mr. Schwab looked straight in her eyes, and said, "It is true. I would like your permission to invite Juha to America." I translated again, but my English being so-so, I suggested we invite Maija to join us. She is fluent in English.

Mother called for one of the other girls to run up to the ticket booth for a while and send Maija down to join us. A few minutes later Maija came over and I introduced her to Mr. Schwab, explaining that she would act as an interpreter. "That is a good idea," he said, knowing how hard it was for me to understand everything he said.

Our sandwiches and beverages arrived. Maija ordered a cup of coffee. The sandwiches were an artistic open face ham and cheese on rye bread. Sliced tomatoes, radishes and twirled slices of cucumber decorated the plates. Mr. Schwab was impressed. I could see that Mother was as nervous as I was. She just nibbled her food, but drank the coffee down fast. While we ate, the conversation was just chit chat, Maija interpreting both ways. After we were finished eating and the table was cleared, the serious part of the meeting began. The Japanese group left, walking towards the tower.

Mr. Schwab began by telling a long story about himself, and the reason for the wish of bringing me to America. Maija kept translating all along.

"I live in Philadelphia USA and am retiring in a few months from the railroad. I have worked for them over thirty years. My wife died four years ago from severe illness. We had been married thirty eight years, without any children." I looked at Mother when hearing this. She was genuinely sad. Her eyes filled up with tears, and she said, "I am sorry to hear this." Maja was translating, as Mr. Schwab continued. "I have traveled for a few weeks and spent some time in Norway and Sweden, before coming to Finland. I intend to do much traveling in the future. I am very lonely and have been so, after my wife's death. My parents were German immigrants and we lived in Philadelphia in the German Town section. They owned a German food market and worked very hard from early morning to late night. They put my brother and me through college. I have one brother, who is a family physician, and also lives in Philadelphia. I attended The University of Pennsylvania and graduated in business management." Maija was busy interpreting. Good thing we had invited her to join us. "The house at home is empty. I am looking for company and at the same time, someone who I can help to excel in life. When I met Juha, this thought grew in my mind. He is a polite and smart young man, hard working and very friendly. He is the type of person, who I wished our son would have been, if we had one." When Maija translated this, Mother's face glowed from pride, and my face reddened. I was embarrassed and self conscious of all this praise. Some of the mischief crossed my mind. I was not a perfect angel by any means.

"Sylvi," he said looking at Mother, "Do you mind if I smoke? That is one of my vices."

"Not at all I smoke also," she said, still trembling lightly. Maija was also ready for a breather, drinking her coffee slowly. Mr. Schwab offered Mother one of his Camels, which she accepted, and they lit up. I could use a cigarette now, but did not dare to ask for one. I had to keep my good behavior intact.

"If you and Juha agree, I would be very happy. As I told him, he would be free to go back home any time, if he did not like it in America. I will arrange for him to start in the local high school. I don't drive, but he is the right age for a driver's license and I would buy a car for him and we could take car trips around the country. There is so much for us to see in my country." Hearing this about a car perked me up immediately. My own car...WOW!

"I can assure you, Sylvi that your son will be in very good hands. You would not have to worry about anything."

A quiet moment commenced, all of us thinking about this phenomenon. I thought that things like this only happened in movies, but this was not a fable, it was true. I still could not fathom this gift. I was delighted and excited. What a man Mr. Schwab turned out to be.

"I am so happy about this offer. Juha would learn so much and perhaps have a much better opportunity in America than here in Finland. He has my blessing. I don't know how to thank you. This all sounds like a dream," Mother finished grabbing Mr. Schwab's hands and holding them for an extended time. Her face shone.

"You don't need to thank me. I will thank you and now the decision is in Juha's hands," he said looking at me intently, waiting for my answer.

"Mr. Schwab, this is a dream for me also. I will accept your invitation to come to America and will promise not to let you down in any way. I am so excited. Thank you." Maija almost appeared exhausted from all the translating she had done, but also totally baffled from this. "I am so happy for you Juha and Sylvi. This is unbelievable," she said.

Mother called Inga and Kari to join us, telling them what just had happened. They both sat wide eyed, but finally stood up and hugged me. Kari said that it sounded scary, America was so far away, but gave me a broad smile. Inga was as surprised as I was, but said, "Juha, that sounds so thrilling. You will do well. We are so happy for you."

"Inga, could you get some paper and a pen, so I can make some notes," Mr. Schwab asked. Maija translated for Inga.

Inga returned with a spiral notebook and a pen and sat down.

"Juha, I need to get your full name and your birth date. Also, your mailing address and your mother's full name." We provided the information to him. Then he proceeded to ask Maija to write down information what was needed from our end. "The first thing, as soon as possible, you should apply for a passport. Your mother probably has to apply for it with you. Once you have the passport, go to Helsinki to the American Consulate and apply for a 'student visa'. By that time I have already contacted them with the school information and my personal information as a guardian." Lastly he had Maija write down his personal address in Philadelphia, with his telephone number, in the event there are problems with the paper work. With the first steps over, I had not woken up. This was not a dream. It was true. I would be leaving for America. He mentioned that it probably would take three to four months for everything to be in order. I would still start school here in the fall, but probably be leaving after Christmas by ship from Bremenhaven, Germany.

Carefully he folded the paper with our information, placing it into his pocket, commenting, "I will mail to you all the tickets from Hameenlinna to New York, where I will meet you."

Mother placed our copy of the information in front of her, keeping a sharp eye on it. She would guard it.

We thanked Maija for her help. She hugged me, before returning to the ticket booth. We sat a bit longer. Everyone was beaming, even Mr. Schwab. After some more coffee, I asked him if he wanted to climb up the tower, to which he answered, "Of course."

"Can I come with you?" Kari asked.

"Sure. Let's go," I said, getting up.

Before we left, Mother approached Mr. Schwab and gave him a hug, saying in English, "Thank you." That must have been her only vocabulary in that language.

We proceeded to the base of the mammoth gray black granite tower. Craning our necks, Mr. Schwab commented, "How in the world could they able to build such a tall massive structure over fifty years ago? This reminds me in a way, of the temples in Mexico, which were built by the Mayans. It is remarkable."

We followed the solid stone steps up to the base of the tower itself. The base was over two stories high. Reaching this point, you could enter the tower through the massive oak doors, or walk around it on a tiled red walkway. We took the walk around and then entered through the doors, where the table and handmade root furniture sat. Mr. Schwab walked to the table, where the open guest book sat. The book itself was massive, thick and very old. He reached for the pen, tied to a long string, and wrote: Laban Schwab, Philadelphia USA. Thank you Finland, July 1954. Glancing up at the top at the looming tower, with sunrays dancing in through windows at every level, he commented again, "This is unreal!"

Slowly we climbed the step all the way to the top. By now we had reached at least seven stories high, from the ground. Other people followed us and others passed us on the way down. The stairwell was broad enough to accommodate two people side by side, with the solid metal handrail following the open side, as the steps spiraled up the rock-solid wall. Looking down at the bottom floor where the guest book sat as a tiny dot. The sight was dizzying. The granite steps showed the heavy use over the years, having worn down in the center.

We reached the top, walking through the doorway into the sunshine. There was a light breeze blowing. The Finnish flag above our heads flapped and danced in the gentle wind. The sight from there was mind boggling. Mr. Schwab was overtaken by the sight. His remarks reflected the grandiose. "I have never seen anything as beautiful as the sight from up here." The landscapes and lakes bent into an artful acrylic painting. The visibility was endless. Aulanko Lake below the tower glittered in the sunshine in deep green and blue color, with small rippled waves lapping the shore. The tall pine and spruce trees appeared the size of bonsai. I kept pointing at various locations in the distance to Mr. Schwab. A few chicken hawks sailed in the light breeze. The restaurant below looked similar to a small doll house.

After a long time enjoying the sights, we departed and began the climb down. Halfway, we stopped at a landing with the same rough furniture, just like down below on the first floor. We sat quiet, without speaking. What a day it had been for all of us.

After saying good bye to Mother, Inga and Kari, we began our trek back to the hotel. Now the walking was not as strenuous, because it was mostly downhill. After stopping for a brief rest at Swan Lake, we reached the hotel in less than one hour.

Mr. Schwab was in a happy mood. It appeared that he was excited about all the plans, as I was. "Thank you, John, I had a wonderful day meeting your family and the escapade in the park and tower. Mostly I can't wait for the day when I will meet you in New York and show you my country. I'm sure you will like it," he said in a broad smile and sparkling eyes.

"I can't wait either. I will not be able to sleep, between now and then. Thank you very much," I said and could not help myself, giving him a strong hug.

We parted company, but before leaving for his room, he said he was thinking of taking the boat trip tomorrow. If it is a nice day, he added.

The rest of the day, I just floated on thin air. I must look on the atlas where Philadelphia is.

35

THAT NIGHT I SLEPT FITFULLY, tossing and turning. In the middle of night, I woke up drenched in sweat after dreaming about crossing the Atlantic Ocean on a small sailboat. The ocean was ugly. I was being thrown around in the little boat in a horrific storm, with huge waves washing over the boat. Flying fish kept leaping on to the deck and cockpit. I was slipping and sliding in the fish slime. The rain was relentless and the wash from the waves was filling the boat fast. I was sinking. The fish were laughing. All of a sudden, a sign was shining on the shore, stating: Welcome to Philadelphia. I was so happy to wake up. A bright beam of light shone through the living room window. I looked out. It was a full moon, smiling at me. Eventually I fell back to sleep, waking up tired in the morning.

At the Aulanko library for the guests, which was very small compared to the city library, I was able to study a world atlas. Without being able to wait to find out where Philadelphia is in America, I rushed there the first chance I could. Mr. Schwab had told me that his city was rather close to New York. Sitting down at the reading table, hands trembling, I turned the atlas pages until I found North America and New York. My finger traveled first north without finding Philadelphia, then south along Atlantic coast, and bingo, I found the city. On the map it looked so close to New York, that it surprised me. In another book I was able to read some history about the city, specifically about Benjamin Frank-lin and the Liberty Hall. Philadelphia was called 'The City of Brotherly Love. I could not wait to arrive in such a friendly city. Philadelphia was waiting for me with open arms. Here I am, thank you for the welcome, I would say upon arrival.

At the front desk they told me that Mr. Schwab had taken the boat trip today on M/s *Aulanko*. The weather was beautiful, warm and balmy. There were only few puffy clouds and a gentle breeze. I hope he will enjoy the trip. His reservation at the hotel was up tomorrow and he would be leaving for Germany for a few days, after that with the ship back home. I would be down at the pier when *m/s Aulanko* returned at seven p.m.

I called Mother's friend who ran a travel agency in Hameenlinna and made an appointment with her for the next day. She would be able to help with the passport and later with the tickets and the itinerary all the way to New York. I briefly explained why I needed her help, and over the phone I could hear that she was spellbound. I wish I could have seen the look on her face. "Juha, I can't believe what I am hearing. I'll see you tomorrow." I was already very ecstatic to be traveling alone from Finland to America. It was a long trip with several different travel modes, but I could handle it. I would become a world traveler which I had always desired to do.

This day turned out to be a very tragic day for the hotel. One lone, thin, gentleman guest from Latvia had entered the roof terrace. A waiter had served him coffee and a croissant. The waiter told the management and police that his customer had acted erratic, spaced out. His eyes were not focused and he had been mumbling to himself. He had only taken a sip of his coffee, and broken the croissant into small crumbs on the table. All of a sudden he was gone. The waiter did not know where he went until later. The man had climbed the iron rungs to the top of the hotel's chimney, which stood in the far corner of the roof terrace. The man jumped head first inside the chimney to his death, and landed in the boiler in the hotel's basement. It was dreadful. Later a suicide note was found in his room. In the note, the thin man from Latvia stated that he was going to commit suicide. He was distraught from his personal life in Latvia, by losing his family in a divorce and his finances were a mess. He wanted to spend his last day in a comfortable and beautiful environment, and had chosen Aulanko for that reason.

The grim news had reverberated throughout the hotel employees and some of the guests, creating a hushed atmosphere. It was a sad day for everyone. The police spent a long time investigating the horrendous tragedy. A repair crew had been called in to dismantle the boiler in the basement in order to reach the dead man. The body was taken to the morgue in Hameenlinna. The mood was in turmoil for a long time afterwards. There was a drawn look on everyone's brow, and the tone was quiet. Things seemed to move in slow motion. Suicide is a terrible thing, but to die the way the Latvian did, was unbelievable.

I took this awful news almost personally. The day before, I was the one who escorted the Latvian man to his room. He seemed nervous. His eyes were watering and red. He did not speak at all. After depositing his one small carryon bag in the room, he uttered, "Thank you" in Latvian, which I understood, because Latvian language was very close to the Finnish language. He did not tip me, which did not bother me, because he was clearly troubled. Today was an endless day. Sad.

Throughout the day I just floated by and did my duties without any fanfare. Later in the afternoon, I was ready for a pork chop diner and ordered it, but it did not make me feel any better. It was perfectly done and presented. It smelled delicious, but my mind was filled with the day's events, which spoiled the enjoyment of my favorite dinner.

Before seven p.m. I was down at the pier, with my three wheel cart. Mr. Schwab would be arriving from his day trip and perhaps some new guests. As I waited for the boat's arrival, I focused into the clear water by the pier. A large school of shiny silvery minnows swam by. There must have been hundreds of these small fish, swimming in an orchestrated swirl, without bumping into each other. I was mesmerized by this sight. How could they harmonize so well? Every fish darted in unison with the group, making circles and turns as one. It was a beautiful sight.

I heard the sound of one horn blow as *M/s Aulanko* was arriving past the peninsula where the sauna sat. The white gleaming ship plowed the water slowly. The engines were humming quietly. As the boat lined up with the pier, I caught the rope thrown by the mate and tied the bow line to the cleats. The stern rope was handled by a second mate. The steps were rolled for the passenger's for debarking.

Men, women and children flowed down the steps to the pier, carrying picnic baskets and souvenir bags. There was a happy glow on everyone's face. Finally Mr. Schwab stepped out. He waved to me. His face was content with a hint of a smile. Dressed in white slacks with a blue polo shirt and his new sneakers, and carrying a small shoulder bag, he had an aura of well being and self assurance. I went to greet him with an outstretched hand. We shook

"Hello John," he said as he embraced me with a big smile. "You were absolutely correct in recommending for me to take this cruise. It was breathtakingly beautiful scenery all throughout the trip. The weather was exceptional. The ride was very comfortable. I had a first class salmon luncheon in the dining room. The service aboard was very professional. The captain even invited me to the bridge where I had a fantastic view. Finland with its lakes is a gem," he said, his tone ecstatic.

"I thought you would like the trip. I am so glad that you did," I said, feeling pleased that I had not steered him wrong. "I am, sorry, but I must help these two couples with their baggage. "Welcome to Aulanko," I greeted them and loaded their luggage on my cart.

We proceeded up the hill to the hotel. Mr. Schwab walked next to me with the guests following us. I was thinking about the awful happening earlier in the day. I did not like the idea of having to tell it to Mr. Schwab, but I must. I rather do it myself, than have him hear it from someone else.

"Mr. Schwab, can we meet in an hour in the lobby? You probably want to go to your room and freshen up?" I asked him.

"Fine, I need to order a light dinner also. See you in one hour," he said, heading for the elevator.

I took care of the new guests, escorting them to their rooms. Mr. Schwab arrived exactly one hour later. I suggested for us to go into the library, where we could sit down and talk. There was no one in the room. Once there, we seated ourselves in comfortable leather chairs, opposite of each other, with low coffee table between us. The room smelled of books and faintly of cigar smoke.

"I hate to spoil your dinner, but I must tell you what an awful happening took place here, earlier in the day," I said in a morose tone. I could tell from his expression that he was expecting bad news. I told him all about the Latvian man's suicide, explaining how gruesome it had been. I explained the turmoil which had taken place all day with the police present and the horrible job in the boiler room in order to retrieve the body. He listened, with his head slightly tilted and his eyes droopy. His face showed agonizing emotion. Even though my English was very poor, it seemed that he understood most of my tale.

When I had finished talking, he took a long breath and said in a low, even tone, "I am sorry to hear such grisly news. I can understand that it touched everyone in the building. I have heard of suicides, but none ever as horrible as this. John, it will take you long time to forget it, but don't dwell with the memory. There was nothing that anyone could have done to stop it," he said, hesitated a moment, continuing, "I am glad that I heard this from you, rather than someone else."

"This was not a happy ending to your enjoyable trip. Sorry," I said.

"Let's forget the whole thing. Nothing can be done about it now. Can you join me for dinner?" he asked.

"Thank you, but I am still on duty. Perhaps a cup of coffee later," I said.

"Okay, I'll look you up after dinner." He got up and gave me a friendly tap on my shoulder. We left the library, and he approached the dining room. Later I would also tell him about the appointment with the travel agency tomorrow.

After his dinner, he found me at the front desk. I had changed from my uniform to casual regular attire. We decided to go out to terrace for coffee. It was a balmy evening. The sun was almost below the horizon. The two ornate marble water fountains were spewing the water high into the air, falling back down into a water fall and cascading into a pool at the base. The fountains were built during the old glory days, when the opulent estate stood here. The sound was soothing. A waiter appeared to take our order. We placed an order for coffee.

"Tomorrow I have an appointment with a travel agent, who happens to be Mother's friend. I called her earlier, and she was so excited to work with me, as to the passport and travel arrangements. Would you like to come along?" I asked.

"My, oh my, you sure work fast. I like that. For some people it takes forever to get anything accomplished, if ever. What time is your meeting?" he asked with a broad smile.

The coffee arrived in a shiny silver pot. The waiter set the cups and saucers in front of us, pouring the strong smelling dark coffee and placing a sugar bowl and cream pitcher and a small silver tray with wafers, on the table. "May I get you anything else?" he asked.

We thanked him, said, "No," and he departed.

"The meeting is at ten tomorrow morning."

"Yes, let's go together. I like to meet her also," Mr. Schwab said. "I am leaving tomorrow on the two clock train to Helsinki. It will give us plenty of time with the agency. We'll meet here at nine and take the bus in town. Okay?"

"Great," I said, thinking about the thrilling journey to America.

We sat there for a while, him telling me about his day trip on the boat. It was so peaceful and relaxing. We could hear the string band playing in the dining room. A whiff of warm evening air rustled the numerous potted fichus trees. The air carried fragrance from the surrounding flower beds and Rose bushes. The coffee was rich and the wafers were sweet.

"See you tomorrow," Mr. Schwab said as we parted much later.

I decided to walk up to the tower and bring Mother up to date on the day's happenings. The sun had settled, creating an eerie feeling on the trail. The trees gave the impression of breathing, in the gentle wind. I had walked this trail so many times, that I could find my way in total darkness. Yet now, it was a bit spooky. Perhaps the dreadful happening today, caused me to be squeamish? When I arrived at the Swan Lake, the three black swans were sleeping next to each other on the shore. Their long necks were folded back with the heads buried into the wings. I walked by them quietly, not wanting to wake them up or scare these beautiful large birds. When I reached the restaurant and entered in through the kitchen door, I saw Mother's back was turned, she twisted around with a frightened look.

"Juha, you scared the heck of me. Next time knock!" she scolded me.

"I'm sorry, I won't do it again," I said walking over to give her a hug "Let's sit down, I have so much to tell you," I said, seating myself on the bench by the kitchen table. Mother joined me, with a coffee cup in hand. She had calmed down by now.

"I don't know if you heard about the tragedy at the hotel."

"No, what happened?"

"A man committed a gruesome suicide." I told her the full story. I was watching her face, which slowly turned into a sad grimace. She did not stop my talking. She had lowered her head. Her eyes were tearing.

When I was finished telling her all I knew, she said in a trembling voice, "That is so sad. The poor man must have had an awful life," she said with a sniffle, continuing, "The hotel must have been in turmoil all day?"

"Yes, it was a chaotic day," I said but told her that I had other news also. Happy news, I added, and told her about Mr. Schwab's boat trip and of our meeting tomorrow with her friend at the travel agency.

"That sure is much better news, than the first part. Why don't you stay here tonight? The girls went home and only Inga and Kari are here with me."

"I will, at least tonight I don't have to share the bed with Kari." I bid her good night and climbed the steps upstairs.

36

IT WAS THUNDERING AND RAINING cats and dogs, when I woke up the next morning. It did not start just now. I had woken up during the night, when a lightening slammed like an explosion, into a nearby tree. The building shook. I laid and listen to the commotion, but fell back to sleep. The tower acted as a magnet for thunderstorms. They were scary. After getting dressed and working my morning foggy mind downstairs, I found Mother making coffee and Inga and Kari sitting by the kitchen table, munching on a sandwich. I sat next to them.

"What a horrible night and morning," Mother said, pouring me and herself a cup of coffee. "The storm had woken Kari, during the night. He was afraid and had moseyed his way to my bed," she said, setting the coffee on the table and ruffling Kari's hair.

"I must get going soon. I hate to walk in this rain storm, but we have the appointment this morning. I need to stop at the house and get changed. Do you have an umbrella that I can borrow? It won't help much. I'll be soaked by the time I get home," I said in a glum tone.

"Have your coffee and a sandwich. I have an umbrella you can take along," Mother said, sliding a platter of sandwiches my way. Inga and Kari sat quietly, still half asleep.

She gave me her sissy looking small umbrella. It was green, yellow and red, with flowers in the same colors. Well, it was better than nothing. "Good luck with your meeting. Say hello to Anja at her travel agency," Mother said. I bid Inga and Kari goodbye, and walked out into the rainstorm. The thunder had moved far away, but I could still hear the rumbling. By the time I reached the bottom of the tower hill, I was soaked. It was chilly. The umbrella was as effective as a fly swatter. Sloshing my way home, I finally made it there in some twenty minutes. Entering into the mudroom, I had to take off all my soaked wet clothes and hang them to dry. Walking naked into the living room, I dried myself with a fluffy blue towel. In my bureau, I found a clean white polo shirt, underwear and a pair of brown slacks. Slowly I was warming up. I slipped my feet into a new pair of sandals. No socks. It was time to continue the trip to the hotel. Luckily I spotted a larger black umbrella in the mudroom. The rain had slacked off to a gentle drizzle, but the sky was still black and threatening. I managed to reach the hotel, dry.

Mr. Schwab was waiting for me in the lobby, at one of the tables. "Good morning John. I am glad that the weather was not like this yesterday, when I took the boat trip," he said looking at me. "You look sharp and dry," he mused. You should have seen me a while ago, I thought. I looked like a wet rag, with an ugly umbrella.

The bus had arrived in front of the hotel, and would leave in ten minutes. I suggested for us to board the bus, which we did. The bus was new with comfortable brown leatherette seats. As we waited for the departure, I did my best in trying to tell him about the busses after the war, with their 'fireplaces' in the back. I don't know if he understood my description in my broken clumsy English. It seemed as if he comprehend most of my explanation, laughing out loud and uttering that he had once read somewhere about this type of propulsion. The bus driver entered, starting the diesel engine and off we went. There were only six other passengers aboard. When we passed our old apartment complex, I did not point it out to Mr. Schwab, because I did not even want to think about that miserable small fire trap of an apartment.

Fifteen minutes later, we had arrived to the city, getting off the bus in front of the hospital. Across the street in a mini mall complex next to a coffee shop sat "ANJA'S TRAVEL AGENCY." The rain had stopped, but heavy black clouds still hung low in the sky. We crossed the street and entered the office. It was long and narrow, with three wood desks, with display racks standing on the floor, with multitude of brochures and pamphlets. It smelled of freshly printed paper. A typewriter and telephone sat on each desk the walls were covered with maps and photographs from around the world. A well dressed middle age lady sat behind the first desk. She stood up, seeing us enter, calling out," Hello, Juha, nice to see you again," as she approached us.

"Hi, Anja, meet Mr. Schwab from America," I said, as they shook hands. Anja had a sunny smiley face. She wore dainty silver framed glasses.

"Follow me," she said leading us to two chairs in front of her desk. "Juha told me the amazing news yesterday. I still can't believe it," looking at me in a broad smile. "What does mother think about this venture?" she asked.

"She is as excited as I am. She told me to say hello to you," I said.

"So, you are headed to New York in a few months." she said to me, and switched into English, which she spoke fluently. Mr. Schwab was happy to hear this. "Juha is a very lucky young man, having met you," she told him.

"Thank you. I am the lucky man from having met him and his family," he answered in an even strong tone. His hands were clasped in his lap.

The first thing which needs to be done is a passport application," she said, opening up one of the drawers of her desk. She pulled out an official looking form and handed it to me. "You need to fill this out and send it off to Helsinki with two passport pictures. It should only take two weeks until you get your passport," she informed, looking both at me and Mr. Schwab.

Mr. Schwab interjected, "As soon as I get home, I will register you with a local high school and fill out the sponsorship papers and mail them to the American consulate in Helsinki. That will probably take one month, before they get them. You will be applying for a student visa, which should not be any problem." He eyed me to make sure that I understood. I nodded. "After, say two months, you will need to visit them in Helsinki and fill out some more papers and your visa will be attached to your passport."

By now I was sure that this was not a dream. I had still had some lingering doubts about all this being a fantasy but now I was convinced that it was true. My God....I must be one of the luckiest youngsters in Finland. I was a bit dizzy with all this paper work.

Anja looked at Mr. Schwab and asked, "If I understand correctly, you will be mailing all the open end travel tickets to Juha? He can then bring them to me and I will get an itinerary together from here to New York. It means for him to take the ship from Helsinki to Stockholm, Sweden. From there you will take the train to Copenhagen Denmark. In Copenhagen he will have to change to a train to Hamburg, Germany, where again he has to change a train to Bremen-haven in Germany, where he will board the ship to cross the Atlantic." That is quite a trip. "Will you be able to do it, without getting lost?" she asked, looking at me in wonderment, with a question mark in her voice.

All I could say was," Don't worry. I will have no problems," sounding confi-dent but in my mind, there were some butterflies dancing in my stomach. Then I thought of a slogan that someone had taught me: 'Where there is a will, there is a way. I have the will.

Mr. Schwab was impressed with Anja's knowledge and her positive attitude and stated, "I can see that you are in good hands with this lady," adding, "If you have any problems, you can get in touch with me," he said handing her his business card. "Thank you Anja."

It was time to leave and we thanked Anja for her help. Before exiting the agency, she collected a handful of brochures, with maps, telling me to read them. "Say hello to your mother," were her last words.

The black heavy clouds still hung but they spewed only a light drizzle. We entered the coffee shop next door. It was a modern glass and shiny chrome con-structed small establishment with four glass covered round tables. The chairs looked uncomfortable. Two attendants were behind the counter. The man was short and fat, with at least several days' stubble on his face. He appeared to suffer a bad hang-over. The girl, perhaps seventeen years old, was skinny with long blond hair and bright blue eyes. She was dressed in a white apron over a colorful summer dress.

With a rosy smile, she asked, "May I help you?"

"Yes, please. Two coffees and two croissants," I said and we walked to one of the tables and sat down. The chairs were not designed for lounging. They were hard, small and uncomfortable. The man delivered our order, slapping it on the table. He looked greasy. A whiff of sweat and alcohol hung in the air. "Anything else?" he growled.

"No," was my short answer. Get away from us, I willed.

Mr. Schwab was enjoying all this in a sly smile. "Not like Aulanko"

"No, that's for sure. Did you see his hairy fingers and the very long finger nails, only on one his little fingers?"

"Yes. He uses it to clean his ears and pick his nose," Mr. Schwab said with a sneer.

"I never heard of such a thing. Gross! What did you think of Anja?"

"I was very much impressed by her. I am glad that I came along, because now I will not have any worries about your travel and the paper work. Make sure you call her if you have any problems," continuing he said, "we better get going soon. I don't want to miss the two o'clock train."

We gobbled up the croissants and finished the coffee. The coffee was good and strong, but I had turbulent thoughts. I was wondering what type of bacteria we caught from the fat man. It was still drizzling lightly, but the sky was slowly clearing. There was a bus stop right in front of the travel agency and ten minutes later, the bus arrived and picked us up for Aulanko. Once we arrived there, Mr. Schwab went to his room to retrieve his luggage. My friend had this bellboy shift, and when the desk received the call from Mr. Schwab that he was ready to depart, the boy scooted up to get the luggage.

He was going to take the hotel cab to the station, leaving us a half hour to sit and talk. We did so in the quiet library.

"I don't know how I can ever pay you back for your kindness. I am so excited about this dream trip and going to school in America. Even though my English is awful, we still seem to understand each other. Give me a half a year and I will speak well," I said, getting up and walking to his chair. I reached down and gave him my strongest hug and uttered, "Thank you."

"John, I am also excited and waiting for your arrival. We'll write back and forth. Okay?" he said with a broad smile. "Thank you for that bear hug."

I carried his luggage to the cab, putting it into the trunk. I told the driver to take the guest to the railroad station. We gave each other the last handshake, for at least for four months. "Have a safe trip to Germany," I said and waved the cab off.

When back home, after my evening shift, I spent over one hour poring through the many brochures and maps that Anja had given me. There was one of New York full of pictures. I could not believe my eyes in seeing the tall skyscrapers. The Empire State building was unbelievable, and the sights from it. There was no brochure of Philadelphia but from what I had read it was a big city with almost one and a half million people. One city, with all these people. Our whole country had only a little over four million. It blew my mind. One brochure was of a ship called *S/S United States*. It was massive and beautiful inside and out. I wondered if this was going to be my ship across the Atlantic Ocean. I hoped so.

Tomorrow I will go to a photographer for two passport pictures.

I was too tired to walk up to the tower, and it was late I slept alone at home.

37

THE NIGHT TRAIN TO OULU was speeding through the late summer landscape. It was twilight. The full moon was hanging low, barely over the tree tops, casting its glow over the newly harvested fields. It became a moon's laser show, when the train plowed through the forest close to the tracks, casting its light in pulsating beams. The steam clouds from the engine added ghostly harmony to the show. I sat glued to the window admiring the sight.

School would start in two weeks. I had taken a leave of absence from the hotel and bid farewell to Mother, Inga and Kari for a week to visit Fammu and Ukki in Oulu. Mother's job at the tower went well and she loved it. Inga and Kari were busy with her. It had been a very active summer for all of us. For me it was important to go and visit my grandparents, before school and the amazing journey to America. I wanted to tell all this in person to them. They would be shocked hearing it. I had not seen them in a few years, so I was really looking forward to this reunion. I had missed them, remembering all the good times we had had and of course Rantala. I wonder if they still had my horse. What about Goya, the parrot? Was she still around? Then of course Rake was also on the top of my visiting list. He was always tall and lanky but by now he must be a tall, thin tower.

I had reserved a second class sleeper compartment. There would only be two of us in the small but comfortable room. He was a middle aged man from Helsinki traveling up to Rovaniemi, which was north of my destination. He was dressed casually but in warmer clothing than I, because where he was going, the cool fall had already arrived. He was a friendly chap, clean shaven but totally bald. His ears were too small to the rest of his face. He had pouty lips and spoke with a slight stutter, noticeably pronounced when he became excited. His eyes shone bright blue.

The train was speeding and clicking on the tracks. We sat side by side, with a small folding table under the window. We had introduced ourselves when I boarded the train in Hameenlinna. His name was Timo Kivi.

"Juha, tell me what you do. What makes you travel to Oulu?" he asked without stutter.

"I am going for a week to visit my grandparents," I said, looking at him and proceeded to tell him about my work at Aulanko, and Mother's at the tower.

"You are lucky, to be in such a beautiful environment. I have visited the hotel a few times. There is nothing in Finland that can compare to Aulanko," he said.

"I'm proud to live and work there. What takes you to Rovaniemi?" I asked.

The train crossed a long bridge, clattering louder. Once across he spoke again. "I am involved with The Santa Clause Village on the Arctic Circle in Lapland. Christmas is not too far away and we have so much to organize and get ready for it. During Christmas time, we receive visitors from all over the world. The foreigners fly in to Rovaniemi and the multitude of Finns either arrive by train or car. You can't believe the huge number of young and old people who come to visit the "true" Santa. On top of it, millions of letters arrive from around the globe, and they all will be answered," he added." He looked tired from thinking about it. The stuttering was noticeable.

"My gosh. I have heard of this village, but never realized how big the operation is," I said bewildered.

"There is so much involved. My main area is the tourism, by organizing airplane charters from around the world. I will be up there for at least a month, meeting with all the parties involved in getting ready for this upcoming Christmas. But after that, I return back to my office in Helsinki. In the first part of December, reindeers with their Lapland herders congregate in the village making the place into a beautiful story book Christmas village," he finished, appearing proud but tired. He dug into his duffel bag, coming out with a bottle of wine and a chunk of cheese. He sat them on the small window table He uncorked the wine and unwrapped the cheese. I could smell the aroma of the strong cheese. He produced two paper cups from his bag and asked, "Are you old enough to have a glass of wine?"

"Yes, I'm few weeks away from seventeen. I'm old enough," I told him, making my tone sound a bit deeper.

He poured a half paper cup for me and filled his own to the rim. "Cheers," he said, breaking off a chunk of cheese. The wine was red. He called it Burgundy from France. I took a sip of it. It was mellow and so smooth. I broke a chunk of cheese, which was strong and pungent, but with the wine it tasted very good. We sat in silence, except from the train's wheels clicking. Outside it had turned into a dark but moon lit night. It had been a long day for me and now the wine was kicking in, making me sleepy. I thanked him and told him that I was ready for bed. "Okay, I'm tired also. It's bed time. Nice talking with you," he said, as I climbed to the upper bunk.

"Good night," I called down to him. The rhythmic sound of the train lulled me asleep in no time.

In the morning, I climbed down. Timo, my travel companion, was still asleep. We would be arriving in Oulu in about half an hour. Quietly I gathered my things, sliding the door open to the hallway and exited the compartment, feeling well rested. Fammu and Ukki would be at the station waiting to greet me. I sat on the small fold down seat, watching the flat landscape slide by. It was a cloudy morning with the sun trying to protrude through the clouds. The ever-present birch trees lined and encircled the farmed fields. Haystacks, built into pyramids, dotted most of the harvested meadows. As the train approached the city, apartment buildings and private homes loomed in place of farms and fields. Soon factories and denser dwellings appeared. As we pulled into the railroad station, which was the old gray wooden building that I had seen many years ago, I gathered my things and walked to the door. The train stopped, with a great huff of steam, I could see Ukki and Fammu standing by the building. I could not help noticing how they had aged in the few years that we had not seen each other. Fammu seemed shorter, perhaps because I was taller, and Ukki's face was thinner and drawn. They were wearing sweaters as it was cooler here than down south. This was my second trip to see them, after Sweden and the short term in the Oulu elementary school after coming back to Finland. I was twelve years old, when I was here last. The sun was peeking out through fast moving clouds. The air was crisp.

"Hello Ukki and Fammu," I greeted them, setting my luggage on the platform, giving Fammu a gentle hug and Ukki a stronger hug.

"We have been waiting for you such a long time. It must be some four years since we saw each other," Fammu said, holding my hand. "You have grown so much. You are a young man by now. Welcome."

Ukki was standing by, looking at me up and down, finally saying, "Juha, you sure look great, tall and strong. I am so glad to see you. Let's go home and have breakfast," he said grabbing one of my bags. His car was parked right in the front of the station. It was a Peugeot, but a newer model since the previous one. We drove only four blocks, stopping in front of a tall apartment building. They had moved since last time. Ukki parked by the building and after retrieving my belongings, we entered and took the elevator to the third floor. Down the hallway, past one other door, with the occupants name tagged by the side of the door, we reached their apartment.

It was bright with large windows, overlooking the city. The smell was of new paint and mortar. Their furniture was the familiar furniture which I remembered. The show piece, which I recall, was a very large living room table, standing on a solid base. The top was an irregular round and well varnished two inch thick slab of a huge tree burl. This was Fammu's favorite evening solitary card table. I don't think a night had gone by without my seeing her sit and play her solitary. At times I had played cards with her. Ukki did not like card games, normally he just sat reading. They had bought this condominium and moved here last spring. It was larger than the apartment during the war, and this building was only a year old. It consisted of three nice size bedrooms, large living room, two bathrooms and a good size kitchen. It was high enough allowing a view of the city. The port of Oulu loomed in the distance, with its tall cranes. The main windows faced south which allowed warm sunshine in.

We sat at the kitchen table. The room smelled so good from the corned beef hash which Fammu was cooking. I was hungry from the trip. Goia's cage sat in the corner of the kitchen. He babbled as always. I scratched his head and he murmured in appreciation in parrot purring.

"So, Juha, tell me everything you have been doing," Ukki said, looking at me across the table. He was holding a steaming coffee cup with both hands. Fammu was standing by the stove, but keeping an eye on us and waiting for my answer. My stomach growled.

"Can I have a cup of coffee also? It smells so good, and I drink coffee at home," I asked, in almost begging voice.

"Of course," Fammu said, pouring a cup for me.

"Thank you Fammu," and then I began to tell them about our life at Aulanko and how much we enjoyed life there. I told them about the awful suicide. "How terrible," Ukki interrupted. I continued by describing how Inga and Kari had grown. I told them about Inga's scary accident with the horse. "My God, she was so lucky of not being paralyzed," Fammu's expression lapsed sad on hearing this.

The hash was ready, Fammu setting a dish in front of us. It looked so good with a sunny side up egg, topping the hash. The aroma was mouthwatering. Toast points decorated the plate. While enjoying the food and coffee, I asked, "Do you still have my horse?"

"No, I am sorry but we had to sell it. There was no one to take care of it at Rantala when we were not there. We spend few weeks off and on there in the summer time," Ukki told me.

"I understand but at least I have such fond memories of him and everything else, especially Stranos, Kollis and everything about the farm. I had not yet told them about the trip plans to America. I would do that in the living room after breakfast. "Fammu, thank you the breakfast was so good," I told her and she returned the compliment with a big smile.

"It is so nice to have you here. Tomorrow we'll go to Rantala for a few days. I am sure you will enjoy it."

I could feel my face light up as I said, "Great,"

Ukki voiced an agreement to the plan, stating, "I enjoy it there so much and would not hesitate to move there altogether, but Fammu does not like the idea." The last part of his comments came in a hushed tone.

After retiring into the living room, we sat around the ornate table talking about everything, including my father, from whom they had not heard anything for a long time. Fammu sighed deeply, when explaining this. "I hope he is well?" is all she could say. Ukki's face showed strain, but he did not say anything. I could see that he was sad.

I had tried to formulate my explanation of the America trip, but could not tell it in any way other than straight out.

"I'm going to America in about four months," I spurted out, in a higher octave voice, surprising myself of this tone.

Silence ensued. Ukki and Fammu looked at each other with puzzled look on their faces.

Ukki was the first to say anything. "You, what...going to America. How? What are you going to do there? Are you going by yourself? It's a long, expensive trip. I don't understand," he was finally able to get out. Fammu was nodding to every question, with her mouth partially hanging open.

Finally Fammu was able to clear her foggy mind, saying, "Juha, I know that you always tell the truth, but this can't be true. It's a joke?" she asked, looking at me.

"It is true. By the time I get back home, my passport should be waiting. I made the application over a week ago. Let me tell you the whole story," I said, waiting for their answer.

"We are all ears," Ukki said.

For the next fifteen minutes, I told them the story of how I had met Mr. Schwab and how he had invited me to his home, in Philadelphia. He would arrange the schooling. He would purchase an automobile and we would travel around the country. I explained that he had met Mother, Inga and Kari and how elated they were after the meeting. Also about the tickets and how he was paying for them. I topped it of telling Ukki and Fammu what a fine gentleman and business man he was. When I was finished, I looked at both of them, sitting still, with hands in their lap, probably still thinking that something was fishy. They still looked shocked.

"I have never heard of anything like this," Fammu said. "I find it hard to believe."

"It is true."

"Are you sure the man is good and not a crackpot looking for a young boy?" Fammu asked, still looking bewildered.

After a long discussion, I think that I was able to convince them that it would be a safe trip and a great adventure to travel to America. "We wish you the best," Ukki said.

Later I tried to get in touch with Rake but he was traveling in Norway on a class trip, which meant that I would not see him. I left my regards with his mother and told her that I would call him in a week. It was too late to leave for Rantala now, so we just relaxed the rest of the afternoon. I played cards with Fammu making her happy to have someone play with her. Later I took a walk around the city. It had changed since I saw it last time. New buildings had been built and others were under construction. I passed the old gray school house, which I hated from all the torment I had received from my class mates. The building was so weather worn that it would not take long for it to collapse. There was only one ruin left from the war bombings. Two smoke stacks, with one leaning precariously, stood in a in a large pile of bricks and mortar with an old rusty truck half buried in the rubble. The sight brought scary memories for me. It stood there as a crumbled monument from the war. All of a sudden, I could taste the shoe string smoke in my mouth which happened in the bomb shelter with Rake. Gross. . . .

It was dinner time by the time I got back. I could smell the aroma of Swedish meat balls, the minute I entered the apartment. Sure enough, Fammu was cooking her famous meat balls. The table in the kitchen was set, ready for dinner. Ukki was already sitting by the table, waiting. Fammu passed the dishes with the small meatballs in a light cream sauce with a side of chopped spinach and boiled potato cubes. The dinner was out of this world. I enjoyed a second helping, telling her that she made the best meatballs I ever had. She beamed in a happy smile. During the meal, Ukki told me that he was partially retired. Every so often he was called to travel on inspection trips to the country side. He enjoyed this arrangement which still kept him busy but not totally tied down.

After dinner, I played cards with Fammu. She could do this hour after hour. It was late when I finally excused myself, telling her I was tired and would like to take a hot bath before going to sleep. I said good night to Ukki.

Fammu showed me to my bedroom and turned the water on in the bathroom. "I hope you sleep well. It is so nice to have you here. Good night."

I took a hot bath, just laying there and thinking about the many things that were happening in my life. I must have dozed off in the tub, because suddenly cold water woke me up. After drying up, I crawled into the bed, thinking about tomorrow's trip to Rantala.

38

RANTALA WAS PEEKING THROUGH THE pine and birch trees. We arrived after a half a hour drive from the city, on a breezy late summer morning. The day was extraordinarily clear. Sunlight lit the clouds to the brightness of a prism. It was noticeably cooler, crisper, here than in South Finland. Few of the aspen leaves were already showed turning color for the upcoming autumn. Ukki drove next to the farm house and parked the car by the kitchen door. He had told me that they had moved downstairs after the Kollis had left.

It was a fantastic feeling for me to be here again. It was like a homecoming, after having spent so much time here. The lake was glistening like a million diamonds with the bright sunshine dancing on the waves. I saw my small boat, dockside, bobbing in the breeze. It was so quiet except the familiar shushing sound from the wind in the tall pines. On the drive, Ukki had suggested that we should heat the sauna tonight. Fammu and I agreed that the idea was great. Now I was looking at the sauna building on the shore, still barn red. Without realizing it, I had missed the Rantala sauna for many years. Taking a sauna here was truly an earthy experience. It must be the handpicked stones that Ukki had collected from our lake, making the steam feel all embracing and smooth. Scanning around, all the buildings looked the same as before. The barn, and the woodshed where Rake and I dried Ukki's tobacco leaves on the roof, stood next to the outhouse.

"Come-on," Ukki hollered, keeping the kitchen door open.

I had become mesmerized with the sights. "Okay, I'm coming," I called as I scooted to the kitchen. The smell of the farm and the barn lingered in the kitchen, leftover from Kolli's days. The furniture from upstairs had been brought down to these quarters. Fammu's piano sat in the living room, close to Ukki's massive oak desk. His gun cabinet stood behind the desk with three shotguns and two rifles. The couches and all other furniture were so familiar to me. One of Strano's violins, rested on a small shelf on the far wall as a center piece for the room. I was touching the furniture, which brought many memories when I was moved from my reveries by a loud honking sound outside. I ran to the picture window, overlooking the lake. A large 'V' shape of some fifty geese flew in formation over the shoreline. They were heading south, for the coming winter. It was a grand sight, but yet discomforting to know that the cold weather was on its way.

"Juha," Ukki called out to me, "We'll have Fammu fix some sandwiches and go out fishing. It's such a nice day and I have not fished in a long time. How does that sound?" he asked.

"That sounds terrific. I have not fished since leaving here. We'll go in my little boat. Okay?"

"Yes," he said, "I have a container dug into the ground with plump worms and the fish should be hungry," Ukki said, laughing like a kid.

Fammu fixed some sandwiches and loaded them into a canvas bag with couple of sodas. "I expect fish for dinner from you guys," she instructed us.

With the bag in hand we strolled to the dock. Right on the shore, Ukki had buried an old wooden barrel. He had filled it with fresh black dirt and mulch, and told me, with hundreds of plump worms. We dug into the dirt and collected a small can full of fat wigglers. Just the food the fish were waiting for, we hoped.

My little boat was bobbing for us. We loaded it with the worms, food and two bamboo fishing rods. These were the same rods which I had used so often.

After stepping aboard, Ukki untied us off the dock. I rowed. It was a short trip to the outside edge of the reeds, where the depth dropped significantly. "The fish follow the drop off, so let's try right here," he said and reached for the anchor in the bow of the boat dropping it into the deeper water. The waves were lapping the boat gently. The sun was shining giving off its warmth. We fished

Tom Sawyer 'style', with a bamboo pole and a cork bobber and plump worms. It was heavenly to be out there fishing with my grandfather.

"Got one," Ukki hollered, delighted, bringing up a good sized perch.

The fish, yellow, red and gray, was thrashing around as Ukki was holding it up on the line.

"Me too," I shouted, hauling in a little bigger fish than his. "Look at this baby," I said holding up my catch. "It's bigger than yours," I taunted him. We hooked the fish onto a stringer which was fastened to the side of the boat and dropping them back into the lake, keeping them alive until it came time to clean them.

This fishing trip, became a memory picture, with grandfather and grandson enjoying fishing together. Ukki sat intently focusing on his bobber, with a relaxed smile. "I like fishing, but don't do it often enough," he said. He told me how sad he was of having to downsize the farm to just a vacation home. The Kollis and Stranos did not want to leave. Stranos had begged for Ukki to help him bring his family to Rantala from Russia and stay there as a permanent caretakers, but Ukki was ready to give up the large farm operation. He was getting tired of the demanding duties, and at times, losses of crops and livestock. Fammu was also ready to slow down. They still kept the small garden cultivated. Fammu also had the berry bushes thriving, collecting blackberries, wine berries and plump juicy raspberries. The surrounding woods were full of blueberries, lingo berries and several species of edible mushrooms. Often they harvested these delicacies which Fammu preserved for the winter. It is said that the cultivated and the wild berries from Finland were superb, due to the clean climate and soil.

We spent over an hour enjoying the gentle rocking of the boat and the bright sunshine. Only a few cotton ball clouds drifted by. Fish were jumping left and right of our boat, creating drifting ringlets on the surface. There was no stopping the hungry fish. Our stringer grew to a point that we stopped fishing and just sat and talked. We enjoyed the sandwiches and drinks, just relaxing. My America trip was a subject which Ukki was keen to learn all about. I told him everything that I knew up to that point, and promised to write often from there. After finally pulling up the anchor, I rowed us back to the dock. Now the worst part of fishing would begin. We kept fourteen plump perch, flopping on the dock. We had discarded the smaller ones. Ukki had constructed a fish cleaning table on the dock. We took turns in gutting the fish and scaling them. It was a messy job, which I never liked. The guts went back into the lake, where the crabs and the crayfish would devour them.

After cleaning the fish and putting the rods away, we carried the 'trophy' fish into the kitchen. As we approached the house, there was exquisite piano music coming through an open window in the living room. Fammu was playing Joseph Haydn, one of her favorite composers. When she heard us enter the kitchen she stopped playing and asked "How did our fishermen do?" She was very pleased when she saw our catch. That would be our dinner in the evening. She would roast the fish in the oven, with her secret flour and spice formula. Perch, though bony, is a delicious fish. It would be a feast.

I decided to take a walk around the farm. My first target was the barn, where I had spent so much time in the past. I entered the stable and Stano's work shop. It smelled of wood and glue. In the shop, I sat down on his bunk bed looking at the multitude of hand tools, saws, chisels plains and clamps, everything placed neatly. Some hung on the walls, others sat on the solid wooden work bench. My truck, which looked so small now, sat under the workbench. It still looked brand new, without any paint fading. How in the world, did I ever fit in it, I don't know. Strano's old tattered sweater, was hanging off a hook by the door. I could still visualize him wearing it as he got out of the car, the day he arrived at Rantala. I could see his drawn face and scared look, not knowing what would happen to him. He turned out to be a gem in every way. He loved it here We loved him. I hope he is happily at home. I sat there for a long time with the memories of those times. I could still picture him working in this room. His scent was floating in the air, his Russian words reverberating through the room.

Next I walked into the stable. My saddle was still hanging off the same wood peg as always. It was light brown, smooth as silk to the touch. Further down the aisle, in the third stall was my horse's stall. It was empty. I missed him. I walked into the stall, still feeling his presence and the sweat of him. I stood there for a long time, thinking back of all the adventures we had together. Hopefully the present owner takes good care of him. When leaving the stable, I turned around and gave it a farewell wave. The rest of the barn, with the cow stalls and the chicken coops on the upper floor felt the same, except empty of the animals. It was as bitter as it was sweet to be back.

The wood shed was waiting for my scrutiny. It had not changed at all. In the corner the tall pile of sawdust buried ice which had been harvested last winter from the lake. Plenty of chopped wood was piled sitting against the wall. The old tractor occupied the center of the shed, sitting on sturdy wood blocks. It looked rusty and tired. On the upper level various types of lumber had been stacked. I continued my musing behind the building where the outhouse was located, close to the long building, where the minks had lived in their cages. It was empty of the minks and cages. It contained only a large mound of cut straw and two clippers. Later I would go and check out Rake's and my sand pit in the woods. I wondered if our secret 'treasure' box was still there.

Fammu had cooked a delicious dinner with our fish. She served them with boiled dill potatoes and fresh green beans. The aroma was heavenly. It tasted as good as it smelled. The fish were superior and fresh. Ukki beamed from knowing that we had caught this dinner. We congratulated Fammu for cooking it. For dessert, she served fresh raspberries with powdered sugar and heavy cream. What a treat!

After dinner, Ukki and I went to heat the sauna. Ukki lit the fires under the two large cast iron pots, and I began to haul buckets of water from the lake for the pots. The hand pump was out of commission. By the time there was enough water, I was exhausted.

"You look tired. It must be like carrying heavy luggage?" he said with a hearty laugh.

"Yep, but so many trips back and forth. The water is heavy," I said. "Why is the pump not working?"

"It froze last winter and I have not had time to fix it. Sorry." It was beginning to warm up in the sauna. "Two hours from now it will be ready," Ukki informed.

"We'll go and rest for awhile," he said and closing the doors tight we headed for the house. I had to take a "bathroom" trip to the outhouse behind the aitta building. Sure enough, my friend, the owl, hooted again after so many years. I hooted back, but must have said the wrong thing, because the owl did not answer.

The sauna was fantastic. Fammu and Ukki had taken it earlier and now I was sitting in the hot room on the upper level, casting water on the hot rocks. The steam shushed like a train hitting me broadside, making me double up with my head between my knees. Wow. . .this is how a sauna should work. There are good saunas and mediocre, but this one was the best. Sweat and tension from my body was pooling at my feet. After about ten minutes of "torture" I scooted out to the dock and jumped into the lake. The lake water was mellow and balmy. It felt so good to just lay in it for a while and cool off. Back in the hot room, I began to sweat again. Now it was time to use the birch "vita" to slap the pores open and relieve them of any remaining dirt. It was a ritual of self torture, which felt great, if you can call torture great. I ran into the lake once more then back to the hot sauna to open the pores again and wash up. Gently, not like the Aulanko matron's harsh treatment. After cooling down in the dressing room, I felt like walking on a cloud. Relaxed and content. The sun was still peeking out across the lake, as I sauntered home. The songbirds were singing in the shore bushes, and several loons called, their age old cries, ever mournful, reverberated across the lake.

Fammu had fixed the small bedroom by the kitchen for me. After a cup of tea and some oatmeal cookies, we all bid good night to each other. I retired to my small room dead tired. After the fishing trip, walking around the farm, the finale of the sauna did me in. I undressed, only leaving my under shorts on and climbed to bed. It was so comfortable on the soft mattress hugging me. Then I heard it. It almost sounded like the Russian planes flying overhead. It was dusk. What is it? I could not see what it was, but it zoomed around me deciding where to land. I turned on the small table lamp next to the bed. Then I saw the 'monster'. It was the biggest cow fly that I had ever seen, circling my head. I tried to catch it, without any luck. I grabbed my sandal, trying to smack it in mid air, but failed. Instead I wound hitting the table lamp, which crashed to the floor, breaking into pieces.

Now I could not see anything. I opened the door to the kitchen, swinging my pillow I was able to chase the miserable thing from my room, closing the door quickly. I'll get you tomorrow, I told myself, falling back into the bed exhausted. Next thing I knew, the daylight woke me up. It was seven o'clock and bright day.

"Good morning," Fammu said, seeing me enter the kitchen. "Did you sleep well?"

I greeted her and told her the story of the stupid giant fly. "I broke the lamp trying to catch it. Sorry," I mumbled.

"I saw it when I walked here and left the door open to outside. After a scuffle with the towel, it flew out. I never saw such a big ugly fly," she said laughing.

Ukki entered, rubbing his eyes, heading for the coffee pot. "Everybody slept well, I hope?" he asked in a rusty voice.

I had a cup of strong coffee also, reminding Ukki about the weak concoction he served me years ago. "You served me only a spoon full of coffee, sugar and the rest, milk." He chuckled.

Fammu suggested for all of us to go into the woods to collect blueberries and lingo berries. Ukki declined, saying that he would go down to the sauna and try to fix the pump. Fammu handed me a large woven wicker basket with a handle and a scoop, with the lip similar to a small rake. She also grabbed the same set up for herself, and off we went. We had to walk only ten minutes in the dry pine needle cushioned woods until reaching the area where the berries were growing abundantly. The lingberries plants were only about seven inches tall, full of dark red berries. The blueberry plants stood about ten inches tall, also full of plump berries. We began scooping them with the 'rake' scoop. Fammu tackled the blueberries and I started to scoop the red berries. It was amazing how fast our baskets filled up with the plump berries. It was so easy to retrieve them this way, rather than picking them by hand. The sun shone through the trees and many different types of birds serenaded us. One was a pesky crow, which dove close to us, trying to scare us away from its domain, and barked at us. It was fun. In about two hours our baskets were full. Few of the plant leaves were mixed in with the berries, but Fammu would sort them out.

"Juha, it is incredible how well the berries grow here," she said on our way back home, with baskets full. I enjoyed this harvest trip very much. It was so peaceful in the woods, and the smell of pine seemed to clear my head into a sharp wave length.

Back home Fammu showed me how to get rid of the leaves which were mixed in with the berries. She placed a large tub on the grass, then scooping up a ladle full of berries, threw them up in air above the tub. The berries fell into the tub and most of the leaves blew away into the grass. "This is the old fashion way of doing it," Fammu said in a satisfied voice. I copied it with my harvest and it was amazing how well it worked.

Ukki came up from the sauna building, sweating and greasy, grumbling, "The damn pump froze over the winter and now it needs to be replaced," and wiped his greasy hands on his pants legs. Fammu gave him an alarming stare, ready to say something, but closed her mouth, when she saw his angry face.

"At least you will be busy canning all those berries," he said, glaring at the two large tubs, half full.

"Let's go inside and eat something," Fammu said," adding, "and calm down," frowning at Ukki.

The rest of the day went by peacefully. I took a walk into the woods, to Rake's and my sandpit. Sure enough, our treasure box was still hidden under the moss lip of the pit. It was all rusted up. I had to force the lid open. Everything we had left in it was still there. The notebook was wet and moldy and so were the few cigarettes. Carefully I closed the lid and put the box back into its hiding place, wondering how many years it would take for it to totally fall apart.

That night I slept deep, without having to fight with the fly. After breakfast, the following morning, we returned to the city. Ukki let me drive through the woods to the main road, commenting how well I drove. I did not tell him that I had practiced driving with the guests cars at Aulanko.

The week went by fast. We had one dinner at my uncle's, without any gas problems. We were served in the casual dining room, without any tension. I watched my aunt's foot. This room had also a bell under the table, signaling for the cook to appear. Some day in the future, perhaps I can have a button under the table?

The evening when I took the night train back to Hameenlinna, was a cold rainy day. Fammu and Ukki bid me farewell, still puzzled about the trip to America. They wished me a safe journey and reminded for me to write to them often. We kissed and hugged each other as I boarded the train. I wonder when I would see them again.

39

I REACHED HOME AT TEN O'CLOCK the following morning. No one was home, meaning that they were at the tower where I would head after getting unpacked and changed. When entering the kitchen, the first thing I noticed on the kitchen table, were two envelopes addressed to me. One of them was a large brown envelope and the other an air mail envelope from America.

My hands were shaking. I was short of breath. Carefully I pried open the large brown envelope and peeked into it. It was my passport...my own passport. It looked so official, with a blue cover and the golden crest of Finland. I opened the front cover and there was my picture with many round government seals. It felt so light and smooth, almost as if it was bound in leather. Now I was holding in my hands the key to my world travels. I was ecstatic. Wow...It gave me the impression of being a significant part of my future. My hands trembled.

Next I looked at the envelope from America. It was addressed to me, from Mr. Schwab in Philadelphia, USA. I used one of the kitchen knives to open it, without tearing it. Carefully I unfolded the letter inside. I had to sit down. I hoped that it was good news. I was afraid. With shaky hands I unfolded the letter with hopes that he had not changed his mind and began to read the short letter.

Dear John:

It was nice to meet you and your family. I had a wonderful trip in Finland and a short stay in Germany. At this writing, I have already sent the student visa application and school acceptance letter to The American Consulate in Helsinki. I have also mailed all tickets with open dates to Anja, asking her to arrange your trip for early part of January next year. That gives you about four months to get everything in order from your end. Plan on visiting the Consulate in Helsinki in about three weeks, with your passport and apply for the visa. By then, they have everything from me. In the next few days, get in touch with Anja at the tourist bureau and ask her to begin making proper reservations from there to here. I hope all is well with you and your family and that you have not changed your mind. I am excitedly looking forward to the day when I meet you again, this time it will be in New York.

Warmest regards.

Laban

I sat a long time, looking at the passport and letter in front of me. It was so hard to fathom that such a miracle had happened in my life. How did I deserve it? Of all the people in the world, I had been chosen. Why? Perhaps God had heard my prayers, but I had never prayed for this to happen. "Thank you God" I spoke out loud. I hope that He heard me. He must have something on His mind to guide me through life. As I sat and mulled this aspect, my trembling had subsided and my mind was clearing into a peaceful emotion. I was jubilant.

The walk to the tower went by fast. I stopped once, next to a large white quartz boulder, which was mother's favorite rock. She would say hello to it every time she passed it, on the way up or down from the tower. I said hello to it for the first time, probably due to the 'cloud' I was walking on. I could not wait to tell Mother, Inga and Kari about these letters and show my passport to them. There was also so much to tell them about my trip to my grandparents.

The restaurant was humming. I had passed two tour busses on the lower parking lot. One group seemed to be elderly people, sitting at the tables, talking loud, and enjoying whatever they were eating. Mother and two girls were behind the counter. Inga and Kari were running amongst the customers, serving them and clearing tables. The other group was a mixture of youngsters and probably their chaperones. They were waiting to enter the tower and horsing around the ticket booth. Maja was busy selling tickets. I waved at Mother and walked in through the kitchen door. Dirty dishes were piled up everywhere. It would be a while before we could sit down and talk, so I decided to give a helping hand and began sorting out the dishes washing them as I went along.

Mother appeared in the doorway, huffing and greeting me in a tired smile. "You can't believe what a morning we have had here. All at once, the place was packed. "My gosh," she said as she sat down at the kitchen table. She smiled and said, "Welcome home. I hope that you had a nice trip? I am ready for a cup of coffee and a cigarette," she said.

Kari ran in with more dirty dishes and growled, "Hi," turning around and running back to the madness.

I poured a cup of coffee for Mother and myself and sat down next to her, giving her a kiss on her tired cheek. I was so excited to show her my passport, which I dug out from my back pocket. "Look, I have my own passport," I said waving it in front of her with a grand smile. "Wait until I translate the letter from Mr. Schwab," I continued excitedly.

"Hi, Juha, how was your trip?" Inga called out in a huff, reaching for the coffee pot and rushing back out, without even waiting for my answer.

"I am dying to hear what your American friend has to say," Mother said in a hesitant tone, looking at me with query in her eyes.

"Well, he has sent the tickets to Anja and the paper work for a student visa to the Consulate in Helsinki. He told me to wait a few weeks, before going to see them. He assures us that everything is in order and that he will be meeting me in New York." I could see Mother's eyes light up and her tiredness dissipate with this sure news. Up until now she had still been somewhat skeptical about all this talk, because to her it seemed as the most unusual happening. I must say that I had also been a bit skeptical but now we all could see that my trip would be taking place.

"Juha, all I can say that you have been blessed. I just hope and pray that your life will benefit from it and that you will strive to achieve high goals. I am still scared," she said, grabbing my head and looking straight into my eyes with the ambivalence of pride and trepidation. "I love you always. I am so happy for you," she whispered, with a single tear running down her cheek.

"Thank you," was all I could say.

"I must go and help the girls, we'll talk later," she said getting up and disappeared into the dining room.

I had to be at work at three in the afternoon and now it was just past eleven o'clock. I approached the sink, full of dishes, and with gusto attacked the mess.

An hour later I was sweating, but proud of my accomplishment. The kitchen was back to normal. Kari still came back with just a few dishes, but his face was beaming and he uttered, "Thanks Juha, I almost fainted with the work waiting for me. This was the craziest morning we ever had. All at once, he whispered, "shit," before running back to the terrace, which by now was almost empty of customers.

About an hour later everything was back to normal. Inga and the Lisa came in to take a break. Both of them looked overwhelmed. Inga's hair was a tangled mess and her face was red and damp from the exertion. She sat down on the bench, and voiced one word, "HUH…" Lisa did not say anything, but appeared bleary eyed and exhausted.

Finally Inga had composed herself and said, "Mom told me that you have some super good news about the America trip. Tell me."

Both she and Lisa sat with their mouths partially open, listening to my news and carefully leafing through my passport. "You lucky skunk," Inga finally said, "How come something like that did not happen to me?" she said, looking petulant.

Later my family and I sat down at a table on the terrace. A multitude of tourists were milling around the outside, snapping photographs and looking at the sights. Only one other table had three elderly persons drinking coffee and eating sweets.

Finally Kari got the whole scoop of my plans. I told them at length about the trip to Oulu and Rantala. Kari became angry when he heard about Ukki's and my fishing trip and mumbled, "How come I never get to go fishing?"

I could not help firing back, "Kari, we are surrounded by lakes. You just have to get up and go fishing. Maybe you and I will do it soon?" He looked happier after hearing this.

"School is starting a week from now," Mother reminded us as if we were unaware of this unpleasant thought. Annukka joined us, bringing a tray full of coffee and scones and a couple of sodas. Her face looked drawn and tired, like everyone else. I could notice her hands trembling and there was no smile, which was unusual, as she was always so happy and bubbly. This morning had taken the toll on everyone, except for me.

"I promise to send everyone cards from New York and from Philadelphia when I get there," I said, looking at each one. They finally smiled.

"I'll give you a list of what I want," Kari said, frowning.

"Okay…we'll see what's on your list," I said, ruffling his hair.

Everyone seemed to come back to earth after being able to relax and unwind from the craziness. Even Inga laughed loud, hearing Kari's comments.

Finally Mother joined the conversation. She had been sitting quietly listening, drinking coffee and was on her second cigarette. "We will be closing down here around the twentieth of September. After school starts, it will be just me and Maija taking care of everything during the week, but you girls can still come to work on the weekends. Okay?" she asked. The girls agreed.

My escapades with Lisa never really got off the ground, between work, travel and the planning for the long journey. Sure, we had gone swimming many evenings in the cold lake and gotten eaten up by hoards of mosquitoes, which was not fun. A couple of times, just her and I disappeared during the day to a favorite spot amongst the boulders, overlooking the shimmering lake below. We talked and messed around just innocently. She was such a stunning beautiful girl that I was wishing to take her along with me to America. I really liked her fresh purity and warm laughter. I would miss her.

It was time for me to leave home, take a shower next door and get changed for work. Mother said that they would come home tonight, instead of staying here. I was glad to hear this. "See you later. Have a good day," I said, waving them good bye.

I was still tired from the train trip and all the work I had done in the kitchen. A hot shower did rejuvenate me somewhat. I still had some time left before having to go to work.

I sat and read Jack London's book called *Adventure*. It is a sad story taking place on the Solomon Islands at a copra plantation. The slavery was horrendous and giving me the chills form the torture and inhumane life of the slaves. After sitting and reading it for some time, I had to lay the book down, because it was turning my mood in a negative direction. Instead I read Mr. Schwab's letter again, twice, bringing me back to the present and a happy frame of mind

I decided to travel to Helsinki the last week in September and ask Mother to come along to the American Consulate, just in case they had any questions for her.

40

IT WAS MONDAY MORNING, THE third day of September, which was also the first day of school. This was my second year in the Lyceum High School and Inga's first year. The Lyceum was the stepping stone for college after three years. A challenging entrance test took place after the last year in middle school. If you passed the test, you would attend it starting in the fall. Inga passed and was accepted, as well as me, a year earlier. If you were not accepted, you would be attending a Vocational High School. She was afraid even though I told her about the school not being any different from her previous one, except harder. Kari was still in the middle school. The morning when we took the bus from Aulanko, it was a cold, drizzly day which echoed with our feelings of having to go back to school. Sitting on the bus my thoughts drifted to America. Actually I had thought about it daily, counting the days when the journey would begin. Now on the bus, I was wondering how the schools were there. It was a scary feeling to start a new school in a different country. It would be hard in beginning because my English was not very good at all. How would my classmates accept me? Would they make fun of me? One aspect did appeal to me. In America you did not go to school on Saturdays, whereas here in Finland we had to attend a half day on Saturday. That stank.

The three of us sauntered slowly in a gloomy mood in the ominous weather toward the schools. From the bus stop in front of the church, it was only three blocks to my and Inga's school and a block farther to Kari's school. The Lyceum of Hameenlinna had a long history, being the first school in Finland to be fully a Finnish language school. All others were still teaching in Swedish but Hameenlinna wanted to express its Finnish independence by opening this school. Jean Sibelius, the famous Finnish composer, year 1876 was one of the very early students there. He was born and raised in the family home, just across the park from the school. Over the years the building itself had grown into a large brick establishment and well respected learning institution. This was my school, even though its history was grand, I was not happy today. It had been an extraordinary summer which I did not want to end. However, now I had something thrilling to look forward to. The trip to America was approaching fast, in January.

Back home later in the day, we sat at the kitchen table with mother, enjoying milk and cookies. Inga had survived her first day at the Lyceum, actually telling us that she enjoyed it. Mine was just the same old thing and when we asked Kari how his day went, he just lifted his shoulders and grunted, "Okay."

"Kari, your birthday is coming up in three days. You are going to be eleven years old, so promise to take school seriously," Mother told him in a stern voice.

"Okay," was his grumpy response.

It was not only Kari's birthday in three days. Mine would be four days after his, and Inga's six days after mine. I was going to be seventeen years old and Inga sixteen years old. All in September, as the saying went, 'Januarys are very cold in Finland. The upcoming Sunday had been designated as a joint birthday party for the three of us. It would be held at the tower restaurant because Mother was still working there another week.

I had made an appointment with Anja at her office for Saturday morning. She had received the tickets from Mr. Schwab and she suggested, that now was the time to begin to make the various reservations and a full itinerary. She asked me to bring Mother along in case she would have some questions. "Don't forget your passport. We need it for the reservations," she advised me.

Saturday morning at nine a.m we arrived at Anja's office. She was already waiting for us with a cup of coffee in hand.

"Good morning Sylvi and Juha. Sylvi it is so nice to see you again. It has been a long time since you and I got together. If I remember right, it was over a year ago when we had dinner together at The Cosmopolitan restaurant. That was the night I had garlic for the first time in my life. It was some Italian seafood dish called *Pasta con Vongole.* It was delicious but when I got home, my husband told me that I stunk. It was the garlic's fault," she said and greeted us with a good laugh. "Would you like some coffee, before we get started with business?" she asked.

Both of us nodded and said, "Thank you, please." We seated ourselves in front of her desk.

As Anja was walking towards the coffee pot, Mother said, "You didn't only have the Italian dinner, but remember all the Italian wine you also had. We had to send for a taxi to take you home," she said rubbing in the memory and giving Anja a wink.

Anja came back with two cups of steaming coffee, placing them in front of us at her desk. "Sylvi, you should not talk like that in front of Juha," she said, looking, embarrassed.

"Sorry. Juha is old enough to understand," Mother said.

"Okay," Anja said after sitting down. "Let's get down to business."

Opening the drawer on her desk, she pulled out a folder tagged: JUHA. She opened the folder setting a stack of tickets in front of us. "The first question is when do you want to leave? I would like to suggest on early January, say the fifth, which happens to be Tuesday, if you agree," she said looking at us for an answer. Mother and I sat quiet for a moment thinking, but there was no reason why this date wasn't as good as any other. In unison we agreed to Anja's suggestion.

"Good," she said. "The ticket for the boat trip to Sweden is from Turku, instead of Helsinki. Turku is on the southwest coast of Finland. The ship leaves for Stockholm, Sweden at eight p.m. and arrives at Stockholm at nine a.m. You will be taking the afternoon train from here to Turku, arriving there at six, giving you two hours before the ship leaves. You have a cabin for the night trip," she explained. "How does that sound so far?" she asked. We agreed, nodding with a smile.

Mother sighed, she was still confused and worried about this unusual awesome event but yet at the same time she was happy for me. "I am going to miss you," she whispered.

"Next leg is a train trip from Stockholm to Copenhagen Denmark. The train leaves at seven p. m. which means that you have all day for sightseeing the Swedish capital. You will have a sleeper cabin on the train and arrive six thirty in the morning in Copenhagen, with a two hour layover for the train to Hamburg Germany, which will arrive in Hamburg at noon. From there, you will take the train at one p.m. to Bremenhaven in Germany, arriving there at about five p.m. Take a taxi to the ship, which will be SS. *United States*. The ship will leave at seven in the evening.. It is the largest, newest and fastest ship across the Atlantic Ocean. By now you must be dizzy from everything I just told you, but don't worry, I will prepare a well organized itinerary for you," she said and took a deep breath after the long explanation, asking, "do you think you can handle all this?"

I thought for a moment. I scanned quickly at Mother who gave me the impression of being totally lost. The coffee cup in her hand was shaking. She looked at me bewildered, when I answered, "Sure, no problem." I said. My stomach dropped, giving me the feeling that the butterflies in my stomach were having a field day. What an involved journey it was going to be. I did not show my nervousness at least I don't think that they noticed it.

We hugged and bid Anja goodbye and thanked her for all the work she was doing on my behalf. "You should hear from me in a couple of weeks with the finished itinerary, and all reservations confirmed," she said, looking at me with a glowing face. "I am so happy for you, Juha and feel sure that you can handle the travel without problems. Just don't get stuck talking to some pretty girl and miss your connections," she added jovially.

Mother wanted to stop at the coffee shop, but after I told her about Mr. Schwab's and my experience with the greasy fat man, she changed her mind. The bus arrived shortly and took us home.

At home we sat at the kitchen table and had a long talk about the journey. It was cool inside, the early fall weather had arrived. Mother had put on her favorite bright yellow woolen sweater. The kitchen window was partially open.

"I would be afraid to travel that far with so many train changes. You speak Swedish, but Danish and German are the languages which could be a problem. Sure lots of people speak English which will help you, but still… dear God, it is long trip," she said, holding my hand, gazing at me with a worried look.

"Mother, don't worry. I can read time tables and if I have problems, someone will help me," I said, sounding as positive as possible. "I am going to be seventeen years old in a few days and after working so long at the hotel, I have learned so much and I am not the least bit scared. It will be an exciting experience and I always dreamt about traveling to faraway places. Please don't worry," I said and this time I squeezed her hand "If I wind up in Istanbul, I will let you know," I joked.

"Don't scare me. That's not funny," she mumbled.

She was smoking, one after the other, with the smoke rising up to the kitchen ceiling. Her voice was garbled and nervous." Juha you are too young for such a trip, and not knowing what is waiting for you. I am truly worried. Mr. Schwab seemed like a fine gentleman, but we don't know anything about him," she breathed out and watching my expression.

"I have round trip tickets and if there are any nasty problems, I will head back home right away. If Mr. Schwab has any ulterior motives, he would not go through with this very expensive proposition. As my guardian, he is responsible for my well being. After getting to know him when he was here, I would have sensed if he was not sincere." I tried my best to ease Mother's concerns. It seemed to work. Her composure became more relaxed and she gave me a broad smile.

"Thank you. You sound so positive. I must say that I also felt very assured of Mr. Schwab, but I can't help still being a little leery about this 'miracle.' Tomorrow is the birthday party for all three of you, and we can combine the celebration also with your upcoming trip," she said, sounding happy and calm by now.

Earlier in the week I had gone shopping for birthday presents for Inga and Kari. I bought Inga a Norwegian hand knitted blue white and red warm wool sweater. It would look sharp on her and keep her warm this winter. For Kari I picked up two books, a Tarzan book and Tom Sawyer. I never saw him read much but I was hopeful that these great books would immerse him into the joy of reading. Although it was not Mother's birthday I also wanted to get her a gift. It was a beautiful gold pennant with a cherry quartz stone on a long gold chain. I hope she will wear it always.

Mother left for the tower and I changed into my bellboy uniform. It was just a regular work day for us, after the morning's excitement. The last words, before leaving, she told me that they would stay up there overnight and for me to come up there around noon tomorrow. Now that school had started, I worked only part time on the weekends and some evenings during the week if needed at the hotel.

It was a slow evening at work giving me time to spend in the library, where I read about American History. At school we studied ancient history, going back thousands of years, whereas American History was very young. In the year 1493, Columbus landed on an island in the Bahamas which marked the anniversary of the discovery of America. Thirteen colonies were founded on the East coast starting in the early 1600s which was the beginning of the USA. It would take me days to cover the written stories of the growth of the country. I skimmed through the chapters, reading about George Washington, Benjamin Franklin, Edison and many more notable individuals. The New York City area was discovered and explored by Hudson, Cabot and Verrazano. Up until this time it was inhabited by native Indian tribes. Over the years it grew to one of the largest cities in the world. I was going there. WOW!

When in bed that evening, I was wondering if there were still native tribes and Indians left in America. I would like to meet some of them.

41

THE BLUE, RED AND WHITE balloons decorated each table on the terrace. They fluttered gently in the light breeze. A hand painted banner hung over the entrance stating 'HAPPY BIRTHDAY KARI, JUHA AND INGA' had been written in dark blue letters. In the center of the terrace, three tables were pushed together, forming one long table. It was covered by a white tablecloth. In the center of the table, on top of a silver cake stand, sat a beautifully decorated birthday cake. A grouping of blue, white and red balloons sprouted from the middle above the cake. Presents wrapped in dark green paper surrounded the cake. It looked so festive. Mother and her helpers must have been busy putting it all together. I couldn't help muttering my favorite expression-"WOW!"

Two tables were occupied by customers. They appeared to enjoy the festivity. The man at one of the tables was playing with his balloon with a big grin on his face. When he saw me walk up to the terrace he hollered, "Come and join the party."

"Thanks. I'm Juha and the other names are my sister and brother. It is our joint birthday party," I said smiling at the man.

The man began to sing Happy Birthday, with the second table joining in. When the song ended, they clapped. Meanwhile, Mother, the girls and Kari had heard the commotion in the store room, coming out and clapping loudly. Mother asked the customers to wait a short while for a piece of the cake. They thanked her and said that they would be happy to join the party.

I had left the house at eleven, without realizing that all this fanfare would take place. It was a pleasant surprise. The weather was cool and the sky crystal clear. It was a sweater day. Fall was arriving with the leaves of the aspen and birch trees changing color, before falling to the ground and leaving the branches cold -naked.

"Juha, come and see the cake," she called out to me. "The hotel's baker created it for us. It is a chocolate layer cake with fresh raspberries and strawberries. Isn't it gorgeous?"

I approached the table with the cake. It was covered in whipped cream with an outline of Finland on one side and America on the other side, separated by blue whipped cream through the center as the Atlantic Ocean. "What a master piece," I burst out. It was gorgeous. The baker had out done himself for this special occasion.

"This cake was baked for all three of you. but I asked him to create the map for your upcoming trip. The baker is a master," she said tapping me on the shoulder.

All of us gathered around the table, including the four customers. Mother lit eleven candles for Kari and said looking at him, "You blow out the candles, because your birthday is first."

Kari looked embarrassed but took in a big breath and blew out the candles. I could see that that his face had reddened. He did not like the attention. The group sprang into singing Happy Birthday again, this time for him. Kari seemed to want to crawl under the table.

Mother sliced the cake into wedges, giving Kari the first piece, then to me and Inga. Next came the customers and after that the girls, Maija and finally herself.

The cake was as good as it looked, tasting almost like a chocolate mousse with fresh strawberries. We sat down at the main table, the customers included. I had requested mother to give me an 'American' slice, which she did. My first bite was somewhere in the area of Philadelphia. It was delicious.

The customers thanked us for an enjoyable time and left to look at the sights. Now it was time for us to open the presents. We would open them in the order of our birthdays. There were so many. Where did they come from? I pondered.

Kari opened his first. "Two books," he said, looking at them nonchalantly, knowing that they came from me. He set them on the table with an empty, non interested look. Next he got a pair of warm winter gloves, giving them the same look, and the last present was a long narrow package. He opened it with care. Now there was a smirk on his face. It was an archery set with a rugged bow and six long arrows. "Oh, thanks, this is nice," he burst out with a big grin, looking around, puzzled, wondering who had given it to him. Mother told him that the gift was from her. "Thanks Mom, I always wanted this," he said, giving her a big smile and extending the bow and drawing the string. "Huh, this is a good bow," he uttered.

Next it was my turn. The first thin package was from Kari. Opening it slowly I thought it would be a small comic book, but no. It was a beautiful brown soft leather cover for my passport, with the golden crest of Finland on the cover. "What a fantastic gift," I burst out." Thank you Kari," I held it up in the air for everyone to see. My second present was from Mother and what a surprise it was for me. It was a gorgeous black Mont Blanc fountain pen in its own velvety box. I had always wanted this pen. "Thank you Mother, I really like it. I will use it to write many letters to you," I said and I hugged her. Inga had bought me a book of American History. This would be my reading on the journey. "Thank you, Inga. What a thoughtful gift," I said and gave her a big smile and an air kiss, across the table.

Now it was Inga's turn to open her presents. She unwrapped my gift to her carefully and holding up the beautiful sweater for everyone to see. She put it on and it fit her perfectly. Her face shone radiantly against the colorful knitting. She thanked me. "Juha, what good taste you have. I love it and it is so warm and soft," she said as she paraded around the table like a model. Mother's gift to her was a new pair of ski pants, in dark red made into a quilted pattern. "Thanks, Mom," she called across the table. Kari gave her the PEPPI LONGSTOCKING in the Finnish version. She held it up promising to read it.

We sat around the table talking and laughing, eating cake and drinking coffee and sodas. The cake tasted like the smooth delicious chocolate soufflé with fresh berries, which I had one day for dessert at the hotel. It had been on a day when the tips were exceptionally good. The soufflé had cost me plenty.

Lisa approached me and timidly handed a small present wrapped in tissue paper. I opened it and to my surprise it contained two small flags, each one attached to a thin wood rod, size of a skinny pencil. One flag was the Finnish white with a blue cross. The second one was the American flag with stars and stripes in red, white and blue. "They are for your desk in America," she said, giving me a hug.

I would have wanted to give her a good kiss, but not in front of everyone so I just kissed her cheek. "Thank you Lisa, I will remember you always when I look at these flags," I managed to say without blushing.

Annukka had been quiet except for her singing the birthday song. She had a strong and beautiful voice, which probably carried across the lake. "I picked out a present for you, but something needs to be done to it before I can give it to you. Perhaps in a week you will get it. I hope you will like it."

"Annukka, I can't wait. It must be something very special. Thank you," I said, giving her also a hug and a kiss on the cheek.

Maija gave me an unexpected gift. It was a birthday card with a crisp twenty dollar bill inside. My eyes must have shown the surprise. I was shocked. That was lots of money in 1954. "Thank you Maija. You should not have done this," I said in a trembling tone.

"I did not know what to get you, but figured that this money will come handy in the new country," she said. I gave her a hug.

A few customers drifted in and out. By now in September, business dropped drastically. One more week and Mother would go back to her job in the hotel. The summer had been very busy. Actually looking at the previous records, this summer bypassed them in sales. Slowly Mother and the girls had been packing up for the closing. Everyone was sad. It had been an immensely great summer for everyone, including Mother.

In a way, this grand birthday party was also a farewell party for the staff. But for us kids it was a reminder that one year had slid by. We all were in a party mood, happy and laughing especially Inga, Kari and I. With all the presents and love, this had been a memorable day. For me it was a combined birthday and a Bon Voyage celebration, which I would never forget. I was wondering where I would be celebrating my next birthday. I hope that it will be in America. With trepidation, I realized that it would not be with my family, I reasoned that some day we would be together for this occasion again. I had been away from home half of my life up until now and oh my, here I go again.

"Mother, I have a small gift for you also," I said, reaching in my pocket for the small gold paper wrapped jewelry box and handed it to her. "Thank you for everything. I hope you like it."

Her eyes lit up with a stunned look. She unwrapped it delicately. Now she was holding the purple colored silken jewelry box in her hand, afraid to open it, scanning each of us in bewilderment. Carefully she lifted the cover, bursting out, "Oh my God. You should not have done this. It is beautiful." Her face glowed from the sight of the cherry quartz gold pennant. Gently she brought it out from the box, dangling it from the gold chain. There was a hush from everyone when they saw it casting golden rays as it swung.

"Juha, this is absolutely beautiful. I will wear it always. I am in a shock," she uttered giving me a strong hug. "Thank you."

"I am glad that you like it. I want this present to be from the three of us for to you for being such a good mother. Thank you," I said as I helped her clasp it around her neck. Everyone came to Mother, looking at it closer. There was much ooing and ahhing.

It was time to clean up. The cake was gone and the table was a mess with wrapping paper and dishes. All of us pitched in and in no time the terrace was back to normal. We left the dancing balloons on the tables for any of the few customers who might show up. The air had chilled since the morning and a stronger breeze blew through the terrace. The girls and Mother had put on sweaters and Kari and I donned on some old jackets we found hanging in the closet. In the latter part of September, the first frosty nights would arrive and not long after that the first snowfall would appear. The day light had become noticeably shorter.

In the early afternoon, Mother decided to close up the restaurant and tower because there had not been any tourists around for several hours. We locked up the business at three o'clock and began the trek home. Maija and the girls walked to the hotel to catch the bus to the city.

To finish off the memorable day, Mother suggested for us to go for dinner at the hotel, which sounded appealing. After getting washed up and changing into proper clothing, the four of us walked to the hotel. There was a small private dining room with a table set up for four, waiting for our arrival. Mother smiled and told us that she had arranged for it earlier in the week. Sly, she had not told this to us. It was another birthday surprise. The table was set with a bouquet of fresh subdued scented flowers. Gleaming silver cutlery surrounded a large base plate at each setting. This dinner was off the menu and served by an old time waiter in the elegant style of the hotel. Kaisa was the busgirl. I could not help feeling odd, sitting there with my family and have her enter the room off and on. The movie night flashed in my mind, hoping that it did not show on my face.

Each one of us ordered something different. I of course had my regular standby, the pork cutlet with roasted potatoes and fresh green beans. Mother ordered a salmon dish, Inga a chicken dish and Kari ordered Swedish meat balls. The hotel sent us a complimentary bottle of a red French wine. Mother gave each of us permission to have a small serving of it.

The dinners were delicious, and perfectly served, not hurried, but in a peaceful and leisurely fashion. The waiter, Carl, attended to us as if we were special guests. For dessert each one of us had a small apple torte with a measured scoop of homemade vanilla ice cream. "I feel like royalty," I said to which everyone agreed. We thanked Mother for a wonderful and unforgettable day.

On the way home, I was reminiscing the terrible time when we lived in the cramped apartment and Mother's awful job at the prison. We ate so much oatmeal and pea soup, that I didn't care if I ever ate it again.

"Mother, our past years here at Aulanko have been like a vacation every day, except of course the school," I said, taking her arm.

"I feel the same way. After that horrible time in the apartment and the prison, this life is like living in the paradise," she said squeezing my arm. In unison, Inga and Kari agreed. The pennant was gleaming in the subdue evening light.

Later, at home, I reminded Mother about the trip to The American Consulate the following week. I was worried, thinking that perhaps Mikko's and my escapade with the police had reached the Consulate. They would not be happy if they found out that I had been involved with the police, even though it was just a prank. I was not a hooligan. I was scared. What would happen if they denied my visa?

42

I<small>T WAS A RAW, GLOOMY</small> day on Wednesday, the last week in September when Mother and I stepped off the train in Helsinki. The Grand Railroad Station is a massive and elegant building in Helsinki, reminding me of a cathedral in Rome, which I had seen in a history book. Once we stepped outside on the street to look for a cab, the elements hit us with a wet blast. We huddled, stooped down under a large umbrella, facing the wind trying to find a cab. Finally a cab pulled to the side of the curb in a large puddle splashing, our feet and legs into a soaking mess.

"Oh shit!" I yelled out. "Look at me. I am a wet mess." I glared at my soaked pants and my shoes felt like they were full of water. "The Embassy won't let us in the door, looking like bums," I snorted.

"I felt like saying the same, but you saved me from the embarrassment," Mother complained, looking down at her soaked clothing. "It's dreadful weather. They'll understand," she said trying to calm me down.

I told the driver, who looked like a gruff farmer from the East, big bellied and flat faced, to take us to the American Embassy on Itainen Puistotie. He took off, growling that he knew where it was.

I emptied my shoes on the cab floor and wrung my pants legs and tried to create a crease in them. No luck. There was nothing Mother could do, except grumble about the puddle. "We surely will make a grand entrance at the Embassy with our appearance."

Fifteen minutes later we arrived in front of a massive old gray building, which was set behind a rod iron fence and trimmed hedging. The taxi driver turned his head towards us and growled "This is the Embassy. It will be thirty marks." We gave him the money without a tip for the misery he had caused. Departing the cab, I slammed the car door harder than necessary. I was mad.

We entered a smaller building to the right, which was the annex entrance to the court yard and the main building. Here a friendly and pretty receptionist sat at a wooden desk, next to the American flag on a stand. She asked us if she could help us. I explained that I was here to apply for a visa to America. She made me fill out a small questionnaire, at the same time making a call telling someone that she was sending a young boy and his mother for a visa application. There was a notable puddle on the floor where we stood. I told the young lady that we were sorry, but that we got soaked on the way over.

"Don't worry about that. It's not the first time. The janitor will mop it up," she said in a cuddly voice and a broad smile. "Now you need to go out again through that door," she said and pointed to a side door. "Walk to the main building and someone will meet you there."

With the umbrella ready, we entered the courtyard. It was beautifully land-scaped with well groomed bushes and hedges. A large circular flowerbed sat in the middle of the yard, all wilted from the cold fall nights. A laid brick walk-way led us to the large oak door in the main Embassy building. Shaking the umbrella before entering, we opened the door. It was solid and heavy but swung soundlessly inward. The first sight greeting us was an enormous American flag hanging on the wall, behind a large desk where a well dressed young man sat.

"Welcome to The American Embassy," he greeted us, standing up and walk-ing over to shake our hand. "So young man, you have come to apply for a visa. Let me call the Consulate general and see if he is available right now," he said and approached the desk and made the call. Hanging up the phone, he told us that it would be about a fifteen minute wait before he could see us. "Please sit down in the waiting area," pointing to a couch and four high back leather chairs in the corner of the room. "May I get you some coffee or cold drinks, while you wait?" he asked pleasantly.

"Thank you very much, but we are fine," Mother answered. Good thing the attendant spoke Finnish and of course English.

"What a welcoming greeting we received," I said to Mother, while looking around the large room. She smiled and I could see that she was pleased with the friendliness and probably thinking that this is how people in America are. Her mind was at ease. She was sitting on the soft light green couch. On the wall above her head, were three large paintings in heavy dark wood frames, of historical American Presidents. I only recognized Abraham Lincoln. The rest of the room was decorated with large photographs of American cities. The walls were painted in a light sand color. The atmosphere was warm and quiet. A hint of old age was in the air.

The phone rang at the desk. After hanging up, the attendant asked us to follow him up a circular broad stairway. His shoes clicked on the steps, but ours did not from being so wet. He led us through a long hallway, atop of a soft light blue plush carpet to the end door and knocked lightly. I was nervous. I hoped that it did not show. My heart was beating louder than normal.

"Come in," came a faint voice from the room.

As we entered the room, we were struck by the opulence and the aura of it. It was a large room with four, at least ten foot tall arched windows overlooking the courtyard. The rain was beating hard against them. An American flag stood next to a long oval glass desk. On top of the desk, there were only two items. One was a red telephone and the other a manila folder. The gentleman sitting behind the desk in a black stuffed office chair appeared very official. He was in his fifties, with thinning gray hair with half moon reading glasses resting on his nose. Seeing us enter, he stood up. He was tall, at least six feet and dressed in a dark pin striped suit, a starched white shirt and a tie with Mickey Mouse pictures. I was tense but the tie seemed to quell some of it away. The rest of the room was furnished with plush and tasteful sitting areas and with book cases lining the walls full of leather backed volumes.

The tall man approached us from behind the desk, extending his hand shaking mother's first and then me. I gave him my usual determined shake, which he returned.

"Welcome, my name is Henry Ashville and I am the Consulate General," he said. "I understand that this young man is planning to travel to America," he continued in English with a questionable gaze at me. Mother introduced us in Finnish.

"Yes sir," I managed to say in clear but shaky voice. He and the surroundings were intimidating and I was nervous in the first place.

"Please be seated in front of the desk," he said as he was returned to his seat. We seated ourselves in two burgundy color leather chairs. He opened the folder, studying it in silence. I was twitching not knowing where to place my wet feet. Mother was more composed.

"I see that you have a sponsor in Philadelphia, a Mr. Schwab. Is he related to you in any way?" he asked, speaking slowly and clearly so that I could understand.

"No sir. He is a family friend," I answered in my broken English.

"He has sent you round trip tickets and he has also registered you in Dobbins's Vocational School. Are you a good student?" He scrutinized me with sharp but friendly eyes.

"Yes sir," I answered, finally able to produce a faint smile.

"Can I see your passport?" he said, extending his hand across the desk.

I had been holding onto it since entering the first building. I handed it to him.

He scanned the few front pages, all other pages being empty. "I can see that everything is in order from your end and the sponsor's in Philadelphia. Are you looking forward to going to America?" he asked

"Yes Sir very much. I am so excited. I can't wait," I blurted out in a higher pitch than intended.

Meanwhile Mother had been sitting quietly, except just nodding the few times when I translated some of the conversation. She seemed relaxed and happy.

"May I keep your passport and in about one week we will mail it to you with the visa? It will come by registered mail, once we are sure that everything is in order," he asked looking at Mother.

I translated to the request and Mother nodded, saying, "Thank you."

"Do you have any questions?"

"No. Thank you," I answered.

"Have a great trip. I am sure you will love our country and do well there. Study as much English between now and then which will help you out in the school," he said standing up saying just one word "*Kiitos*" which is thank you in Finnish. He spoke as much Finnish as Mother spoke English. He walked us to the door, making a last comment, "Good luck." We shook hands and walked the long hallway to the steps. I felt so good. In fact I wanted to slide down the wide smooth wooden banister. When I mentioned this to Mother, she gave me a dirty look and growled, "No."

At the reception building we asked the young lady to call for a taxi. Ten minutes later, it arrived and asked the driver to take us to Stockmann Department store, where we would have lunch and perhaps do some shopping. Stockmann was built in 1930 and has become an internationally renewed shopping experience. Over the years it was modernized and brought up to high standards, with goods from around the world. On the second floor, there is a cozy café and restaurant, next to the Academia book department. This was our destination for lunch and browsing. We could take the afternoon train back home, giving us plenty of time for a leisurely lunch.

The taxi navigated past many street cars, which were running throughout the city. The rain had subsided to a raw and windy drizzle. When we sat down at one of the restaurant's tables, looking at the menu, we began talking about the morning's experience.

"Juha, if the people in America are as nice and friendly as the ones we met, I am so glad for you. Here in Finland everyone seems to carry a chip on their shoulder and are generally very gruff. You are so lucky to be able to see the world," Mother said, looking at me over her menu.

"I was so nervous when we arrived at the Embassy, but everyone was cordial and helpful, that by the end I felt so great. It also looks that there are no problems in getting the visa. I'm very happy now," I said smiling. "We better order."

Mother ordered a shrimp salad dish and I ordered a smoked salmon platter. We were sitting by the window, overlooking the broad boulevard teaming with people under umbrellas. Some of the city noise reached us. The street cars with their bells were clanging. Their wheels screeched as they navigated a curve on the tracks. It was illegal to use car horns, unless absolutely necessary. What a difference this was from New York, as I would find out later, where there was a constant honking of horns, especially from the hoards of taxi drivers.

Our lunch arrived. The waitress set an appealing dish of smoked salmon in for me and delicious looking dish of shrimp salad for Mother and coffee for both of us.

"I love salmon," I said, "especially cold smoked with its trimming of chopped eggs, onions and capers."

"I know you do, my shrimp salad is out of this world," she said between the bites of her shrimp dish."

After lunch we did some shopping. I bought a pair tan colored corduroy slacks for the long journey. Mother went to the women's department to buy some personal things. For Inga and Kari we bought a box of Fazer chocolates each. Fazer and the Swiss chocolates have been competing with each other for many years as being the best chocolates in the world. As far as I know, our chocolates are the best. Come to think of it, I had never tasted Swiss chocolate. We caught the three o'clock train back home.

This day had been one of the better days in my life. I was good to go with the escapade to America. At his point I was counting the days

43

WINTER ARRIVED EARLY. THE FIRST snowfall blanketed the ground in the latter part of October, the nights dropping to freezing temperature. The daylight was slowly becoming shorter and it would not be long before the sun rose late in the morning and then dropping below the horizon in the early afternoon. The long winter was on its way.

School went well for all of us. Mother was back working in the hotel. I was counting the days when my trip would begin. The passport from The American Embassy arrived with the student visa stamped on one of the empty pages. I read it over and over. It looked very official. I was good to go. I hid the passport under my mattress for safety.

One Thursday morning Kari said, "I'm not going to school," pouting he added, "I'm sick."

Mother felt his head, "You don't have a fever."

"Yah...but my stomach hurts." He looked miserable, with his hands on his stomach.

"If you are really sick, stay home, but if you are pulling my leg, I will be very mad at you," Mother said, in a threatening tone, "Go back to bed and no playing around," she commanded.

"Kari, this gives you a good chance to open one of the books I gave you," knowing that he had not opened neither book I gave to him on his birthday.

"Okay," he said, crawling back to bed.

Inga and I walked to the bus. "He did look sick," Inga said. It had snowed during the night as we walked in the dark, the snow crunching under our feet. The stars and a quarter moon lit our trek. The sun was still asleep. "I agree, he rarely misses a day," I confirmed.

The Lyceum was hard. There was tedious amount of homework every night. We had a different teacher for each class. I found the classes interesting, especially Geography and Mathematics. In the history class, we were studying ancient Greek mythology, spending a couple of days learning about Zeus and his off springs. This subject I found to be very interesting, yet tedious subject. It was followed by Plato and Aristotle, which turned out to be boring except for Plato's description of the lost Atlantis. In the year 355 B.C. he wrote about an island nation west of the Pillars of Hercules in the Atlantic Ocean. It, according to him, it was far advanced city with a large civilized population. At some point the island was devastated by earth quakes and sank into the ocean. Now that was attention-grabbing to me and I made a mental note to read about Atlantis in the future." I had hoped to maybe find it one day."

Closer to Christmas we all, Kari included were busy in the hotel with various parties. The tips were great and I was happy to work any hours when needed. I even bought some black market dollar bills from other tip employees. It was a brisk business to sell dollars to the highest bidder. One day just before Christmas there was a registered letter for me from Mr. Schwab. It was on the thick side. After opening it carefully, I was shocked. The letter contained a short note, wishing us a happy holiday and a safe journey. My hands were shaking when I counted the small stack of money also enclosed inside. The total came to three hundred dollars. I could not believe my eyes. With the money he sent and what I had collected over time, I now had three hundred and ninety dollars. That was a small fortune. I was now covered for any unforeseen problem during the journey. When I showed the stack to Mother, Inga and Kari, they could not believe their eyes. "You lucky skunk," Inga said in a sullen smile. But they all were happy for me. I hid the money inside the passport under the mattress.

One week before Christmas, the hotel held their annual Christmas party for the employees and their families. The dining room was closed for regular business. There must have been close to two hundred of us. The dining room was festively decorated with Christmas trees and garlands. Red candles with poinsettias adorned each table. A full musical band from Helsinki had been booked, playing Christmas music and dance tunes throughout the evening. People danced. I danced, but did not know what I was doing. I stepped on many toes, but had a good time. The dinner was buffet style with ham and trimmings. Each table had been provided with two bottles of French wine and cocktails were available at the bar. The partying lasted until midnight, with everyone having a festive and good time. I drank wine, more than ever before, and by midnight I was drunk. I had problems in walking a straight line home. I had to navigate with one eye closed. The next morning I woke up with a terrible hangover. This was my first hangover. Never again I told myself, swallowing two aspirins and nearly throwing up. After a few more hours of sleep, I felt somewhat better.

Anja had called and left a message for me to come and see her at her office, which I did the following day after school. She looked as chipper as always and the office had been decorated for Christmas with a tall Christmas tree standing in the middle of the room. It was decorated with colorful brochures from around the world.

"Hello Juha, Merry Christmas," she greeted me.

"Merry Christmas to you also," I said, sitting down by her desk

"Well, I have your itinerary and all reservations confirmed for your trip. You will be leaving soon, in fact January the fifth. You must be so thrilled and suffer travel fever."

"Thanks, I am ready to go."

"Let's go over everything," she said setting a pile of tickets on the desk. "First look over the itinerary and if you have any questions, let me know."

I studied the sheet carefully and found everything in the order, just as we had talked about a few months back. "No questions. It seems perfect," I said with a smile and feeling on top of the world. I had never ever been so energized as now. I was holding my future in my hands. "Fine, now let me show you all the tickets," which she did from beginning to end. "Make sure to keep them in a safe place. I suggest that you make a list of everything when you get home today of all the items you need to take along and double check everything before you leave the house on the fifth. That way you will not forget anything," she told me in a parental tone.

"Okay, that's a good idea. I will do it."

Anja placed all the tickets and folded itinerary into a canvas pouch with a zipper. She walked around the desk. I stood up and she grabbed me in a powerful hug, giving me a kiss on my forehead. "I am so joyful for you. Here are your tickets," handing me the pouch and continuing, "Bon Voyage!"

I placed the pouch inside my shirt, for safe keeping and bid Anja good bye.

I felt like singing on the bus back home. I slid my hand inside my parka and felt the pouch with the tickets against my skin under the shirt. I could not wait to show them to my family.

Fifteen days and twelve hours were left before my trip would start. WOW!

44

THE SHIP'S ENGINES HUMMED QUIETLY and I could feel a constant gentle vibration under foot as I was standing aboard *SS. Scandia* at the docks in Turku. We would be departing in one hour for Stockholm. It was seven p.m. as I leaned against the railing, watching the commotion on the dock. I had arrived by train from Hameenlinna and boarded the ship two hours before departure. It was freezing cold. Ice had formed on the wall of the dock and on the multiple pilings. The ship was a large passenger vessel and a ferry boat for cars and trucks. People were boarding on the broad gangway and automobiles were entering into the belly of the ship through a driveway in the aft. It was too cold to stay outside any length of time so I decided to go inside to look around. I had found my cabin for the night earlier and left my suitcase and backpack on my bunk, but all the important papers and monies were well tucked inside my shirt in the pouch which Anja had given me. There were two bunks in the room, but my roommate had not yet arrived.

What I had so often thought was a long dream, but now the reality was setting in. The first leg of the trip had begun and I was on my way. It was still unbelievable, but true.

The last two weeks flew by fast. We had celebrated Christmas at home. Mother had cooked a delicious ham dinner on Christmas eve, with roasted potatoes and fresh broccoli and for dessert ice cream and cake done by the hotel. After dinner we opened the small pile of presents laid under the Christmas tree. Two packages had arrived a week earlier, one from Fammu and Ukki and the other one from Far and Mor in Sweden. The gifts from them consisted mainly of winter clothing, sweaters, gloves and scarves. Kari received a blood red knitted ski hat from Fammu, which he promptly gave to Inga. "I will not wear this sissy hat, you can have it," he growled. Mother received a beautiful knitted sweater from Fammu and Ukki. It was patterned in blue, white and yellow colors. She loved it. From Sweden came chocolates and chewing gum with some more gloves and scarves. I had bought Inga a diary bound in leather with a lock and key clasp.

"Oh Juha, I always wanted this. Thank you. I will keep it locked so that Kari can't read my secrets," she said smiling, holding the book against her chest.

Kari's main gift was a new pair of skis, which I brought in from a hiding spot in the breeze way. The gift was from mother and me. "Thank you. My old skis were like two flat planks. This is great," he said holding the skis in the air with a broad smile. Mother had gotten me a new backpack and a good size luggage for the trip which I needed badly. I could not wait to start packing. Kari got me a copy of Horatio Hornblower for reading during the trip. He had inscribed the inside cover page: *"From your brother Kari. Good luck always."*

"Thank you Kari. I will treasure this book forever," I told him, meaning every word. It was a great Christmas. On Christmas day, we attended the Lutheran church in Hameenlinna and had lunch afterwards in a small cozy restaurant.

On New Year's eve, we all worked at the hotel which was packed with customers. I did my old fun job again, which was selling balloons throughout the night. With a pocket full of money, I was dead tired by one o'clock in the morning but happy as a lark. The next day I counted my earnings which were unreal. I gave the whole lot to Mother, but kept two one dollar bills which were mixed in the pile. Mother promised to put the monies in the bank. This time there was no need for me to explain how I had earned so much. She knew my trick from the previous time.

Finally the morning of January fifth 1955 arrived. That night I had slept restlessly, waking up several times, to check the clock. All the packing had been done over the few previous days. The suitcase was heavy, stuffed mostly of clothing and a present from mother to Mr. Schwab. It was a gorgeous thick 'Iittala' glass vase. Iittala glass was world renowned artistic glass, sold in the finest shops around the globe. We hope he will appreciate this beautiful hand blown piece of art? The backpack had mainly a few clothing items, the pile of brochures from Anja and two of my books. Mother insisted that I pack a pair of slippers into it also.

The day before, we had arranged for the hotel taxi to pick us up at noon for the trip to the railroad station. The train would arrive at one o'clock for the trip to Turku. All four of us piled into the taxi and the luggage went into the trunk. At the station there was time for us to sit and have coffee and doughnuts. My family seemed sad and yet happy about my journey. Now we had reached the climax after many months of planning and waiting. Before the train's arrival we stood on the platform, hugging and kissing each other.

"I still can't believe that this is happening. I am so happy and excited for you and will miss you very much. I hope that we will see each other in a year or two, no more," mother said holding my hand.

"I will miss all of you. Here I go again, after Oulu and Sweden. I will write often and send some presents from America," I promised, seeing each one looking sad. "Be happy. Who knows? Maybe you will come and visit me some day." I said, trying to lighten their gloom.

"Send me a pair of cowboy boots," Kari said in a pleading voice.

"Okay Kari, I will," I said as the train was pulling up. After the last hugs and kisses, I boarded it. When the train pulled away, I was waving to them. I wondered when we would meet again. I had a sinking gut feeling, as if I was deserting my family again. Yet, my outlook for the future remained positive, knowing that this trip had been arranged by God and he would guide me always. I felt sad and glad at the same time.

The ships horn blew three long deep blasts. It was time for us to pull out from the dock. I defied the cold air by bundling up and going back to the deck. The men ashore released the thick ropes from the dock cleats and the ship was free. Slowly, we pulled away into the open harbor, and slid by Turku into the ice laden Bothnian Sea with the next stop being Sweden. The ship knifed through the ice floats picking up speed. I was frozen again and had to retire inside.

After stopping in my cabin for a comfortable sweater without meeting my roommate who had deposited his belongings on the other bunk, I returned up to the dining room deck. I faced a huge dining room with an enormous double buffet. The smell of the food jolted my stomach. I was famished. The clanging of dishes and subdued background music invitingly added to the atmosphere.

My ticket included the cost of the buffet. I found a seat with several Finnish men and joined their table. They were rowdy and half drunk by then, swearing and laughing out loud at some stupid jokes.

"Look, we have a young gentleman with us. You pigs behave," one of the men commanded.

"Shut up Erkki. We are the gentlemen and he's just a hooligan," one of the men hollered, laughing hoarsely, with a toothless grin.

"Piss on him. We are here having fun. If he does not like it, piss on him, again."

One of the burlier unkempt men coughed up and belched loud. "He can move, if he doesn't enjoy our jolly company," he roared looking at me with piercing watery eyes.

I got up and went to the buffet table, loading up with a plate full of shrimp. These were whole shrimps, with the head legs and tail. I found a table with some old ladies, who invited me to sit down. Peeling the delicious shrimps, one of the puny old ladies asked me where I was going.

"America," I answered.

They looked at each other, hesitating, until someone else spoke, "This ship goes only to Sweden. Not America. You must be on the wrong boat?" she said seeming puzzled.

"No, well, I will travel to Germany and catch the ship across Atlantic there," I answered in a kind voice.

They appeared to be still confused, until one of the 'smarter' ladies said, "I know, that's the country where my son caught the claps in Hamburg. Young man, you don't want to go there. The women are dangerous. Mark my word," she croaked, almost spitting up a mouth full of food.

What is wrong with these people on this ship? I wondered. Are they all nuts, or am I unlucky in finding a decent table? *"Mamma mia!"* I said out loud, which was a saying I had learned from some Italian tourists at the hotel. I went back to the buffet table and collected a plate full of food. I looked around for an empty table and saw one in the far end of the dining room. I rushed to it before anyone else claimed it. Just as I sat down, a young lady, perhaps two to three years older than myself, asked if she could join me.

What could I say except, "Yes please," and she sat down.

She was a petite, pretty girl, with sparkling blue eyes and a long blond ponytail. Her plate contained only a few select items compared to mine, which was loaded with food.

"My name is Asta and I am on my way to Rome, Italy to attend The University of Rome. Where are you going?"

"I am traveling to America. My name is Juha."

"Wow- I always wanted to go to America," she said with a sigh. "What is that awful banging on the ship's hull?" she asked, looking worried.

"The ice breakers have been busy all winter keeping the frozen shipping lanes open to Sweden. The loud notice is from thick ice flows hitting the side of our ship. Don't worry, the hull can cope with it," I explained and assured her.

"I hope to visit Italy some day. I understand that it is a beautiful country. I am sure you will enjoy your stay there," I said looking into her bright eyes.

"Thanks. Let's eat," she said, forking a tiny morsel into her mouth.

I looked at my huge pile of food. My eyes were bigger than my stomach. There was no way I could finish what I had piled on my plate. I picked and picked without making a noticeable dent into my selection. "I am crazy, but everything looked so good and I did not want to miss anything," I said to Asta, who was staring at my progress in a crooked smile.

"The trick with buffets is that you go back and forth sampling different items," she advised, watching me.

"You are correct. I just got carried away," I said, while chewing a piece of beef.

After dinner we parted, wishing each other a safe journey. I hung around the salons and several bar rooms. A band was playing in one of them with the dance floor packed with people dancing. A few drunks seemed to have passed out on the lounge chairs. At home I had heard that these boat trips were a drunken brawl, because the liquor was much cheaper than ashore. At the duty free shop, business was brisk with liquor sales. I bought a bar of chocolate, and munched it as I walked around. I wondered how much bigger the SS *United States* was compared to this ship. I hope that it was much bigger.

By now it was almost eleven o'clock. I was tired from the long day and disturbed sleep the night before. Walking to the cabin in the long narrow hallway, I could not wait to lie down. When I opened the cabin door, I saw my roommate sound asleep. He was an elderly man, snoring lightly in his bunk. I got undressed and slipped between the covers. Our cabin was located on the outer wall of the ship. A constant banging and scraping sounds from the ice flows against the hull, did not keep me awake, but lulled me to a deep sleep in no time.

45

"**W**AKE UP YOUNG MAN! WE are in Stockholm," the cabin attendant said in a surly voice, shaking my shoulder at the same time.

I opened my eyes confused. He repeated himself. Finally it started to dawn on me that we had arrived in Stockholm and the ship was already tied dockside. "Thank you. I slept like a rock," I said, sitting up on the bunk, rubbing my eyes. The man stood by the door, keeping the door open, but advised me to get up and leave the ship. "We need to clean this room, now," he barked.

I jumped up, rushed to the bathroom, did my business and got dressed. All this took only a few minutes. I had no packing to do, except a couple of chocolate bars, which I stuck into the back pack. The long corridor was empty of passengers as I made my way to the upper deck, where the gangway led to the terminal. Good thing the man had woken me. It would have been awful to wake up and find out that I was still on the ship, but now on the way back to Finland. It was almost ten o'clock. We must have been docked for an hour already.

The passport control was a breeze and now I was back in Sweden where I had left some nine years earlier, but this time on a different mission. I took a taxi to the railroad station, where I checked my luggage in the storage area, but kept the backpack on me. The train to Copenhagen did not leave until seven in the evening, giving me plenty of time to roam around the city. I found a telephone booth at the station and decided to call the Westholms, with whom I had not talked in so many years. Mor answered the phone and was so surprised to hear that I was back in Sweden. After a long pleasant conversation, I told her about my trip to America. She was astonished and wished me well. Their son was five years old and growing fast. Far was in town and I sent regards to him and promised to write to them from America. I felt so good having called them.

Now I had the whole day ahead of me to stroll around the city. My first destination was the 'old town.' Walking leisurely and crossing several bridges of the city called "The Venice of the North' I arrived in the historical district with narrow cobble stone streets, flanked by very old, three to four stories high, brick buildings containing stores on the street level of every description and many small intimate restaurants and coffee shops. I browsed inside a leather goods shop and bought a new, sharp brown leather wallet. My old wallet was ratty. At the station I had changed forty dollars into Swedish kronor, for lunch and light shopping. The next stop was a small coffee shop. I was hungry, ready for food and lots of coffee. The coffee in Sweden was always rich and aromatic, imported from Columbia. I devoured an open face ham sandwich rapidly, washing it down with the good brew. While sitting in the café, I emptied my old wallet's contents into the new one, ditching the old one into a trash can. Now I felt like a new person after food, coffee and a spiffy new wallet.

Still moseying around trying to kill time, I spent a good hour in a large book store, and bought an imported magazine from America called Life. I entered the same gun shop where Ukki and I had visited years ago. The inventory appeared to be modernized and the store had expanded. The shop brought happy memories about the previous trip. After stopping for another coffee and leafing through the magazine, I began slowly drift back to the station. The weather was cold but warmer than in Finland. There was also much less snow accumulation here than back home.

There were still two hours left to wait for the train departure to Denmark. I sat in a rather comfortable waiting lounge, surrounded by other waiting passengers. The building was an old dome shaped structure. The many announcements about train departures echoed in the building. People went and others arrived. It was fun to sit and relax and people watch. From the backpack I retrieved Kari's gift, Horatio Hornblower and started to read it. The book turned out to be very adventurous, making the time pass by fast. Half an hour before my train's departure, I found the track where the train was already waiting. Many passengers were boarding and I did also after finding my coach number on the ticket. Once aboard, I found my sleeper compartment. It was a second class meaning that there would be only two of us for the trip. Setting the suitcase under the lower bunk and the backpack on the floor, under a small fold up table by the window, I sat down watching the people parade by. It was a very comfortable cabin with a soft cushiony bunk, in the typical gray and black upholstery. Blue and yellow striped curtains, the Swedish colors, surrounded the window. A fold down sink was attached to the wall. Bathrooms were in either end of the coach.

The train blew the whistle and departed at seven sharp. I was still alone wondering if someone else would join at the next stop. It was great to have the cabin all to myself. The upper bunk remained as a backrest for the lower bunk where I sat. It would be turned up if someone else arrived. Night had set in. It was dark outside. The half moon was hanging low over the horizon. I decided to take a stroll to the dining car and get something to eat. It was three coaches away. Walking through the rumbling connectors from car to car was daunting and noisy. The dining car was old and elegantly appointed with starched tablecloths and napkins with gleaming silverware. On each table, a lonely bright red rose sat in a small crystal vase. Only a couple of tables were occupied and I sat down at a small table for two. A waiter appeared immediately with the menu and asked if I would like to have something to drink. I ordered a bottle of Swedish beer and studied the menu. The prices were high. The cheapest dinner was Swedish meatballs, which I ordered when the waiter arrived with the beer. Eventually the dinner arrived. It was good, but could not compare to Fammu's meatballs. They were not as moist and flaky as hers. I took my old sweet time in eating and enjoying the beer, finally returning to my compartment. The beer had relaxed me and I was tired from all the walking earlier. It was time for bed. I turned on the reading lamp and crawled under the covers. We would be arriving in Copenhagen at six thirty in the morning. My reading lasted only some ten minutes, after which time I fell asleep. About two hours later, there was commotion in the cabin which woke me up. The coach attendant secured the upper bunk for a gentleman waiting in the hallway. Once done, the man entered, I said hello and turned to face the wall and fell asleep again immediately.

At six thirty, the train rolled into the railroad station in Copenhagen, Denmark. Here I had a two hour layover for a train to Hamburg, Germany. I had breakfast at the station restaurant, relaxed in the lounge and before I knew it, it was time to board the train to Hamburg. We would be arriving there at noon. It was a sparkling clear day. No snow appeared anywhere. I sat by the window watching the landscape as the train sped by, faster than the Finnish or Swedish trains. There were five other people in this day compartment. They spoke Danish and German, which I could not understand. It was almost a four hour trip and I did some more reading.

We arrived in Hamburg at the colossal railroad station a few minutes past noon. It was the busiest station I had ever seen. I had to present my passport at the gate before entering the station. I had always heard of the delicious German beers, which of course I had to taste. I sat at a barstool in the station pub and ordered a glass of local draught beer. The bartender set a glass of beer with a hefty head of foam in front of me. I took a big swallow of the amber color beer and it tasted superb. My upper lip was decorated with the foam. I drank it up quickly. It was true why people raved about German beer. I had to scoot off to find the train for Bremenhaven, which would leave in twenty minutes. If I would miss this train, I would also miss the ship. After careful navigation, I found the platform where the train sat and double checked with the conductor if this was the train to Bremenhaven. "Yes," he assured me. I boarded the train and found a window seat for the three hour trip.

Pulling out from Hamburg, we passed countless huge factories and in the background large tall gray colored apartment buildings. The scenery was dank and smoky. It seemed to take forever before some open landscape appeared with a few farm houses here and there. The sky was overcast, lending to the gloomy sight. Up north, everything seemed so pristine, but here in Germany it was just the opposite. Even the trees looked straggly. The train sped by many small communities with more factories and the same murkiness. I thought that I was lucky not to have lived here. I sat with some Germans, two men and two women, speaking in German. They didn't pay any attention to me, which was fine. After a while, I dug out my book and sailed on the Pacific Ocean with *Horatio Hornblower*.

Before I realized, we had arrived at Bremenhaven. After getting off the train, I went outside of the railroad station to find a taxi. That was no problem. There was a long line waiting for the passengers off the train. All I had to tell the driver was, *SS United States*, and off we went. It was about a fifteen minute ride to the shipping terminal. Several other taxies were following us, with the same destination. I did not see the ship yet because it was on the other side of a large three story terminal building.

A long line of ticket checkers were stationed behind individual booths. I waited a short time to reach one of them. It was a pleasant young lady with a big smile, who greeted me.

"Hello. Welcome to *SS United States.* May I see your ticket and passport."

I handed them over to her. She called a gentleman behind her, who came over to inspect the visa. He looked at me up and down. "All is in order," he called out to me and the attendant. Meanwhile I was sweating, hoping that nothing was wrong.

"You may leave your luggage here," attaching a sticker with my cabin number on it, continuing, "it will be delivered to your state room. Have a good journey." She handed

my passport and a ticket stub back, and added, "Here is a brochure of the ship, showing the different decks and your state room."

"Thank you," I muttered almost tongue tied and nervous. I looked around to find the way to the ship, finally seeing a line of people in front of a broad doorway stating, "ENTRANCE TO SS UNITED STATES"

I joined the line with an enormous feeling of accomplishment and optimistic forward thoughts of the future.

46

W HEN I FINALLY ENTERED THE glass enclosed gangway to the ship, I
could not believe my eyes. The colossal and majestic passenger liner
was docked in front of us. It was the grandest ship I had ever seen.
From the brochure I had read that it was almost a thousand feet long, with a
beam of over one hundred feet. Two enormous smoke stacks, painted red, towered skyward emitting dark gray smoke. The hull was painted black with white
trimming. The line of boarding passengers was moving slowly with everyone
admiring the sight. The brochure stated that *SS United States* was a luxury liner
built in 1952, and designed to be the fastest passenger liner on the Atlantic crossing. I could not wait to board it.

At the entrance, we were greeted by officers who checked our tickets and
passports. Visitors were allowed to accompany their families or friends, receiving a special pass. They were to debark one half hour before departure. The officer who was checking my ticket told me that my cabin was on deck five, pointing
the way to the elevator. At this point we were on deck eight. When I stepped
off the elevator on my deck, I had to stop and scan the several hallway signs
with arrows pointing to cabin numbers. This was the third class, which held
the most cabins. I found my directions and walked the long, burgundy color
carpeted hallway until I reached my cabin. I stopped to double check the cabin

number with the ticket. This was it. The door was open to the hallway and I stepped inside the small room. There were four bunks in the room. Two against one wall, a lower and upper, and the same on the opposite wall. In between the bunks stood a tall bureau with four drawers. A small bathroom was located on the left side. A comfortable upholstered chair with a small table sat in the far corner, with a reading lamp attached to the wall. There would be four of us sharing the cabin.

My suitcase and two others sat in the middle of the room. My bunk number was one of the upper ones on the far wall. I threw the backpack on the bunk, retrieving the pouch with the passport and monies, and slipped it inside my shirt.

"Hello," someone said behind me. I turned around and faced a clean shaven middle age man in casual clothing. He extended his hand for greeting and stated, "My name is Carl Johanson from Stockholm."

I shook his hand and introduced myself in Swedish. "Nice to meet you I am Juha from Finland." He was trim with light blue eyes and a friendly smile. His light hair had receded to almost baldness. He located his bunk, setting the hand luggage on it.

"I am glad to find that you speak Swedish. What a gorgeous ship this is. It is my first time across the ocean. What about you?"

"This is also my first trip across. I was shocked when I saw the size of our vessel. Hopefully the weather is good, but I am sure this ship can handle anything that ocean dishes up," I said, moving my luggage aside.

In stepped another man. He was short, overweight, dressed in a rumpled suit. He reminded me a little of Stranos, the Russian at my grandparents' farm. In broken English he told us that his name was Hugo from Romania. Carl and I introduced ourselves to him in broken English. He found his bunk and arranged his belongings on it.

"I am going up and look around the ship. See you later," I said and stepped into the hallway. People were streaming in looking for their cabins. There was barely room in the narrow corridor to pass each other. I took the elevator to the highest deck which was deck twelve. When I stepped off the elevator into a wide paneled room with doorways leading to the outer deck, I took the doorway leading to the dockside. A light cool breeze greeted me. Good thing I was still wearing the parka. I walked to the highly varnished teak railing and looked down. I could not believe how high up I was. The crewmen on the dock looked like miniature workers. They were loading the belly of the ship with boxes after boxes which most likely were food supplies and other necessities. I walked forward to the bow, until I came to a tall rod iron gate pained white, with a plaque stating: "First class only." It was locked, but through the webbing I could see the bow of the ship, far away from where I stood. It was monstrous. The bow sat at least four stories high above the water level. It would plow through anything, I was thinking. I wanted to climb over the gate, but there was no way I could do it so I had to give up the idea.

Other passengers were also up and about. A few women and children were admiring the sights also. I walked towards the aft and discovered that the walkway led around the corner where you had the view of the stern and the harbor to the left. Here again I had to stop and admire the sights of this enormous ship. The two tall massive smoke stacks loomed behind me reaching high into the sky. Continuing my walk around I was now on the open harbor side. Other large ships were docked on the opposite side of the harbor. I could smell the diesel fuel emanating from the ships. Tug boats hustled in the harbor. The Bremenhaven skyline was visible on the horizon. It would take me several days to discover everything about the ship, inside and outside. One thing I had learned from the brochure was that the ship could carry almost two thousand passengers. After leaving Germany, we would make a short stop in Le Havre, France and Cobh, Ireland to pick up more passengers, before heading across the open Atlantic to New York.

Back inside, I walked down a wide stairway to the next level. There I was greeted with signs "First Class only" and more locked doors. At the next level down, the same thing. Finally, when I reached deck eight, it opened up into a huge dining room to the left and an equally large bar room to the right. Dinner would be served half an hour after departure. I had an assigned table number. I wonder who my table mates would be. Doorways also led to the outside deck. I took a peek down and faced a long row of large life boats sitting in their cradles on the deck below. There were ten on this side and ten more on the harbor side. I hope we never need to use them, thinking of what had happened to the Titanic.

The loudspeaker blared with an announcement, "Attention!" All visitors must leave the ship now. We will depart shortly." The announcement was repeated three times. I wondered why they let visitors aboard in the first place. It would be so easy to just stay aboard for a ride to New York. In fact, a day later I learned that a German man had done just that, claiming that he did not hear the announcement. Having no passport, the ship was obligated to haul him on a round trip back to Germany. He had been supplied with a cot somewhere on the ship and fed him throughout the round trip. Once I saw him sitting in the bar, happy as a lark. Perhaps they put him to work in order to earn his keep?

At seven p.m. sharp, the loud steam horns blew three long blasts. I could feel the vibration of the engines revving up as I ran to the outside railing to watch the departure. The thick ropes were let loose from the dock cleats and we began moving slowly towards the open waters. I stood there for a long time in mesmerized thoughts about the exciting future, watching the shoreline slowly disappear as the ship approached the English Channel. The next stop would be France in the middle of night.

I made my way to the cabin. Carl was there changing his clothing for dinner and that was what I was going to do also. "Well my friend, here we go. Let's hope that the Atlantic is kind to us," he said, pulling a turtle neck sweater on.

An announcement blared throughout the ship. "Everyone is to report on deck seven with their life jackets on, for emergency exercise within fifteen minutes." We followed the order and scrambled to the deck, where we were instructed what to do in the event there was an emergency alert. Everyone listened to the instructions which took about twenty minutes. The last advice was to study the procedures, including your life craft number, which were posted on the inside of the each cabin door.

"I have been walking all over the ship. I can't believe how huge and nice it is," I told him, at the same time changing into the new corduroy slacks, a new white shirt and a dark blue V neck sweater. My scuffed shoes would do.

"Carl, what is your dining room table number?" I asked.

He pulled out his ticket and found the number to be fifty three. "What's yours?"

"I am glad. Mine is the same number. Probably Hugo's also?"

"Let's go for dinner, if you are ready," Carl said.

We took the elevator up and walked into the dining room which was half full by now. The hostess at the door pointed us into the direction of table fifty three. It was half way through the giant room, close to a large window overlooking the sea. The table was set for four. Hugo was sitting there already, greeting us with a "Hello."

"Looks like our cabin has this table," Carl said as we sat down. "Perhaps we will pick up the fourth person in France or Ireland."

The table was set with base plates, shiny utensils and a water and wine glass and crisp linen. A large menu sat at each place setting with a colorful picture of our ship on the cover. It was also dated January fifth 1955. They must print the menus daily, I surmised. When I opened it up, I was amazed of the selections available. Several appetizers, six dinner entrees and a good selection of desserts and wines were listed. The food was part of the ticket, but wines and other liquors were extra. As I was reading the menu, the waiter appeared at our table, bowing introducing himself as, "Luigi." "Gentlemen, welcome. I will be your waiter for breakfast, lunch and dinner throughout the voyage. May I suggest a bottle of wine?" he asked.

We talked it over and decided to order a bottle of Merlot. "Good choice," Luigi said trotting off to fetch the wine. Carl offered to pay for tonight's wine and we would be taking turns each dinner. I was trying to decide what to order. It was hard, because everything sounded so good. Finally I chose a shrimp cock-tail for appetizer, roast beef for the entrée. Carl and Hugo experienced the same dilemma as I had in choosing, but lastly making up their minds. Each one of us ordered something different.

Luigi came back with the wine, uncorking it and offering for one of us to taste it. Carl lifted his glass. He tasted it and nodded his approval. Luigi poured some in each glass. We gave him our dinner orders. "Thank you," he said and disappeared.

By now the room was full, with happy chatter and laughter sounding throughout the room. Soft dinner music filled the background. I was elated sitting here. I felt like royalty, traveling in luxury to America. In a way I felt selfish by not having my family here to share this with me, but as the faith had its way, I had been chosen. I would write home and share my experience with them. Hugo interrupted my thoughts, by stating in very broken English, "I never thought that we would be treated this well." We agreed with him.

Luigi returned balancing a tray with appetizers and hot rolls, placing our orders on top of the base plate in front of us. My shrimps sat on a bed of crushed ice. Hugo had ordered herring in sour cream, and Carl a cup of onion soup, with a crouton topping. Every dish looked first class. This reminded me so much of Aulanko Hotel. A floating Aulanko. I was very hungry and the shrimps disappeared quickly. After the dishes were cleared our entrees arrived. Here again, the food was arranged on the plates looking eye appealing and smelling appetizing. When I bit into my beef, it just melted in my mouth. We all agreed that this was fine dining. Carl had a chicken dish and Hugo had opted for salmon. I glanced out the window and in the dusk, I could see the calm sea, and the long rolling swells. Aboard the ship you barely felt them. Satisfied and full, the three of us sat chatting with coffees in front of us. I was surprised to see Hugo ladle four spoons of sugar into his coffee. The man had a sweet tooth. None of us ordered dessert. After Luigi had cleared the dishes and served the coffee, he bowed again and said, "See you at breakfast. Have a good night."

The food and the wine had made me feel mellow and content. I still had some more exploring to do so I excused myself, saying, "What a great dinner. I am going to go and walk around. See you in the cabin later," and headed to the deck. The cool air felt good. I stood against the railing looking at the long shallow swells. It was almost dark but crystal clear. The stars were already visible with a half moon hanging just above the horizon. A few gulls were following the ship barely having to flap their wings, but gliding in the slip stream of the ship. It was so peaceful. I was so happy, calling out to the gulls and telling them thus. An old lady gave me a big smile, after hearing my uttering. "So am I," she said and smiled some more before walking along.

Inside I stopped at the bar and listened to a live band for a while. Couples were dancing. I did not dare to ask anyone to dance with me, remembering the clumsy effort I had done at the Christmas party. It was fun to just watch. I found another smaller lounge, which was a sitting room with one wall covered by a book case, filled with books. At one table six men sat playing poker, puffing on big cigars. A few people had dozed off in the comfortable chairs. On the next level down, I discovered a boutique store, selling some clothing, souvenirs and post cards. I bought eight postcards showing the New York skyline, with the Statue of Liberty in the forefront. These I would write aboard and mail them from New York. This would allow me to be a step ahead with writing. Finally I worked my way down to my cabin. Hugo was asleep already, but Carl was probably enjoying himself in the lounge. It was past ten o'clock. It had been a long day. I was dead tired. After brushing my teeth, I crawled into my bunk, which was comfortable and soft. The gentle ships motion lulled me to sleep almost immediately

It must have been around one a.m. when there was subdued commotion in our cabin. We must have stopped in Le Havre. I woke up, looking with one eye at a man who had entered the cabin. He must be the fourth passenger with us, I surmised. I watched him unpack some of his luggage, and quietly get undressed for bed. His bunk was under mine. I fell asleep again very soon.

The next morning we met him. The new passenger was getting dressed. I was awake first. The man was tall and thin, seemingly in very good shape, a runner or soccer player I assumed. When he saw me sit up on my bunk, he looked at me and said, *"Je m'appelle Claude."*

"I have no idea what you said," I answered, in English, looking at him, puzzled.

He pointed at himself, repeating twice "Claude."

I followed his example, pointing at myself, "Juha," and pointed at Hugo and Carl, naming them. In Finnish I told Claude that it is nice to meet him. He looked stunned with his mouth open. I can play that game also. I had heard that the French people were snobbish and refused to speak any other language even if they knew how.

Carl greeted him in Swedish, and Hugo followed in Romanian.

The poor man looked taken aback. His mouth was contorted. From there on, he communicated with us in broken English, just like we did. See, I thought.

The ship's engines quieted and we seemed to have stopped. I got dressed quickly and ran to the elevator taking it all the way to the deck twelve. Running to the outside deck, I saw that we were close to a rocky coast line. A motor vessel was approaching the ship, and maneuvering itself next to an open large hatch, near the water level. Ropes were thrown from the small boat and pulled snug against our ship. Once tied up about a dozen people stepped aboard. This must be Cobh, Ireland? This was our last stop, before the open Atlantic Ocean.

We met each other again at our table. Claude had been the missing puzzle, but now we were all here. Luigi approached with a coffee pot in hand, greeting us, "Good morning gentlemen," he said and poured coffee for each of us. "Breakfast is served buffet style, help yourselves," he said pointing at a long colorful buffet table. The dining room was less than half full. We were the early birds. I piled my plate with scrambled eggs, sausages, toast and fresh fruits. Everyone else came back with full plates. The food was delicious. Carl seemed a bit under the weather. Too much partying last night he told us. Claude had just a small collection on his plate, of mainly fresh fruits. I was afraid that he was ready to do some pushups right next to the table.

We sat and ate some more. The conversation was hit or miss but somehow we understood each other. Claude excused himself, explaining that he was going out to jog on the deck. The motion of the ship had changed noticeably. As we were rounding the southern point of Ireland and approaching the open

Atlantic, the gentle swells had changed into good size waves. The ship had begun a rolling motion as the waves stuck it broadside. Later in the morning, the rolling and pitching grew to the point of having to depend on hand holds in order to move around. Few of the passengers already complained about sea-sickness. I was on the upper deck hanging onto the railing and watching the sea become angrier. The sky was ominously overcast in heavy ugly gray cloud. This was the North Atlantic in dead winter, which was known to be the stormy season. I was hoping that it would not get any worse, but it did to the point of being scary.

By lunch time the dining room was less than half full. Only Carl showed up at our table. Luigi came over and I asked him about the storm. "This is nothing, yet. I am sorry to say but we are in for a severe storm by tomorrow. The Captain had informed all employees to secure any loose items and furniture tonight after dinner. The Captain will also make an announcement to the passengers later today. What you are experiencing now is just a small baby storm, but it will grow fast. Sorry," he said looking at us. "Can I get you anything for lunch?"

Carl ordered a beer and a ham sandwich and I ordered the same. Luigi went to fetch our lunch.

"What he told us sounds scary. I hope not to get seasick. What about you, Carl?"

"I feel fine now, but later I don't know. At least we are on board a safe ship," he said in hesitant tone.

Our lunch arrived. A few of the passengers had to rush out without finishing their lunch, looking pasty. I had to hold on to my beer bottle so it would not tip over. Even now the rolling and pitching seemed to have increased. A few items fell to the floor at nearby tables. This was bad, but Luigi's storm sounded awful.

After lunch we walked down to our cabin. Extra heavy ropes had been strung in the hallway for handhold. This alone gave me goose bumps. Hugo and the French man stayed in their bunks, looking pale and sick. I felt fine and Carl seemed to feel all right. In a way of being here on the fifth deck was more comfortable than the first class up high above. There they could feel the ship's swaying and rolling more than down below where we were, closer to the belly of the ship. Not that I would not have enjoyed the first class amenities, but I was very pleased with our cabin and the good food and service.

Hugo was awake and I asked him, "Would you like some food?"

"Don't say that word again, because I will vomit."

"OK, just a friendly gesture. You should go out on the deck and get some fresh air. That would make you feel better."

"I feel like dying," he muttered.

Wait until tomorrow I thought. Then you surely will feel like dying. To me this was exciting, but yet I was concerned about what was coming in the next few days. I had never been seasick, but would my luck hold up on this trip?

I climbed into my bunk and fell asleep from the lulling of the ship. At dinner time Carl and I entered the dining room, which was almost empty. Luigi came running over, explaining that tonight they were not able to serve dinner, but the Chef had fixed containers of food to go. Each one of us got one and we proceeded to the deck, sitting down on benches secured to the wall. The ocean was wild by now. The waves almost reached deck eight where we sat. The wind was whipping hard. A spray of cold ocean water reached our feet, when the ship heaved to our side. The turbulent ocean was showing us its might. It was frightening. We had to go back inside. It seemed to get windier, and the ship was listing more with each wave. Ropes had been strung everywhere for hand hold. Back in the cabin, Hugo and Claude were still laying in their bunks.

I asked Hugo, "Do you want anything? I can go back up and get it for you."

He moaned, with a look of a ghost. "Get me a bucket, please." Claude said he wanted one also, giving us a withering gaze.

There was a stack of buckets in a special rack in the hallway, close to our cabin. I brought back one each. I was surprised that I had no ill feelings. The turbulence in the cabin was much less than up above where Carl and I had been. Carl seemed to feel fine also. Down here I could feel the tremors of the ship mixed with the rolling. I hoped that the ship could take it and no icebergs, please.

A half an hour ago, the captain had made a statement over the ship's loudspeakers: "I wish to announce to our passengers not to worry. I am sorry, but we are in for two days of stormy January weather. Please be careful when walking about the ship. Food and drinks will be available any time, served in containers. Do make the best of it. Your Captain"

Okay, I will not worry. My dream of the storm in the sailboat and the flying fish came to mind. Perhaps tomorrow's dinner was pan fried fresh flying fish?

For the next two days we were tossed around as if we were inside a washing machine. The ship rolled and heaved as the waves battered it relentlessly. I could not imagine that the magnitude of the waves which were able to toss this huge ship as it did. At times I felt queasy, but luckily not seasick. The hallways stunk. The elevator stunk and everywhere else the same thing. People had thrown up everywhere. The crew was busy mopping up the mess. I had slept well, even so at times I felt like I was rolling out of my bunk. The rocking and rolling felt like being in a crib.

On the second day of the storm, which had noticeably increased into a fury, I made my way up to the bar. There were windows overlooking the bow. I could not believe what I saw, hanging onto the handrail with white knuckles The waves were monstrous, washing over the ship, every time we slipped into the trough and began the climb up the towards the next white capped crest. It was a rollercoaster ride. The sky was black. The bar was open and I decided to have a bottle of beer. There were only three other men in the large lounge, besides the bartender.

The bartender handed me the bottle and said, "Sorry, but no glass. Hang on tight. I have been bartending on the ship two years and every winter we experience storms, but this one will go down in the record books. It is the worst that I ever experienced."

"I hope that the Captain knows what he is doing?" I could not help being worried.

"He is the best ever," the bartender assured me, hanging onto the bar.

In the morning of the third day, just after waking up, I sensed that we had survived the worst of the storm. The ship was still heaving but the motion was gentle compared to the previous days. Even Hugo displayed a tired smile. He gave the impression of having lost several pounds. Claude was equally below par, in a droopy facial expression and needing a shave. They had not eaten anything, only drinking a few bottles of water. Their only escape from the bunks had been quick bathroom trips.

"Guys, we are through with the terrible storm. Get dressed and come up to the deck for a while, and get something light to eat. That will make you feel better." They agreed. "I'll meet you on deck eight," I said and left them. Carl was up and about somewhere. The ship had come alive. People were milling around, some looking tired and weak. The dining room was open again. It felt so good after the harrowing ordeal. Carl was sitting at our table and I joined him. Luigi ran over and took my breakfast order. "We are back to almost normal," he uttered before running to fetch my food. I did not want the buffet but just a simple ham omelet and toast. It was January the tenth, meaning that tomorrow morning we would arrive in New York. I was thinking about the future with intrepid determination. America was the land of opportunity and I had every intention of grabbing hold of it. Hugo and Claude joined us for the first time after the farewell dinner four days ago. Even Claude, who was tall and skinny, showed some weight loss. Both of them went to the buffet for only toast and fruits, sitting down and devouring their pickings

The following morning brought gentle rollers and bright sunshine. We should be arriving in New York in about one hour. After breakfast the four of us decided to go out on the deck to watch the arrival. It was chilly outside, but the bright sunshine buoyed our anticipation of reaching New York. I could see land on the starboard side, but it was still far away. We moved to the port side to get the full benefit of the sun.

It did not take long before the skyline of New York City loomed ahead. It grew taller as the ship entered the channel to the harbor. The sight was majestic. The dark green Statue of Liberty stood graciously welcoming us to America. The Empire State building stood in the center of Manhattan Island, surrounded by other skyscrapers. I was mesmerized by the grandeur of the city.

Chills were running up my arms. I was so excited to finally arrive here, after so many months of planning and after the storm of storms which we went through. I felt a tear running down my cheek. The sight was breathtaking.

Two tugboats appeared. Lines were heaved aboard after which they took over and guided our ship to the pier. Docking the ship was a slow motion operation but finally we were tied up and the gangplank was extended.

The luggage was to be placed in the hallway, where they would be picked up and delivered to an area inside the terminal. I was dressed neat in my new slacks with a white shirt and blue sweater. We said good bye to each other with everyone wishing each other well. It was too warm to wear the parka, which I attached to the backpack and headed up for debarking.

There was a long line of passengers exiting the ship. I fell in line. Now I had time to think about meeting Mr. Schwab, after so many months. Over the months I had promised myself not to let him down, after the miraculous invitation which he had extended to me on the park bench at Aulanko. No, I was a Finn with integrity and internal fortitude. The line moved slowly. I was nervous about meeting him again. The thoughts of what the future in America would bring, revolved in my head.

After a seemingly long time, I arrived at the passport control and passed through a doorway to America. In the huge crowd of passengers and greeting friends, it took me a while to spot him. Actually we spotted each other at the same time. He was dressed in a dark pin stripe suit, with a white shirt and a blue and white tie. The Finnish colors He looked the same as I remembered. We met each other with a bear hug.

"John, welcome to America. I hope you had a pleasant journey," he said, in a big smile.

"Thank you Mr. Schwab. I am so happy to be here. The ride was a bit bumpy. I will tell you all about it later." I said in genially broad smile.

After finding my luggage, we proceeded to flag a cab to the Grand Central railroad station. I was bewildered by the tall, tall buildings and the loud traffic. Car horns blew everywhere. The sidewalks were packed with foot traffic. I had never seen anything like this in peaceful Finland. Neon lights everywhere. Craziness! I loved it.

"I heard on the TV about the terrible North Atlantic storm, wondering how you were coping with it. I was worried," he said looking at me. "By the way, from here on you can call me Laban," he added

"TV, you have one? I have never seen a TV," I spurted out excitedly.

We arrived at the station and caught the train to Philadelphia.

This was the day when my colorful and exciting life in USA began.

* * * *

EPILOGUE

LIFE IN AMERICA WAS WONDERFUL and exciting, fulfilling all my expectations. The people were friendly but it seemed as if everyone was in a rush somewhere. The city traffic was mind-boggling. The weather was almost spring like, compared to mid winter in Finland. I took a subway ride for the fun of it north, where eventually I got off somewhere and took the next train back downtown. I had never ridden a subway before. It was exciting to see so many black people. I had seen only a couple of them in Finland. My life was turning a new page. Just walking in the crowd in downtown Philadelphia was an adventure in itself. On the third day, early in the morning, I stood outside a small jewelry store on Market Street, looking at the window display, when a burly salesman came out and dragged me in to the store. He wanted to sell me a men's 'diamond' ring, set in 'white gold' for one hundred dollars. I told him no, but he insisted that I must have it. I could not get out of the store. After haggling back and forth and in order for me to escape, I bought the 'fine' ring for three dollars. What a country. I got a beautiful ring for only three dollars. When I showed the ring to Laban, that night, he laughed very hard. "It is a piece of junk," he said and handed it back to me. I sent it to Kari, inside his cowboy boots.

Laban lived close to the center of Philadelphia in a spacious new condominium, on the fifth floor. It overlooked a nearby park, with naked trees. The

Delaware River loomed in the background. The condo consisted of three good size bedrooms and two full bathrooms. The living room was furnished in a comfortable soft seating mixed with a touch of antique American pieces. Large picture windows allowed sunshine in through gray colored slatted blinds. A big TV was against the wall in front of a wraparound couch. It was so exciting to finally see the black and white shows. I was glued nightly to this amazing box and watched show after show. The kitchen was modern with the latest appliances. My room held wide book shelves, a desk and a double bed with a matching bureau. It was cozy.

My high school was a Vocational School, located eight blocks away. It was a huge gray building. The first day I stepped into the school building, there was lots of snickering about my clothing, which was totally different from what the students wore. It embarrassed me and told Laban about it, who suggested that we go shopping right away for new casual clothes. The next day no-one made fun of my attire. I had been assigned to the Electronics Department, besides the regular high school subjects. That spring I learned how to build a radio from scratch. I loved it. The following year, I graduated.

After taking driving lessons and the required driving test, I got my driver's license. We shopped around for a car and finally bought a 1952 blue Ford. I was as proud of this car as Ukki had been of his. Laban and I traveled often to the sea shore and Pocono Mountains. In July we took a long trip to Canada with one of his friends, Horace Jenkins. In Quebec we stayed three days at the famous Fontainebleau Hotel and had dinners at some of the finest restaurants. We continued the scenic leisurely trip along the Saint Lawrence Sea way to Perth peninsula, and eventually back home. It had been a magnificent trip. Having been the only driver in the car, I had logged over one thousand miles on this trip.

Later the following summer, I returned back to Finland to fulfill my required army duty in October. For eleven months I had been assigned into the communications regiment, mainly listening to Morse code hour after hour. Most of the time I was daydreaming and at the same time writing down the Morse messages. It was outright boring.

The homecoming, after two years had been a joyous occasion. Mother looked well and happy, still working the summers at the tower. Inga had grown up to be a beautiful young lady, and Kari a solid strapping young fellow. I told them all about America, which they never got tired of hearing. Their life had continued more or less the same way as it was when I left.

One day the following June, Laban showed up at my army barracks totally unexpected holding a certificate in his hand. He had approached The Finnish Army headquarters in Helsinki, requesting a two weeks leave for me to be his 'guide' in Finland. Somehow he had been able to convince them to issue it. Needless to say, my buddies were not very happy of my good fortune. We traveled throughout Finland and stayed at home at Aulanko for two days. Mother was happy to see him again, thanking him for taking such care of me.

One thing led to another. Laban had retired and decided to travel throughout Europe, Africa and South America for a year or more. He told me that his friend Mr. Jenkins, who had become my friend also, would extend the same invitation and sponsorship as Laban had done, after my army duties. This incredible news put me in very in high spirits. I was going back to America. Mr. Jenkins was in the same lonely situation as Laban and would welcome me for company and arranged for continued schooling. Mr. Jenkins was one of the finest men I have ever met. He was a Christian Science Practitioner. Our neighbor at Aulanko was a Christian Scientist, only one of the few in Finland, and she had often talked to Mother and us children about this religion, so we had some understanding about it. The last time I heard from Laban, he was in Egypt, and leaving shortly to travel in Brazil, South America. I wondered if I would ever see him again.

It was in August when I repeated the same long journey to America aboard *SS United States*. I felt at home aboard the ship. The trip was uneventful. The ocean was calm and sunny, nothing like the first trip. It was a pleasure cruise.

Mr. Jenkins met me in New York and we traveled back to Philadelphia. He had arranged for room and board for me close to Temple University and signed me up to start there in September. I had a small room on the second floor of an old row house, sharing the house with other students. Mrs. Ange, the landlady, was a short and outright fat woman. She also had a large black and fat mixture of a dog sharing the house. All the furniture was old and run down. There was only one bathroom on the second floor, which everyone in the house shared. Often Mrs. Ange had trouble making it up in time and the steep steps told the story. The house was not clean and the dreaded dog's hair was everywhere. Mrs. Ange fed us but most of the time we had no idea what we were eating. My student friends, at the dinner table, snickered that we were eating dog food. I never knew for sure. I attended Temple University, which was only three blocks away from the house, studying business and accounting.

Mr. Jenkins had an office in the center of the city and a small efficiency apartment for the weekdays. The weekends I spent with him and his brother at their large home in Gwynedd Valley which was over half an hour train trip north from Philadelphia. The house was a massive very old stone building, with a caretaker's home next to it. They had a part time cook, who came daily to cook very good dinners. She was a pleasant woman, nothing like Mrs. Anderson in Sweden.

On the weekends we took trips into the country side and often to the Amish community. Mr. Jenkins asked me to call him Horace and his brother Bill. Horace was brilliant. He even studied Finnish and in a short time, he was able to speak simple sentences. He was a member of The New York Athletic Club. At least once per month we took the train to the club, enjoying their lavish sauna, steam room and swimming pool. Afterwards we sat for a leisurely delicious lunch in the dining room.

Horace was an amazing man. He wanted for me to learn to fly. He enrolled me for flying lessons at a nearby airfield in Gwynedd Valley. When I met my flight instructor, Mr. Black, for the fifth lesson, he asked me, "Are you ready to solo today? In my opinion you are doing so well in handling the airplane and you are welcome to take off alone, if you feel comfortable in doing so." He patted me on my shoulder and smiled. "Normally I would not let any student solo until after at least ten lessons, but in your case I feel that you are ready."

I was elated and speechless for a moment and answered him in a confidante tone, "Yes, Mr. Black. I am ready. Thanks."

As we walked over to the old two seat Aeronca plane, sitting on the grass runway, next to a short paved runway, he told me to only do 'touch and go' flying on the first solo trip. After pre inspection of the plane, I climbed aboard and turned the switches on, calling out through the open window, "Contact." He gave the propeller a quick turn and the engine started. Moving aside he gave me a salute and waved me off.

I taxied to the end of the pawed runway, stopped and revved up the engine, checking the gauges. All looked normal. There was no other air traffic around so I took off gaining enough speed for liftoff. I felt like a bird, taking its first flight from the nest. It was a magnificent feeling. I was whistling and singing. For one hour I flew around the airport and preformed touch and go landings on the grass runway and the paved one. This was one of the highlights of my life.

Back home I was beaming from ear to ear when I told Horace about my exciting day. He was surprised to hear that I soloed so fast. "Next week I will fly over the house and flap my wings for you," I told him.

Close to Christmas Horace told me that we would be taking a car trip to Miami to visit one of his good friends. On the way we would celebrate Christmas in Georgetown South Carolina, as guests of Colonel Montgomery's daughter, Hope. They owned a large plantation just outside of the town called Mansfield Plantation. On the third day, we reached the entrance to the plantation and drove two miles, past a string of small white wooden buildings, which Horace informed me were the living quarters of the black help. We reached the main mansion where a tuxedo attired black man welcomed us. After our introduction, he pointed to a close by large brick building and told us that it was the North Guest House, reserved for us. "Please get refreshed and return for refreshments with Madam Hope," he advised us.

I drove next to the building, not believing that this gorgeous large building was our 'guest house.' Inside it was appointed with beautiful antique furnishing with the walls decorated in oil paintings of Southern motif. There were four bedrooms and two full bathrooms. After taking a long hot shower and stretching out on the bed to get the kinks out from the long ride, I changed to the best clothes which I had brought along. Horace was sitting in the living room reading, already changed and ready to return to the main building and greet Madam Hope.

Entering the main building the smell of coffee hung in the air. The servant led the way to the large living room, where a frail looking middle aged woman sat, overlooking the vast expanse of fields beyond the picture window. Hearing us arrive, she stood up and approached us. She was beautiful, graceful and regal. Horace walked up to her and gave her a gentle hug and kiss on her cheek. "Hope, you look wonderful. Thank you for your invitation. I am so happy to see you again," he said, turning towards me and introducing me to her.

She gave me a hug and a kiss and said, "Welcome. Any friend of Horace is also a friend of mine. I hope you will enjoy your stay here."

I was tongue tied from her and the opulence of this place, only able to utter, "Thank you Madam Hope."

"Forget the 'Madam' business, just call Auntie Hope," she said with a broad smile.

We enjoyed a delightful afternoon of coffee with pastries with her description of the Plantation and her father, Colonel Montgomery. She was a sweet lady, with sparkly hazel eyes and a genuine happy laughter. Time flew by and I felt so content in this peaceful aura.

"We must drive to Georgetown," Horace said after returning from Auntie Hope's "You need a tuxedo for the Christmas dinner tomorrow night. We'll go and rent one right away."

I mumbled, totally baffled, "Tuxedo?"

In the town we found a tuxedo rental shop. I tried on several and finally settling on one which fitted perfectly. Black shoes were needed also. I looked at myself in the store mirror and could not believe that it was me. I had never before worn a tux, as they called it. The shopkeeper told that I looked like a young movie star. I did not say anything, but agreed with his comment. Horace was pleased with the outfit also. In Finland we wore sweaters at Christmas. This dinner must be something special, I decided.

Christmas Eve, we entered the mansion dressed to kill. There were several other guests present, men in tuxedos and the ladies in long gowns. Hors oeuvres' were passed by two servants. The atmosphere was festive. I had never experienced such a well to do crowd. They were all pleasant and several of the guests inquired about life in Finland. I don't know why, but I felt very comfortable in this crowd. The butler announced that the dinner will be served.

There were total of sixteen dignified people sitting at the dinner table when the appetizers arrived. I was sitting next to Horace looking at my platter of something. I whispered into his ear, "What is this? I had no idea. There were six wiggly gray things on a seashell.

Horace whispered back to me, "They are raw oysters. Just taste one. They are delicious," he said with a smile. I watched how the other guests handled these gray slimy looking things and finally got the nerve to fork one into my mouth. It sort of slid into my stomach, but I was not sure it would not come back up. Somehow I finished all of them, but still felt queasy. After the servants cleared the dishes, elegant empty china dishes were placed in front of each of us, for the main course which had arrived. I was —horrified. Horace told me that it was rare duck. The servant came next to me holding the silver platter low and all I could see was bloody meat. He placed two thin slices of the bloody duck on my plate. First the oysters and now bloody duck. Everyone else at the table was oohing and ahing, except for me - and I had to wear a tuxedo for this! Vegetables arrived by other servants, at least they looked edible. I made a show of enjoying the dinner, but my stomach was doing a "fox-trot'. The guests were smacking their lips and congratulating Auntie Hope for a marvelous dinner. I did so also, but in my mind it was a fib. I could not believe what I had just eaten. The dessert was a delicious raspberry chocolate mousse. Different wines had been passed along during the dinner, but Horace and I declined the offer.

Back at our guest house, I couldn't help from telling Horace that this was the worst Christmas dinner I ever had. I added though, "It was interesting and memorable."

Horace sort of agreed with me, but did not express it as vividly as I had spoken. He just laughed it off.

We left the next day, after thanking Auntie Hope for her wonderful hospitality. My tuxedo was left with the butler, who would return it back to the store after Christmas.

In two more days we reached Miami and visited with his friend and family. After sightseeing and me taking dips in the ocean, our long trip back home began. I did still meet Auntie Hope twice in the spring, when she had moved back up North to their mansion in Adressan, off the Main Line in Philadelphia. This was the mansion where the movie *Philadelphia Story*, with Grace Kelly was filmed. Both of our visits were elegant luncheons and with long walks through the mansion which was just mind blowing. The opulence of this mansion was unbelievable. My mind traveled back home to Finland and found it hard to accept the fact that a 'bellboy' was experiencing such grandiose and lovable treatment. It seemed like a dream.

Late that summer I met my sweetheart. Paola Barboni who was born in Pescara, Italy. They had endured the terrible war time with the Nazis for many years. She emigrated to USA four years earlier with her mother and sister. They were American citizens because the mother had been born here. Her father and two brothers followed two years later, as immigrants. Paola and I hit it off immediately. I guess you could call it ' love on the first sight.' She was beautiful and still is after over fifty years of marriage. Six months later we were married, in a simple ceremony at her parents' home in New Jersey, right outside of Philadelphia. We found a small apartment on Spring Garden Street in Philadelphia and moved in. Now I had to stop school and find work, which I did with some friends' help. I became the Assistant Internal Auditor at The Benjamin Franklin Hotel in the center city. We lived happily but very frugally. I visited with

Horace a few times after the marriage, but sadly Horace passed away the following spring. My memories of him are etched in my mind forever, as the smartest and warmest person I had ever met.

Our son, John Claus was born about nine months after our marriage. Two years later our daughter, Laila was born in Alexandria, Virginia where we lived at that time. Lewis Hotel School had brought us to Washington DC area. I never finished the school but accepted a position at the famous Jockey Club which had just opened. It was in the Fairfax Hotel, on Massachusetts Ave. owned by Colonel Gore, Jimmy and Louise Gore. There was one more person from the Gore family. The Colonel's grandson a youngster Al Gore was also present. I became very close to the family, who lived in the Hotel. I was only a few years older than Al, and we became good friends. My duties were the daily accounting and purchasing just about everything needed for this classy restaurant, which had become the 'In' spot in DC. President Jack Kennedy was always escorted in through the back door. Everyone who was famous in DC to Hollywood considered Jockey Club as their club. My wife and I were sent to The 21 Club in New York for two days, to come back with ideas from there. Jockey Club was a take-off from 21 Club. After three years with this famous restaurant, I began my Country Club career.

Over the years I became a Certified Country Club Manager, running some of the finest country clubs in US.

My first private club position was as The General Manager of Baltimore Yacht club. It was a year round position with many banquets throughout the winter months, and very busy with boating activities in the spring through late fall. Our housing was provided on the premise. We stayed five years. My ambition was to 'climb the ladder' and we moved to the Mainline of Philadelphia, becoming The General Manager of St. David's Golf Club. I was also deeply involved with The Club Managers Association, attending week long conventions with Paola throughout the country and at least two seminars per year in different cities.

Our next move, I would rather like to forget and Paola feels very strongly likewise. We bought a small resort with several cabins in Northern Minnesota. She, having grown up in the sub-tropical part of Italy, and now living through brutal winters here, was devastated. It was colder with more snow up here than I had experienced in Finland. The one and only good thing that happened at the resort, was the birth of our third child, a beautiful little girl, Claudia. She was baptized in the smallest church I had ever seen, called *Suomi* church. Suomi, in English is Finland. There was a tiny community of Finns in the area.

The children, Johnny and Laila loved it at the resort, and Claudia was growing up in the wild. The summers were beautiful but life was hard. It was time to sell the resort and I accepted a General Managers position at Rolling Green Country Club in Minneapolis, which was heavenly compared to the resort. We bought a beautiful new home close to the club.

At Rolling Green I met President Ford. He came to play golf in a large fund raising golf tournament. I shared my office with him. On my desk there had been installed a red telephone with direct contact to The White House. CIA agents had been at the club for two weeks prior to his arrival. Each employee was investigated by them and FBI and once cleared, received an official button to wear on their lapel. I had become a US citizen two years earlier, and still have my button as a memento. During the time at this club, I became a Certified Club Manager, at our yearly convention which was in Los Angeles that year. One year the week long convention was in London, England, where Paola and I attended, extending the trip to a three week journey to Sweden, where my brother lived, then to Finland to my Mother and Inga, who was by now married with two children. The next stop was Pescara, Italy at Paola's parents who had moved back to their home country from New Jersey. It was an unforgettable trip.

Time had arrived again to 'climb the ladder'. This time I received an invitation for an interview at one of the finest Country Clubs in the country, The Westwood Country Club in St. Louis, Missouri. It was huge and elegant. US open golf tournament had been played there the previous year. Paola and I flew there to meet with the board of governors. The meeting went well and three days later I received an official letter from the Club President, offering the position as The General Manager at Westwood. I accepted and we moved again, this time to an even larger home, almost around the corner from the club. The position was very demanding, yet gratifying. The staff of the whole operation reached up to two hundred employees at times. I had my hands full, but proficient help surrounded me.

During this same period, a very sad happening took place. In the fall of 1977 I received news that Mother had died. I was heartbroken upon hearing this. I had just visited with her one month earlier, and to this day I miss her terribly. At least I still have my happy memories of her.

By 1980 I was burnt out from club management, from the long hours and weekends. One thing led to another, for a long haul, without climbing. We purchased a shell of a closed up restaurant in Fairhaven, Massachusetts, close to Cape Cod. Within one year, with Johnny's help we opened it, naming it The Pasta House Italian restaurant. It did not take long, until it became famous of fine food and ambiance. Paola was the person who designed the menu and taught the kitchen staff all about Italian cooking. She had always been a wonderful cook, but only at home. She was scared and had nightmares of cooking huge quantities in huge pots. She worked hard and long hours in the kitchen. It was not an easy task to achieve, but in short order her reputation spread and the Pasta House became a landmark. Johnny and Laila were also very much involved in the daily operation. Our seating capacity was over one hundred customers with a large bar and lounge. It was hard work, but with persistence we grew to become the finest Italian restaurant south of Boston. Claudia attended college and graduated in textile field. Often she could also be found helping out at the restaurant. We were featured in several newspaper articles, magazines, radio and TV interviews.

Life in Fairhaven was very nice. Our home was only three blocks from Buzzard's Bay facing the Atlantic Ocean. It was great for swimming and fishing. Both Laila and Claudia got married during this time. Our son in laws Richard and Ross were fine men. Claudia and Ross had three children, making Paola and I into proud grandparents. Laila and Richard unfortunately were not able to have any children, but are happily married. Johnny remains as a bachelor.

While enjoying our life during this period there was, however, also some very grim news. My sister Inga was diagnosed with incurable liver cancer. Paula and I visited her in the hospital two weeks before her death in 1993. I can still see her happy, smiling face in old photographs and in my mind. And when I think of her, and Mother, and others that I have lost, I can't help but wonder, shall we all meet again someday?

After twenty-three years we sold The Pasta House and moved again, for the last time. Claudia and Ross with the children had moved to Summerville, in the outskirts of Charleston, South Carolina. After visiting them, we decided to follow them. The climate was so enhancing, especially for Paola, from warm Italy, that we fell in love with the area. I also had enough of snow by now. We bought a comfortable smaller house very close to the grandchildren and retired.

A very sad happening took place in 2009 at Myrtle Beach. Ross and his friend had taken a trip there to play golf, where he was murdered by a gunshot by an crazed individual. The police caught the killer and locked him up. At the first court hearing the judge set the bail for $250,000 but someone paid a cash bail of $25,000 and the man was let out. The official hearing is still pending. It was a heart breaking episode in everyone's life. It was a shock. Claudia and the children were devastated and also the rest of the family and friends.

We miss you, Ross.

I contribute everything in our life to my higher power, God. There were many mistakes which we endured, but these were self inflicted, selfish and wrongdoings mainly on my part. There were so many people in our lives who helped us along to achieve what we did and what became of us, but I still look up to HIM as the originator of it all.

As I had learned in Finland, America was the land of opportunity." This was true. I am so happy to be able to state that it is a fact, once we stop and listen.

Thank you for reading my story.

Acknowledgments

SPECIAL ACKNOWLEDGMENTS GO TO EDITOR MIKE VALENTINO, who molded and assisted me in every stage in preparing my book for print. Without his knowledge and hard work it could not have happened.

There are many others who contributed their ideas and help with the preparations. In the beginning stages, I owe special recognition to Ms. Kimberle Unger, who extended her talents with the story. Thank you, Kimberle.

The cover design was a creation by Mike Corathers at Printing Associates, in Summerville, South Carolina. He came up with the stunning front and back cover.

My friend and author James Nicholson contributed very helpful ideas and suggestions. I thank him of all the pestering I did.

CreateSpace publishing Co., who created a first class printing project, advised me every step of the way. Thank you.

Lastly, but not least, my wife Paola deserves hugs and kisses for putting up with me while I was glued to the computer key board, day after day. I love you and thank you for your patience. The rest of my family also deserves my gratitude whose love sustained me through all this.

John Raikkonen
Summerville, SC

Made in the USA
Charleston, SC
06 July 2015